The factory question and industrial England,
1830–1860

The factory question and industrial England, 1830–1860 addresses the con-
tinuing controversy over industrialisation. It investigates different perceptions of the 'factory system' either as a threat or as a promise, and the
contested meanings of waged work in industry. Making use of a great
variety of sources, such as sermons, medical treatises, fictional and
visual representations, Robert Gray places the languages of debate in
their cultural contexts, paying particular attention to the shifting constructions of class and gender in the rhetoric of reform, and the ambiguities and tensions inherent in 'protective' legislation. He then relates
patterns of conflict over factory legislation to the features of specific
industrial towns. The combination of regional, cultural and textual
analysis makes this book a coherent and original contribution to the
study of industrial Britain in the nineteenth century.

The factory question and industrial England, 1830–1860

Robert Gray

University of Portsmouth

PUBLISHED BY THE PRESS SYNDICATE OF THE UNIVERSITY OF CAMBRIDGE
The Pitt Building, Trumpington Street, Cambridge, United Kingdom

CAMBRIDGE UNIVERSITY PRESS
The Edinburgh Building, Cambridge CB2 2RU, UK
40 West 20th Street, New York NY 10011–4211, USA
477 Williamstown Road, Port Melbourne, VIC 3207, Australia
Ruiz de Alarcón 13, 28014 Madrid, Spain
Dock House, The Waterfront, Cape Town 8001, South Africa

http://www.cambridge.org

© Cambridge University Press 1996

First published 1996
First paperback edition 2002

A catalogue record for this book is available from the British Library

Library of Congress Cataloguing in Publication data
Gray, Robert Q.
The factory question and industrial England, 1830–1860 / Robert
Gray.
      p.   cm.
Includes bibliographical references and index.
ISBN 0 521 49659 4 (hc)
1. Factory system – Great Britain – History – 19th century.
2. Industrialization – Great Britain – History – 19th century.
I. Title.
HD2356.G3G73   1995
338.6'5'0941–dc20   95-37611   CIP

ISBN 0 521 49659 4 hardback
ISBN 0 521 89292 9 paperback

It is just possible that the principal actors in the stirring scenes of these times were they now to read their own speeches, as then reported, would do so with astonishment.

'Alfred' [Samuel Kydd],
The History of the Factory Movement (1857)

If I was in solitary confinement I could write a history of my life, and I could show up the factory system then.

Charles Aberdeen, victimised card-room worker,
giving evidence to the Factory Commission, 1833

Contents

Illustrations

Tables

Acknowledgments

Research towards this book was supported by a Nuffield Social Science Research Fellowship; an honorary Simon Fellowship at the University of Manchester provided kind hospitality and an academic base in cottonopolis. Return visits there were facilitated by generous support from the Faculty of Humanities and Social Sciences, University of Portsmouth.

Various libraries and archives and their staffs have made this study possible. It started with browsing among the Parliamentary Papers in the Frewen Library at Portsmouth, and I have depended throughout on the efficiency and courtesy of the staff there. Richard Oastler's own collection of pamphlets, and much else of relevance, are to be found in the Goldsmiths' Collection, University of London, and I owe a special debt to Angela Whitelegg and her colleagues. Reference libraries and local archives are an indispensable resource for a study of this kind, especially Manchester Central Library, Bradford Library, Bolton Archives and Tameside Archives, Stalybridge. Thanks also to Dr Williams Library, the John Rylands University Library, Manchester, and the British Library.

This book owes much to colleagues at Portsmouth. Graham Davies and Sue Harper read the entire manuscript. I am profoundly grateful for the constructively critical attention they brought to this task, and not least for their generosity in undertaking it at a time of the academic year when they had many other things to do. I would also thank Ena Ainsworth, John Oakley, Ken Lunn, Sylvia Taylor, Dave Andress, and other colleagues or former colleagues, for intellectual, material and moral support. I am grateful to Fergus Carr, for the interest he has taken in this work, as well as for all he has done in his capacity as Head of School to facilitate serious scholarship. Carol Parker and Robin Prior took much time and trouble preparing the diagrams; I would also acknowledge the cartographic skills of Bill Johnson, and the help of the University photographers with some of the illustrations. Our students, whose contribution is often greater than we, or they, realise, have been a source of ideas and encouragement.

In the wider research community, I am particularly indebted to Patrick Joyce for the stimulus of his own work, for consistent encouragement and

for prodding me to write. Clive Behagg and Donna Loftus share interests
in many of the themes of this work, and I have benefited greatly from discussion with them. John Seed, Pat Hudson, John Saunders, Rob Sykes,
Neville Kirk, Simon Gunn, Catherine Hall, Joan Mottram, John
Pickstone, Michael Winstanley, David Walsh, Michael Rose and Alan
Fowler all helped with discussion, advice and in some cases sharing
unpublished work. A 1983 History Workshop session on 'the history of
work', and a subsequently convened research group on this topic helped
focus my ideas, and I am indebted to Keith McClelland, Richard Whipp
and other participants. I have also benefited from opportunities to discuss
my work at Social History Society conferences, and at various other
venues. I would like to express my thanks for useful and searching comments by an anonymous reader for Cambridge University Press. The
book is better for this attention, and I alone bear responsibility for its
remaining shortcomings.

This book incorporates material from articles in P. Joyce (ed.), *The
Historical Meanings of Work* (Cambridge University Press, 1987), pp.
143–79; *Social History* 16, no. 1 (Jan. 1991), pp. 19–43; and *Gender &
History* 5, no. 3 (spring 1993), pp. 56–80. I am grateful to the editors and
publishers for permission to re-use the material.

My greatest debt is to Joan Gray, for tolerating me and this book, for
reading successive drafts of key parts – and sometimes for reminding me
that there was more to the nineteenth century than factories, workers and
inspectors. But also for making everything else possible.

General note

Throughout the text of this book I have followed the general practice of capitalising references to 'Liberal', 'Evangelical', etc., where an identifiable organised grouping is involved, and using lower case to refer to movements and ideas in a more generic sense. Lower case is used for generic references to the factory acts, the campaign for a ten-hours bill, etc.; capitalised references indicate a specific Bill or Act.

Introduction

The factory, the forge and the pithead do not nowadays cast quite such a long shadow over the historiography of nineteenth-century British society. Industrialisation and class are familiar themes in British social history, but they have also to some extent become unfashionable ones, with revisionist historiographies of economic growth, the apparently diminished impact of industry and a general emphasis on gradualism and continuity, in social and cultural as well as economic terms.[1] The argument of this book begins from the assumption that, whatever the net contribution of industry to the longer-run growth of Britain's economy or to the social identities of Britain's peoples, the nineteenth century was marked by changes in employment relations and working lives. There was a process of invention, not just of machines, but of ways of life understood as 'industrial'. The formation of cultures of industrial work remains an important part of British historical experience. Capital, labour, work, wages, consumption – the very categories of economics and economic history – were themselves products of cultural changes.[2] In this book I explore the making of these contested meanings.

Industrialisation has to be considered as a cultural transformation. My argument is in part a critical response to recent historiography. A powerful trend in economic history has downplayed the 'industrial revolution'. Economic growth has been seen as more modest than had been supposed; while the role within this of factory-based production, or other

---

[1] See esp. N.F.R. Crafts, *British Economic Growth during the Industrial Revolution* (Oxford, 1985); R. Floud and D. McCloskey (eds.), *The Economic History of Britain since 1700* (Cambridge, 1981). It should be emphasised that debates on these topics are partly a matter of emphasis; for a critical overview, P. Hudson, *The Industrial Revolution* (London, 1992). An important recent interpretation emphasising continuities centred on 'gentlemanly capitalism', empire, finance and the service sector is P.J. Cain and A.G. Hopkins, *British Imperialism: Innovation and Expansion, 1688–1914* (Harlow, 1993).

[2] For the cultural construction of waged work, see, e.g., P. Joyce (ed.), *The Historical Meanings of Work* (Cambridge, 1987); W.R. Reddy, *The Rise of Market Culture: The Textile Trade and French Society, 1750–1900* (Cambridge, 1984).

1

new technologies, has been similarly qualified.[3] In social and political terms, it is suggested that essentially 'pre-industrial' elites retained their dominance, while the expansion of the 'middle classes' showed similar characteristics, based not predominantly in industrial entrepreneurship, but in commerce, services and opportunities created by largely independent processes of urban growth.[4] At the same time, the story of popular protest was less the making of any particular class than a series of localised protests, contingently unified by a consciousness of political exclusion. This politically defined conflict has been argued to be prior to, and independent of, the social relations of industrial capitalism.[5]

Industrialisation and class, and the break represented by the 'industrial revolution' have thus become less distinct. The once-powerful figures of the 'new' industrial entrepreneur and the 'new' industrial worker have been lost in a larger and more crowded panorama of British society, peopled by aristocracy, 'gentlemanly capitalists' and allied professional elites at the top, plebeian classes beneath; privatised and aspirant middle classes are uneasily poised, precisely, somewhere in the middle. There are, of course, some factory chimneys somewhere in the picture, but they are less prominent than in earlier pictures.

The present study once more gives prominence to the factory, industrial employers and industrial workers. These are seen as important, not only in themselves, but in the way their activities and aspirations impinged on other groups, forming the material of social debates, occasional political intervention and continued philanthropic *angst*. In giving renewed attention to these issues, I have no wish to reinstate a teleological reduction of everything else to an effect of industrialisation and class. The first half of the nineteenth century was marked by transformations in a number of spheres. Indeed part of my purpose is to investigate how ideas and cultural forms derived from diverse sources influenced relations and identities in industry itself.

---

[3] See works cited above, n. 1; for a discussion of uneven development and the labour process, P. Joyce, 'Work', in F.M.L. Thompson (ed.), *The Cambridge Social History of Britain, 1750–1950* (Cambridge, 1990), vol. II.

[4] Cain and Hopkins, *British Imperialism*. For studies of the middle class in industrial regions, S. Gunn, 'The Manchester middle class, 1850–1880', PhD, University of Manchester, 1992; T. Koditschek, *Class Formation and Urban Industrial Society: Bradford 1750–1850* (Cambridge, 1990); R.J. Morris, *Class, Sect and Party: The Making of the British Middle Class, Leeds, 1820–1850* (Manchester, 1990); J. Smail, 'The origins of middle-class culture in Halifax', paper at symposium on 'Conflict and Change in English Communities and Regions', University of Liverpool, 1995; R.H. Trainor, *Black Country Elites: The Exercise of Authority in an Industrial Area, 1830–1900* (Oxford, 1993).

[5] E.F. Biagini and A.R. Reid (eds.), *Currents of Radicalism: Popular Radicalism, Organised Labour and Party Politics in Britain, 1850–1914* (Cambridge, 1991) ; G. Stedman Jones, *Languages of Class* (Cambridge, 1983).

This cultural perspective leads back to some of the 'traditional' themes of the industrial revolution. As recent critics have pointed out, the term 'industrial revolution' is used in varied senses.[6] It may indicate acceleration of economic growth; the specific impact of new technologies and forms of work organisation, such as the factory; or a series of wider economic, social and cultural changes, roughly equivalent to some notion of 'modernisation'. It may also indicate social problems thought to be associated with some or all of these processes. Contemporary, or near-contemporary views often elided these definitions into some grand sweep of historical change, regarded with varying degrees of enthusiasm or apprehension. Innovations in communication, including new printing techniques and new media as well as transport methods, were among the ways this impinged on people not directly engaged in industrial production. It is neatly captured in Peacock's satire on 'steam intellect'.[7]

The focus on the machine and on the steam-engine as prime movers and regulators of the industrial process was a powerful one. Perhaps in keeping with the 'spirit of the age', it provided (and to some extent continues to provide) a technicist explanation for complex social changes. As recent scholarship has emphasised, key regions of rapid industrialisation were by no means confined to factory-based industries, but also included the expansion and intensification of workshop and domestic production. Here, and equally within the factory itself, changes in the organisation of work and the sub-divisions of labour were as important as machinery. As research on the labour process, in Britain and elsewhere, has indicated, the factory was simply one form of a wider disciplining and intensification of labour. 'Productivist pressure', with or without the aid of machinery, was common to factory, workshop and domestic industrial locations.[8] But the factory (together with other

---

[6] J. Goodman and K. Honeyman, *Gainful Pursuits: The Making of Industrial Europe 1600–1914* (London, 1988), pp. 1–2.

[7] Thomas Love Peacock, as quoted in E.P. Thompson, *The Making of the English Working Class* (Pelican edn, Harmondsworth, 1968), p. 805; see also H. Jennings, *Pandemonium: The Coming of the Machine as Seen by Contemporary Observers* (Pan edn, London, 1987), for perceptions of technological change; G.N. von Tunzelmann, *Steam-Power and British Industrialisation to 1860* (Oxford, 1978), for an economic analysis of the uneven and less than spectacular achievements of the steam-engine.

[8] See A. Cottereau, 'The distinctiveness of working-class cultures in France', in I. Katznelson and A.R. Zolberg (eds.), *Working-Class Formation: Nineteenth-Century Patterns in Western Europe and the United States* (Princeton, 1986), pp. 121–3. On change in British workshop trades see C. Behagg, *Politics and Production in the Early Nineteenth Century* (London, 1990); M. Berg, *The Age of Manufactures, 1700–1820* (London, 1985); as Landes has recently pointed out, 'revisionist' writers often exaggerate the stagnation of non-factory sectors: D.S. Landes, 'The fable of the dead horse; or, the industrial revolution revisited', in J. Mokyr (ed.), *The British Industrial Revolution: an Economic Perspective* (Boulder, Colo., and Oxford, 1993), pp. 156–7, note.

glamorous applications of steam-power, notably to transport) came to stand as a potent symbol of industrial change, whether viewed as improvement, immiseration or some ambivalent mixture of the two. While the role of the factory and the machine were exaggerated and mythologised, they were also, as Pat Hudson has argued, 'symbolic of so many other changes attendant on the emergence of a more competitive market environment and the greater disciplining and alienation of labour'.[9] Downward revision of estimated industrial growth and the undoubtedly narrow base of the factory sector would, if anything, make this cultural imagery of modern industry all the more deserving of historical analysis. The very limitations of industrial productivity required greater numbers of workers, and in that respect could actually *increase* the social impact of industrialism. If images of 'industrial revolution' sometimes reduce diverse processes to the remorseless expansion of mechanised factory production, the origins of this elision remain worthy of study.

There are a number of reasons for continuing to see what contemporaries often called the 'factory system' as a significant development in early and mid-nineteenth-century Britain. The economic weight attached to the industrial sector is a matter of continuing debate, and it is certainly as well to resist any hardening of recent revisions into neo-orthodoxy. The case has been well argued by Pat Hudson, who suggests that structural transformations might not be expressed directly in increased growth-rates, but nevertheless establish preconditions of later growth; the periods of most dramatic change (and disturbance) are not necessarily the periods of most rapid growth in quantitative terms. She also draws attention to the relevance of specific regional experiences of concentrated industrial and urban growth, which may justify much of the 'traditional' emphasis on a dramatic – or even, in some respects, a catastrophic – transformation.[10]

Such unique regional experiences of industrial and urban expansion and change provide the framework of this study. I focus on the 'factory districts' of Lancashire and the West Riding, and on the development there of conflicts over work conditions and employment practices, which were expressed in attempts to impose regulated working hours. The debates associated with these struggles extended into changing definitions of the nature of work, the claims and limits of the employment contract and of employers' authority.

What was often referred to as the 'factory question' focused attention on problems and conflicts associated with concentrated regional experi-

[9] Hudson, *Industrial Revolution*, p. 218.   [10] Ibid., esp. ch. 4.

ences of rapid industrialisation. It was in the shape of this 'question' that such experiences impinged most often on public debate. The early 1830s saw the emergence of a popular short-time movement demanding a regulated ten-hour day for juvenile workers, and latterly for adult women; this was implicitly, and sometimes explicitly, envisaged as extending in practice to adult men. The ensuing struggles and debates provide the organising theme of this book. This has been extensively treated, from a variety of viewpoints, and some brief comments on the existing scholarship may bring out more clearly the distinctive approach of this book.

The factory acts constitute a classic case-study in state intervention in the framework of economic and political liberalism. Among the issues raised were the definition of market relations and their individual agents, the appropriate boundaries (whether legal, customary or moral) of employment contracts, the stabilisation of the family, education and the reproduction of wage-labour. This was expressed in reinterpretations of political economy, for example in J.S. Mill's celebrated codification of the permissible exceptions to the rule of non-interference, as well as in arguments on 'higher than commercial grounds' about endangered childhoods, physical and moral deterioration and the need to reconstitute a properly ordered family life. These debates have long preoccupied economists and historians of economic thought, notably in A.P. Robson's valuable study of the forging of a new policy synthesis incorporating factory regulation along with free trade.[11] More recently, 'neo liberal' interpretations have suggested that the ameliorative effect of legislation at best gave marginal reinforcement to the benign processes of an expanding market economy, in which more efficient labour markets produced preferences for fitter and better educated workers. At worst, legislation represented the levying of monopolistic quasi-rents by skilled workers in collusion with those employers who were advantaged by lower compliance costs.[12] These issues have perhaps acquired renewed topicality with the current trend, in Britain and elsewhere, towards the de-regulation of markets.

Marx, in his prolonged critical dialogue with political economy, took up the themes of 'human capital' and industrial efficiency, as well as the image of the large factory as the exemplar of rationalised, disciplined labour. The detailed regulations of hours and working arrangements 'by the stroke of the clock' were 'by no means a product of the fantasy of Members of Parliament. They developed gradually out of circumstances

---

[11] A.P. Robson, *On Higher than Commercial Grounds: The Factory Controversy, 1830–1853* (New York and London, 1985); see also A.W. Coats (ed.), *The Classical Economists and Economic Policy* (London, 1971).

[12] C. Nardinelli, *Child Labor and the Industrial Revolution* (Bloomington and Indianapolis, 1990). I comment further on de-regulation in the conclusion to this book.

as natural laws of the modern mode of production.' There is however some tension in Marx's account between these inherent requirements of modern industry and the moment of class struggle, which brought about their 'formulation, official recognition and proclamation by the State'.[13] Marx seems to have seen working-class pressure and state intervention as countervailing forces, which imposed discipline on individual capitals in the ultimate interest of capitalism as a system. These comments have been much discussed and elaborated in more recent theoretical writings about the capitalist state (though that discussion sometimes seems to proceed on the odd assumption that an acquaintance with the text of *Capital* is a sufficient encounter with the real history Marx was trying to comprehend).[14] The impact of legislation on the labour process and on the social reproduction of labour-power is among the important issues raised in Marx's analysis, and I have taken it up in the present work.

The historiography of factory reform has perhaps been most strongly influenced by late Victorian and Edwardian perspectives, which retained their influence down to the extension of the 'welfare state' after 1945. These views were shaped by the context of political democratisation, the growth of labour politics, the expansion of the national and local state and debates surrounding 'collectivism'. Of varying political persuasions, these accounts have in common a somewhat Whiggish view of constitutional progress and social evolution, which achieved some rational control over the chaos of economic and social change and the excesses of *laissez-faire*. As the Hammonds confidently asserted: 'the English people began to devise constructive institutions, such as the Civil Service, the Trade Unions, and the system of Factory Law'.[15] Successive extensions and consolidations of legislation, from its initial application to textile factories, could be readily placed in a perspective of gradualist progress. Within this, differing importance might be attached to working-class pressure (the Hammonds' 'trade unions'), the administrative zeal of officials and politicians ('the civil service' and the 'system of factory law') or to an enlightened public opinion.[16]

Views of factory regulation as part of a broad-based enlightened consensus can in fact be traced back to the immediate aftermath of the battles of the 1830s and 40s; the benefits of legislation came to form part of a

---

[13] K. Marx, *Capital, vol. I* (Pelican edn, Harmondsworth, 1976), pp. 394–5.
[14] B. Jessop, *The Capitalist State* (Oxford, 1982); for an analytic inventory of Marx's and Engels' own views, see P. Phillips, *Marx and Engels on Law and Laws* (Oxford, 1980).
[15] J.L. Hammond and B. Hammond, *The Rise of Modern Industry* (6th edn, London, 1946; orig. edn 1925), p. x. Cf., e.g., J. Morley, *The Life of Richard Cobden* (10th edn, 1903), p. 303, and the views of Alfred Marshall, quoted by Nardinelli, *Child Labor*, p. 105.
[16] B.L. Hutchins and A. Harrison, *A History of Factory Legislation* (3rd edn, London, 1926); M.W. Thomas, *The Early Factory Legislation* (Leigh-on-Sea, 1947).

conventional wisdom in the rhetoric of workers' representatives, prominent employers and politicians across a spectrum of opinion. The
construction of this view, with its ambiguities and its silences, will be one
problem addressed in this study (see especially chapter 8 below). Within
this framework, Tory–Evangelical influences have often been singled out
for emphasis in historical retrospect. There has been a particular focus on
the role of Lord Ashley (subsequently Lord Shaftesbury), that mid-
Victorian icon of patrician Christian benevolence. This can also be linked
to a wider social interpretation, emphasising the landed gentry as a
counterweight to industrial capital, taking opportunistic 'revenge' for the
repeal of the corn laws, but also acting as bearers of a more deeply rooted
ethic of social responsibility. In addition to the role of Ashley, this interpretation rests on the flamboyant Tory populism of Richard Oastler, and
the activities of G.S. Bull and a few other Anglican clerics.[17] The links
between Toryism and factory reform have been reinforced by the creation
of 'retrospective Tories' from certain local radical activists who subsequently aligned with the Tories, with the decline of Chartism and the
squeezing of the space for an independent radicalism.[18]

The 'Tory–Radical alliance' for factory reform may thus be in large
measure a retrospective construct. Recent studies have placed more
emphasis on the popular radical elements in short-time activity, its base in
working-class organisations and links to Chartism.[19] Propertied advocates of the ten-hours bill included independent radicals like Fielden,
functioning as parliamentary spokesmen for popular radicalism, and to
some extent for Chartism. Fielden's death rendered him unavailable for
reconstruction as a 'retrospective Tory' (though his family did follow this
kind of trajectory); but, as Stuart Weaver has argued, Fielden's politics
belonged as much to the radical edge of Liberal Dissent, as to some
incipient Tory populism.[20] In recent scholarship the factory movement
has appeared more clearly as an episode in the making of the working

---

[17] See J.T. Ward, *The Factory Movement, 1830–1855* (London, 1962). On key figures, C.
Driver, *Tory Radical: The Life of Richard Oastler* (New York, 1946), remains indispensable;
G.B.A.M. Finlayson, *The Seventh Earl of Shaftesbury* (London, 1981), is the most recent
scholarly biography, earlier studies include one by the Hammonds; B. Hilton, *The Age of
Atonement: The Influence of Evangelicalism upon Social Thought, 1785–1865* (paperback
edn, Oxford, 1991), for an important reappraisal of evangelical thought, as well as of
many other themes relevant to this study.

[18] J.R. Saunders, 'Working-class movements in the West Riding textile district, 1829–1839',
PhD, University of Manchester, 1984, pp. 360–1.

[19] Ibid., ch. 5; R.A. Sykes, 'Popular politics and trade unionism in south-east Lancashire,
1829–44', PhD, University of Manchester, 1982, pp. 425–37; S.A. Weaver, 'The political
ideology of short-time', in G. Cross (ed.), *Worktime and Industrialization: An International
History* (Philadelphia, 1988).

[20] S.A. Weaver, *John Fielden and the Politics of Popular Radicalism, 1832–1847* (Oxford,
1987).

class. I certainly see it in that way myself. But I have also tried to take seriously the frequent cross-class appeals of its rhetoric, and to explore the
construction of wider alliances, whether with Tory or Liberal elites. I
would argue that gender, patriarchy and languages of 'patriarchal protection' were important dimensions of this process.

Feminist perspectives have drawn attention to the patriarchal, as well as
class, interests involved in reshaping divisions of labour and labour processes. 'Protective legislation', of which the early factory acts were a key
instance, has been viewed in this light.[21] The regulation of women's
employment is seen as reinforcing job segregation and their marginalisa-
tion in the 'public' sphere of the formal economy. Short-time agitation
helped construct the 'male breadwinner' ideology, in which the
Evangelical values of patrician reformers like Ashley converged with the
exclusionist interests of male workers. The much-discussed social settlement of the mid-century then appears as a negotiated collusion of organised male workers, employers and the state to subordinate and exploit
working-class women.

Contemporaries and some of the earlier historians were aware of this
dimension, although they also noted the tactical use of protected workers
as stalking-horses, in campaigns 'really' aimed at shorter hours for the
men.[22] Such tactics would seem to undermine the logic of excluding
women from factory work altogether. This apparent contradiction indicates the importance of looking closely at the construction of gender and
class in specific contexts, and taking account of varying practical implications. Pervasive concerns, across class divides, to restabilise a form of
patriarchal nuclear family did not necessarily lead to coherent or consistent strategies or programmes. The most extensively discussed case is that
of the 1842 Mines Act, and this does not necessarily provide an appropriate model for the factory acts, which were themselves variable in their significance.[23] The debate on the Mines Act does, however, provide a very
important model in its attention to the complexity of alliances around
class and gender issues, and to regional and local variations. Finally, fem-

[21] W. Seccombe, 'Patriarchy stabilised: the construction of the male breadwinner norm in
nineteenth-century Britain', *Social History* 11 (1986); M. Valverde, '"Giving the female a
domestic turn": the social, legal and moral regulation of women's work in British cotton
mills, 1830–1850', *Journal of Social History* 21 (1988); S. Walby, *Patriarchy at Work*
(Cambridge, 1986); and *Social History* 13 (1988), thematic issue on 'gender and employment'.
[22] Hutchins and Harrison, *History of Factory Legislation*, pp. 65–6, 109–110.
[23] A.V. John, *By the Sweat of their Brow: Women Workers at Victorian Coal Mines* (paperback
edn, London, 1984); J. Humphries, 'Protective legislation, the capitalist state and
working class men: the case of the 1842 Mines Regulation Act', *Feminist Review* no. 7
(spring 1981), and subsequent debate, ibid. no. 9 (autumn 1981).

inist work has indicated the importance of taking languages of social enquiry and intervention seriously; for men and for women, a patriarchal rhetoric was, after all, part of the *substance* of the matter. My emphasis on the varied, sometimes incoherent, practical effects of such rhetoric should not be taken to imply that it is irrelevant, or the simple epiphenomenon of a struggle whose essential meaning is to be sought at the level of class analysis.

This study will therefore examine the variable and contested meanings of the factory question, and the construction of these meanings in specific contexts, in both time and space. I argue that this is related to the wider construction of 'industrial England' as a functioning society, marked by particular patterns of social difference and conflict.

I have also set out to examine factory regulation as an episode in the formation of the early and mid-Victorian 'liberal state', and of the imagined imperial Britain, in which industrial England occupied an important place. Historians have long debated the nature of the Victorian state and the respective contributions to it of Benthamism, Tory paternalism, Evangelical zeal and administrative pragmatism.[24] More recently, Mandler's important study has sought to recover the active contributions of a specifically Whig aristocratic paternalism and interventionism.[25] One issue is that of continuity and change in governing elites. The continued aristocratic presence at the political centre, and in much of the administrative state, might reinforce a thesis of 'gentlemanly capitalism' and the limited impact of industry.[26] On the other hand, attention has also been drawn to the role of key individuals identified with rationalising liberal reform, and linked to middle-class networks in manufacturing towns.[27] Such figures are perhaps best defined in terms of their rather precarious claims to professionalism.

The extent to which these professionalised intellectuals were enabled to take agenda-setting initiatives is one important issue in the analysis of state formation. Factory regulation provides an illuminating case-study.

[24] See esp. P. Corrigan (ed.), *Capitalism, State Formation and Marxist Theory* (London, 1980); O. MacDonagh, 'The nineteenth-century revolution in government: a reappraisal', *Historical Journal* 1 (1958); H. Parris, *Constitutional Bureaucracy* (London, 1969); D. Roberts, *Victorian Origins of the Welfare State* (New Haven, 1960); G. Sutherland (ed.), *Studies in the Growth of Nineteenth-Century Government* (London, 1972).

[25] P. Mandler, *Aristocratic Government in the Age of Reform: Whigs and Liberals, 1830–1852* (Oxford, 1989).

[26] See Cain and Hopkins, *British Imperialism*, esp. ch. 3, for a recent interpretative synthesis along these lines.

[27] R. Johnson, 'Educating the educators: educational experts and the state, 1833–1839', in A.P. Donajgrodzki (ed.), *Social Control in Nineteenth-Century Britain* (London, 1977); F. Mort, *Dangerous Sexualities* (London, 1987).

Continued organised pressure, from both employers and workers and their allies, and considerable sensitivity about intervention in labour markets and the workplace, made the issue a thorny one. From the Factory Commission of 1833 onwards, it also provided one sphere of activity for an identifiable group of liberal 'experts', who attempted, with mixed results, to articulate versions of factory reform inflected by their own agendas (especially regarding education). Factory regulation thus exemplifies both the appropriation and partial redefinition of a social issue by a network of intellectuals, and the other forces which limited their practical influence. Socio-legal studies of factory act enforcement have made illuminating contributions here, raising issues about the practical reach of official schemes of reform and the redefinition of agendas through conflict and bargaining.[28]

Concerns with language are relevant to these problems of class, gender and state formation. The 'linguistic turn' in social history forms part of the context of this work. The short-time movement has an obvious bearing on 'languages of class'.[29] I shall give sustained attention to languages of radical constitutionalism and popular evangelicalism (of the Methodist, rather than patrician Anglican variety). Both of these combined an address to working-class people with cross-class moralising appeals. The factory movement is of particular interest for the mobilisation of such languages to address employment relations. Radicalism and evangelicalism were also of course gendered languages, and I investigate the complex and often ambiguous positioning of class and gender in ten-hours rhetoric. Finally, it will be necessary to consider the relationship of popular rhetorics to other, less confrontational languages of reform – whether of patrician Evangelical, enlightened Whig or Benthamite derivation – and to the pressure of the state and its agents in establishing a preferred language of public debate. This, too, is to be seen as a complex process, as the site of contestation and renegotiation rather than as the imposition of a single, all-encompassing authoritative discourse.

A range of discourses influenced people's understandings of industrial change. Sermons, journalism, medical tracts and various fictions have to be read alongside the parliamentary and extra-parliamentary speeches, offi-

---

[28] P. Bartrip and P. Fenn, 'The evolution of regulatory style in the nineteenth-century British factory inspectorate', *Journal of Law and Society* 10 (1983); W.G. Carson, 'The conventionalization of early factory crime', *International Journal of the Sociology of Law* 7 (1979); S. Field, 'Without the law?: professor Arthurs and the early factory inspectorate', *Journal of Law and Society* 17, no. 4 (1990), pp. 445–68.

[29] Stedman Jones, *Languages of Class*; see also J.W. Scott, *Gender and the Politics of History* (New York and Oxford, 1988). Weaver, 'Political ideology of short-time' emphasises the radical language of working-class short-time activism.

cial reports, pamphlets and placards that more directly addressed the factory question. I have tried to identify the inter-textualities involved in this range of cultural representations, and the appropriation and transformation of language and metaphor. In charting such shifts, it is important to pay close attention to the adaptation of language in different contexts, to consider language use and language users, as well as the formal characteristics of particular discourses. The cultural competences of different publics affected the possibilities of appropriation. It is worth noting that, for working-class publics, these competences were by no means inconsiderable.[30] It is also important to realise that the available evidence, especially regarding popular political and cultural expression, constitutes a series of fragmentary traces of a wider linguistic field. The popular meanings of the factory question were, for example, conveyed in the visual imagery of banners, none of which survive (though descriptions of them do).[31]

Attempts to establish specific discourses as preferred ways of talking about particular topics involved an anxious policing of the boundaries, and rarely went uncontested. This policing is to be seen, for example, in the concern of less outspoken reformers to dissociate their views from the 'excessive' language of popular figures like Richard Oastler. There are some grounds for regarding the second quarter of the nineteenth century as a period of some cultural uncertainty, when discursive hierarchies were unsettled and open to challenge. The years around the mid-century, on the other hand, show signs of a process of greater settlement. In this sense, it is possible to adduce cultural evidence for the much-debated thesis of a mid-century diminution in social conflicts. As Samuel Kydd put it in his near-contemporary account of the factory movement: 'It is just possible that the principal actors in the stirring scenes of these times were they now to read their own speeches, as then reported, would do so with astonishment.'[32] This shift should not, however, be taken to imply

---

[30] Cf. S. Harper, *Picturing the Past: The Rise and Fall of the British Costume Film* (London, 1994), 'Introduction'. On nineteenth-century working-class cultural competences, esp. B. Maidment (ed.), *The Poorhouse Fugitives* (paperback edn, Manchester, 1992); C. Steedman, *The Radical Soldier's Tale: John Pearman, 1819–1908* (London, 1988); D. Vincent, *Literacy and Popular Culture* (Cambridge, 1989).

[31] See below, ch. 1 n. 71; ch. 8 n. 36.

[32] 'Alfred' [Samuel Kydd], *The History of the Factory Movement*, 2 vols. (1857), vol. II, p. 59. For the debate on mid-century transition, see, e.g., J. Foster, *Class Struggle and the Industrial Revolution: Early Industrial Capitalism in Three English Towns* (London, 1974); R. Gray, *The Aristocracy of Labour in Nineteenth-Century Britain, c. 1850–1914* (London, 1981); P. Joyce, *Work, Society and Politics: The Culture of the Factory in Later Victorian England* (Brighton, 1980); N. Kirk, *The Growth of Working-Class Reformism in Mid-Victorian England* (Beckenham, 1985); H.J. Perkin, *The Origins of Modern English Society* (London, 1969); T.R. Tholfsen, *Working-Class Radicalism in Mid-Victorian England* (London, 1976).

the disappearance of social tensions, or their containment within some dominant discourse. In so far as there was wider acceptance of an authoritative language of debate, it simply altered the terms of conflict.

These issues are examined in the local and regional context of the factory districts of Lancashire and the West Riding, the classical territory of the 'industrial revolution'. This was the main regional base of the ten-hours campaigns, as well as of much other social protest, and the main referent of the imagery of industrialism circulated among a wider public. The economic and social development of these areas has been widely discussed, but a brief outline may be useful at this stage. Here, and throughout the book, I focus on cotton in Lancashire and adjoining parts of Cheshire and Derbyshire, and wool and worsted in the West Riding of Yorkshire. In 1850, these districts accounted respectively for 80 per cent of all cotton operatives, 50 per cent of all woollen operatives and 89 per cent of all worsted operatives in the United Kingdom, as enumerated in returns collected by the factory inspectors. Cotton, most of it in Lancashire and adjacent counties, was the biggest branch of textiles, accounting for over half the UK total of operatives.[33] Silk (in Cheshire) and flax (in Yorkshire) accounted for appreciable numbers of factory workers; and several firms in fancy woollens and worsteds specialised in varieties of mixed fabrics. Statements about the limited extent of factory production have to be set in the context of this marked regional concentration. Hundreds of thousands of potentially aggrieved, or even simply demoralised, factory workers constituted a social fact of some significance.

There were also of course substantial textile industries elsewhere in the United Kingdom, the largest numbers outside the north of England being in Scotland. I therefore refer advisedly to 'industrial *England*'; the phrase is not intended as a surrogate for industrial Britain. It was however a British parliament that deliberated on legislation applicable throughout the United Kingdom, and I do touch on Scottish contributions to the terms of debate at that level.

Economic change was associated with increasing regional specialisation, and complex differences within the major industries and regions.[34] In cotton, spinning, the most thoroughly mechanised industrial process, became concentrated in south-east Lancashire, while power-loom facto-

---

[33] Calculated from returns of numbers employed, etc., PP 1850 (745) XLII; and see D.T. Jenkins, 'The validity of the factory returns, 1833–1850', *Textile History* 4 (1973).

[34] The following discussion draws especially on: D.A. Farnie, *The English Cotton Industry and the World Market, 1815–1896* (Oxford, 1979); P. Hudson, *The Genesis of Industrial Capital: A Study of the West Riding Wool Textile Industry, c. 1750–1850* (Cambridge, 1986); Joyce, *Work, Society and Politics*; Kirk, *Growth of Reformism*; J.K. Walton, 'The north west', in Thompson (ed.), *Cambridge Social History*, vol. I.

ries superseded handlooms in a belt further north, round Blackburn, Burnley and Accrington. However both spinning and weaving were to be found throughout the cotton area; many large ('combined') firms incorporated both processes. There were also local specialisations in finer or coarser yarns and fabrics. Manchester and Bolton were centres of fine spinning, whereas Oldham, the Ashton and Stalybridge area and Blackburn were engaged in the expanding, and fiercely competitive, medium and coarse sectors. Bolton, an old mercantile town eclipsed by the rise of Manchester, also specialised in fancy goods, retaining handloom weaving and elements of the merchant-manufacturing tradition. Oldham was characterised by the proliferation of small and medium-sized spinning concerns, as well as some bigger ones. The Ashton–Stalybridge district and Blackburn were both notable for the rise of large combined firms.

The spinning-mule, the prevalent type of machine adopted in the Lancashire cotton region, was one of the celebrated inventions of the late eighteenth century, and became something of a symbol of the industrial supremacy of the region, or indeed of the nation.[35] Adult male mule spinners, the most important organised group of factory operatives, were struggling to consolidate their position as skilled workers within the factory, and to impose male control of the trade. They retained responsibility for hiring and supervising the piecers who assisted them; these, too, were increasingly male, and the most suitable (or best connected) of them would eventually be promoted to spinner. Attention has focused on mule spinning, either as a technological achievement or as the site of industrial conflict. This can obscure the continued use of the throstle, a development of Arkwright's spinning-frame. This machine, tended by female and juvenile workers, was particularly adapted to the spinning of stronger coarse yarns for warps. It should also be noted that the actual spinning was only the last of a series of processes in the mill. These preparatory processes (carding, stretching, etc.) accounted for a substantial part of the work-force, many of them women and young workers. Power-loom weaving, which expanded rapidly from the 1830s, was a major sector of female employment, and the best-paid work for women.

The West Riding of Yorkshire was associated with the wool and worsted sectors. The woollen districts stretched in a wide arc, from north of Leeds to Huddersfield and on to Saddleworth; the worsted district lay to the north of this, round Keighley, Bradford and Halifax. Calderdale (the rural part of the huge parish of Halifax, extending towards

---

[35] The selective nature of representations of industrial work is discussed in ch. 5, below.

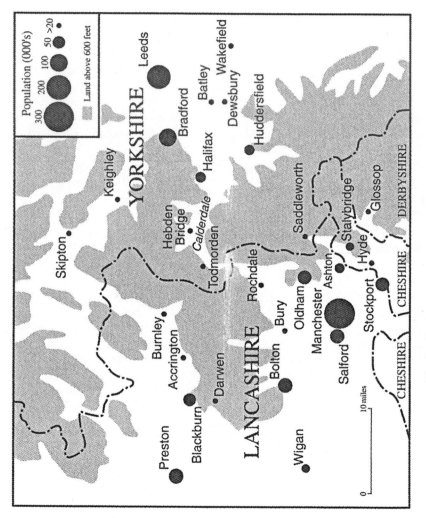

Textile districts of northern England, c 1851

Population (000's)

300
200
100
50
>20

Land above 600 feet

YORKSHIRE

Leeds
Bradford
Batley
Wakefield
Dewsbury
Halifax
Huddersfield
Keighley
Hebden
Bridge
Calderdale
Todmorden
Skipton
Saddleworth
Stalybridge
Glossop
Hyde
Ashton
DERBYSHIRE
Burnley
Accrington
Darwen
Rochdale
Bury
Oldham
Manchester
Stockport
CHESHIRE
Salford
Bolton
LANCASHIRE
Preston
Blackburn
Wigan
CHESHIRE

0   10 miles

Todmorden and the county boundary) was an area of mixed industrial composition, with local concentrations of wool, worsted and cotton; Saddleworth was also a mixed area, with wool and cotton. In the woollen district, heavy woollens were concentrated round Dewsbury, fancy cloths round Huddersfield. Towns like Leeds and Huddersfield developed as merchanting and finishing centres for a dispersed rural manufacture, and retained their specialisation in finishing. Woollen cloth manufacture involved a complicated mix of mill, workshop and domestic processes. Some firms incorporated more of these processes into integrated factory units (including the employment of hand-workers on the factory premises); others provided mill services for the domestic clothiers. Worsted underwent a rapid transition to mechanised spinning, using spinning-frames with a juvenile and female work-force. The preparatory worsted process of combing employed large numbers of adult men as out-workers, as did handloom weaving. The mechanisation of weaving, and later of combing, was a protracted process.

The experience of work varied, both between and within the main industrial sectors. Factory labour could have different meanings, and the definition of the factory as a distinct type of workplace was itself a construct of the debates considered in this book. Out-work and artisanal trades also underwent varied patterns of change. Factory and non-factory work should be seen in their interrelations, rather than as polar opposites. Many working-class people had some experience of both. Changes in the age and gender composition of the labour-force were an important issue in debates about the factory. In the 1850 returns, the proportion of adult men was greatest in wool (40 per cent), lower in cotton (30 per cent) and lowest in worsted (18 per cent).[36] Employment of very young children was probably declining by the 1830s (though unevenly; child labour remained more prominent in worsted than in cotton). There was a corresponding growth in teenaged workers of both sexes and in adult women (who unfortunately cannot be distinguished in the official returns which, characteristically, combined all women aged thirteen and above into a single category, reflecting the legislative treatment of women as 'young persons' from 1844). Age and gender composition also varied within industries between types of mill and districts. While the employment of very young workers is often associated with particular technologies (such as the early water-powered 'Arkwright mills'), there is also evidence of variations between districts employing similar technologies.[37] The most widely circulated image of the factory child was probably that of a scavenger or piecer in the spin-

---

[36] Factory returns, 1850.   [37] See below, ch. 6, table 6.1 and text.

ning-room. But in fact children might be employed at a wide range of tasks, and technology was only one variable affecting labour recruitment practices.

The factory question has often been treated, both by contemporaries and historians, as part of the debate about working-class standards of living. This book makes no claim to contribute to that long-running controversy. It does however depend on the simple observation that there was a widespread sense of deterioration and insecurity in the second quarter of the nineteenth century, across the textile districts. Much of the evidence considered below cannot sensibly be interpreted on any other basis.

The various factory towns and districts thus had distinctive characteristics, and it will be argued below that these had some relevance to struggles over factory regulation. Places which might look alike to outside observers had strongly marked local characteristics. This localism was in some ways reinforced by the expansion of industry, which absorbed growing populations that would otherwise have dispersed through migration.[38] Local distinctiveness was composed of the *longue durée* of land tenure and inheritance patterns, manorial or ecclesiastical governance and cultural tradition, as well as the make-up of industry. Continuity and change were interdependent processes, and it was often through these existing institutions and practices that industrial capital established itself. The sense of place, which defined the subjective reality of localities, was fluid and variable, differently understood by different social actors, or in different social contexts. Popular understandings of locality diverged from administrative boundaries, civic definitions of community by would-be local elites, or the maps of itinerant officials, such as factory inspectors. The 'township', a word whose etymological roots refer to a collectivity of people rather than to a demarcated space, was one characteristic focus of organisation, especially where industrial settlements expanded in distant parts of large straggling parishes.[39]

Various networks linked localities to each other, and to a wider world. Contemporary observers were sometimes bewildered by the juxtaposition of what they took to be the leading edge of industrial technology,

---

[38] P. Hudson, 'The culture of industrialising communities', paper at symposium 'Conflict and Change in English Communities and Regions'; I am much indebted to papers and discussion at this symposium.

[39] R. Pearson, 'Knowing one's place: perceptions of community in the industrial suburbs of Leeds, 1790–1890', *Journal of Social History* 27 (1993); I owe the point about the 'township' to Steve Caunce, comments at symposium on 'Conflict and Change in English Communities and Regions'.

strongly linked to world markets, and intense popular attachments to local identities and traditions.[40] Modernity was not all of a piece. Enlightened professional men and employers could be seen as agents of improvement in this respect, cultural brokers between the locality and wider networks of the nation-state and the world market. But the Methodist circuit, Chartist agitation and the ten-hours movement itself also linked localities to wider networks, on rather different terms.

I am particularly concerned with these processes of mediation. The resources of language considered in this study resonated within industrial localities, while representations of the factory districts contributed to the image of 'industrial England', part of the imagined liberal and progressive nation of the mid-century years. Whatever conclusions are to be drawn about the impact of the industrial revolution, it certainly produced types of community, patterns of class relations and of popular culture which retain a unique historical significance. The meanings of 'class' have often been bound up with regional identities associated with 'industrial England'.[41] This found condensed expression in the conflicts and debates considered in this book.

[40] See, e.g., description of Oldham, in *Penny Magazine*, supp. , June 1843, pp. 241–3.
[41] See P. Joyce, *Visions of the People: Industrial England and the Question of Class, 1840–1914* (Cambridge, 1991).

Part 1

Voices in a debate, *c.* 1830–1850

1   Factory slavery

Attempts to regulate factory employment can be traced back, almost to the beginnings of factory production itself. The restructuring of labour markets and employment relations during early industrialisation was accompanied by a series of overlapping debates about protective labour laws, the poor laws and statutory or customary controls over wages, prices and commercial practice.[1] Such debates involved a shifting balance of propertied interests, patrician notions of enlightened benevolence and pressure from below by working communities. The issue of factory children, and by implication of the broader regulation of factory production, arose in this context. During the first three decades of the nineteenth century, campaigns for regulation involved the Lancashire mule-spinners, in conjunction with merchants, professional men and some 'enlightened' manufacturers.[2]

In the 1830s, these concerns were crystallised in a new way, to constitute the 'factory question' of the early Victorian period. This was no doubt a function of the increasing extent of the factory textile sector, including its development in the West Riding wool and worsted industries.[3] But the emerging factory movement was not just a reflex of growth in the size of the population affected. Like other popular causes, the factory movement was driven by responses to the economic insecurities that accompanied industrial growth, cyclical fluctuations and conflicts over control of the labour process. It also had political and cultural

---

[1] See D. Gregory, *Regional Transformation and Industrial Revolution: A Geography of the Yorkshire Woollen Industry* (London and Basingstoke, 1982); I. Prothero, *Artisans and Politics* (London, 1979), chs. 3, 9; A. Randall, *Before the Luddites: Class, Community and Machinery in the English Woollen Industry, 1776–1809* (Cambridge, 1991); J. Rule, 'The property of skill in the period of manufacture', in Joyce (ed.), *Historical Meanings of Work*.

[2] J. Foster, 'The first six factory acts', *Bulletin of the Society for the Study of Labour History* 18 (spring 1969), p. 5; A. Fowler and T. Wyke (eds.), *The Barefoot Aristocrats: A History of the Amalgamated Association of Operative Cotton-Spinners* (Littleborough, Lancs., 1987), pp. 2–3, 30–1; R.G. Kirby and A.E. Musson, *Voice of the People: John Doherty 1798–1854* (Manchester, 1975), ch. 10.

[3] See Gregory, *Regional Transformation*; Hudson, *Genesis of Industrial Capital*.

dimensions. The articulation of the factory question occurred in an expanding public sphere based on new social constituencies in the industrial districts. In that context, working-class men claimed a voice alongside their recently enfranchised middle-class counterparts.[4] These publics had some access, directly or indirectly, to decision-making processes in the reformed political nation. At the same time, a wider cultural circulation of themes and images from the debate about the factory helped establish the place in that reformed nation of distinctive 'industrial' interests and problems.

Factory reform was one of a range of issues, campaigns and pressure-groups proliferating in the 1830s and 40s. All of these claimed a language of reform, Christian benevolence and social and moral order.[5] Among the plethora of issues, what distinguished the factory question was its popular implantation in industrial communities, expressed in the existence of short-time committees, but equally on Chartist and trade union platforms and from the pulpits of popular preachers. The specific demand for a ten-hour day distinguished this popular movement from other, less contentious projects to reform factory conditions. Employer interests, which perceived themselves as threatened by ten-hours agitation could exert some influence in governing circles, based on the claim that industry was vital to the nation's wealth and power. Factory regulation therefore became the site of protracted controversy, resistance and negotiation. In the process the terms of debate were themselves contested and transformed.

In the chapters comprising Part 1 of this book, I outline some of the positions in these debates, their sources and wider cultural resonances, as they emerged in the two decades after 1830. The early ten-hours movement had a number of strands, loosely held together by rhetorics variously composed of popular radical ideas of citizenship and labour as property, patriarchal values, evangelical religion and patrician philanthropy. This chapter will examine the role of working-class radical perspectives in short-time campaigns, constructions of class identities and gender difference in the rhetoric of those campaigns, and the significance of the references to 'slavery' that recur in these debates.

---

[4] On the notion of a working-class public sphere, see G. Eley, 'Edward Thompson, social history and political culture', in H.J. Kaye and K. McClelland (eds.), *E.P. Thompson: Critical Perspectives* (Cambridge, 1990).

[5] See, e.g., P. Hollis (ed.), *Pressure from Without in Early Victorian England* (London, 1974); D. Turley, *The Culture of English Anti-Slavery, 1780–1860* (London, 1991).

Work, gender and short-time agitation

Recent scholarship has emphasised the basis of the short-time movement in working-class organisations, drawing on the networks of popular radicalism, Chartism and trade unionism.[6] In the Lancashire cotton region, the mule spinners were joined by male power-loom weavers, card-room hands and others in a network of short-time committees. In the West Riding, short-time organisation was based on adult male skilled and supervisory factory workers in wool and worsted mills, as well as hand-loom weavers and woolcombers. The county provided the bulk of operative witnesses at Sadler's parliamentary committee (1832); adult male workers giving evidence included fifteen woollen workers (cloth-dressers, slubbers, etc.) mainly from the Leeds and Huddersfield areas, six from the worsted industry (combers, weavers, a woolsorter and an overlooker), five (mainly overlookers) from flax mills, and four outside textiles, giving evidence as parents or (like many weavers and combers) former child workers.[7] It is also likely that the formal short-time organisations were only one aspect of activity to regulate hours. Something of the range of that activity, from petitioning and parliamentary lobbying to workplace resistance to extended working, strikes, mass pickets and crowd violence, should become apparent in the chapters which follow. The demand for a standard working day was never far from the preoccupations of all forms of popular protest in the factory districts, and probably embraced a broader range of workers than those well-organised trades which constituted the public face presented by the movement to parliamentary elite opinion.

The specific demands and aspirations of differently situated occupational groups coalesced in the ten-hours campaign. Given this diversity, it is likely that shared programmes were interpreted in differing ways; ambiguities in the language of factory agitation provided space for diverse interpretations. The debates themselves helped construct notions of the factory as the site of a shared work-experience, as much as they reflected some pre-given commonalty of experience. What was common to the experience of industrial work was not its location in any particular type of productive unit, but the intensification and commodification of labour and the consequent effects on living standards and work-practices.[8] An

[6] See works cited above, n. 2; also: Saunders, 'Working-class movements', ch. 5; Sykes, 'Popular politics and trade unionism in south-east Lancashire', pp. 425–37; Weaver, 'Political ideology of short-time'.

[7] Select Committee on Labour of Children in Factories, PP 1831–2 XV (hereafter cited as 'Select Committee 1832').

[8] Cottereau, 'The distinctiveness of working-class cultures in France', argues this in a French context.

overblown and malign 'factory system' came to stand as a unifying metaphor for a range of problems. The demand for a regulated working day was a consistent theme in workers' responses to these pressures. The strategic importance attached to the factory as a distinct type of workplace was itself a product of the consequent debates.

Industrial change was associated with crises of gender and class relations, and struggles over factory regulation can be seen in the context of a gendered class consciousness. I propose to discuss this, first, from the standpoint of the specific adult male occupations, which dominated formal organisation and the public representation of working-class interests; then to place this in the context of wider communities and the survival strategies of working-class families, from which the analysis of discrete occupations may be an artificial abstraction. In this widened field of vision it is essential to recognise the significance of the formal and informal economic activities of women. This leads on to a discussion of the gendered class consciousness manifested in factory agitation, and of languages of patriarchal protection, which were a site both of class identity and of negotiation with other classes.

Mule spinners, the biggest and best-organised adult male factory occupation, were concerned to control fluctuations in output, investment and employment. Increased job security and control would consolidate their position as artisans within the factory – a consolidation associated with the further masculinisation of piecing, and thereby of the recruitment of future spinners.[9] At the same time, the spinners' position was threatened by the increased size of mules, self-acting machines, 'double-decking' and other practices which tended to raise the ratio of spindles to operatives. Such threats were exacerbated, especially during cyclical downturns, by the availability of trained senior piecers forced to await promotion to spinner. Short-time working, and to some extent the restriction of juvenile and female workers, were stratagems to mitigate these problems.

In the West Riding woollen industry, factory production had grown by the piecemeal aggregation of processes into the mill, with complex and variegated patterns of factory, out-work and artisanal workshop labour.[10] The position of skilled woollen workers as artisans within the factory was perhaps more clearly defined than in the case of the cotton mule spinners. The consequent conflicts over wages and working practices were espe-

---

[9] Fowler and Wyke (eds.), *Barefoot Aristocrats*, chs. 1–3; M. Freifeld, 'Technological change and the "self-acting" mule', *Social History* 11 (1986); W. Lazonick, 'Industrial relations and technical change: the case of the self-acting mule', *Cambridge Journal of Economics* 3 (1979).

[10] See Hudson, *Genesis of Industrial Capital*; Saunders, 'Working-class movements'.

cially sharp in the Dewsbury heavy woollen district. As one employer stated in reply to a questionnaire from the Factory Commission (1833):

N.B. No regulation or Act of Parliament is necessary because the Union among the workpeople dictates to us the wages we are to pay, the men we are to employ, and, if they desired it, would dictate the hours of labour also. Our servants are our masters, and the situation of employer is become exceedingly unpleasant.[11]

In the Leeds and Huddersfield districts, the mechanisation of finishing processes was associated with intensification of male teenaged labour, and threatened to disrupt the balance between factory processes and the domestic clothier. Sadler's witnesses – by no means all of whom were simply recalling conditions in their own childhoods – went into considerable detail about these changes. In cloth-dressing, 'the work is very laborious at the gig, and it is necessary to be uncommonly careful'.[12]

In the worsted sector of the West Riding, it was the out-working preparatory process of combing, as well as weaving, that constituted a basis for adult male operative organisation. Weavers and other out-workers in the worsted and woollen districts were concerned to defend domestic production against the enhanced bargaining-power of large-scale factory enterprises, and the threat that de-skilling would 'DRIVE the Weaver from his Loom, and the Comber from his Shop'.[13] This defence of domestic manufacture was inseparable from anxieties about the factory employment of out-workers' children, and the future viability of the producer household. The large millowner could be seen as a 'monopolist', as more processes were incorporated into woollen mills and the balance of power in worsted shifted to the mechanised spinner. Factory owners also functioned as merchants in the putting-out sector, driving hard bargains and adopting aggressive new marketing practices. Richard Oastler often expressed this view of the millowner as monopolist: 'the common people here say "The Factory System has *robbed* us of *our* capital, *our* trade, and *our* labour"'.[14] Dependence on children's factory earnings, and the consequent draining of labour-power away from the domestic manufacturing household may have added to this image of monopolistic engrossment.

Demands for factory regulation must therefore be located in relation to the working-class family and its survival strategies, not merely to the discrete employment situations of individual (mostly adult male) workers.

---

[11] Royal Commission on Employment of Children in Factories, Supplementary Report, PP 1834 XX (hereafter cited as 'Factory Comm., Supp. Report'), employer questionnaires: West Riding, C.1, p. 87 (J. Nussey, Batley); cf. C. Behagg, 'Controlling the product: work, time and the early industrial labour-force in Britain, 1800–1850', in Cross (ed.), *Worktime and Industrialization.*   [12] Select Committee 1832, q. 1587.
[13] *A Conversation between George Hadfield and Charles Comber,* Oastler coll. broadsides, Goldsmiths' Library.   [14] R. Oastler, *A Letter to Mr. Holland Hoole* (1832), p. 9.

Employment patterns in some cases cut across sectoral differences, and a compartmentalised account of differing industrial structures may distort the complex mosaic of activities (including informal transactions and unwaged labour, especially by women) that were undertaken by labouring households. In regions of mixed industrial composition like Calderdale, the children of woollen weavers might be employed in worsted or cotton throstle-spinning mills; the fathers or husbands of factory workers might also be employed outside textiles altogether, for example as miners.[15] Publicly expressed concerns about the health and morals of child and juvenile workers could be related to anxieties about their future earning-power (and for girls their eligibility as 'respectable' wives and home-makers) on leaving the mill in their later teens. Factory agitation involved a series of community responses to the impact of factory expansion, affecting artisans and out-workers as well as those directly engaged in factory work; many, perhaps most, adult workers in the textile districts had in any case spent some time in the factory as children.

In this defence of a 'family economy', gender divisions were central to the articulation of class interests: 'Work and family were not separate spheres but interrelated concepts with the need for remunerative work vital to maintain a particular household order.'[16] The unfolding debate on the factory was to be strongly inflected by values of 'separate spheres' – the institutional separation of 'home' and 'work' and the designation of the latter as a properly masculine sphere. Working-class adult men were also enabled to position themselves as political protagonists, and as upright independent citizens seeking decent livelihoods from their honest toil. But the reality was a network of interdependencies, in which the contributions of all household members were crucial, and such unwaged activities as child-minding were closely geared to the exigencies of waged work in industry.[17] Survival strategies could entail the involvement of family members in a variety of different formal and informal economic activities. The 'family economy' rarely dovetailed neatly with a single source of employment, whether in factory or domestic sectors. Even the image of the weaving household working as a team may be misleading; individu-

---

[15] See, e.g., comments on labour recruitment in notebook 'Mytholmroyd Mill', Fielden Papers, W. Yorks. RO, C353/341; Gardner and Bazley, MS return of hands employed, 15 April 1844, Haggas Bryan Coll., Bolton Archives, ZHB/1/5, gives husbands' occupations of married women employed.

[16] C. Evans, 'The separation of work and home?: the case of Lancashire textiles, 1825–65', PhD, University of Manchester, 1990, p. 25.

[17] M. Anderson, *Family Structure in Nineteenth-Century Lancashire* (Cambridge, 1971).

als might take in separate pieces of work and deal with different employers or middlemen.[18] In the factory, the undoubted significance of kinship in employment rarely incorporated a complete nuclear family, but links between mothers and children, older and younger siblings, fathers and sons, uncles and nephews and more distant kin. The idealised family economy implied the economic power and authority of the husband and father. But this authority might co-exist, in a greater or lesser degree of tension, with the need for independent initiative by other family members. In addition to their own economic activities, women must often have negotiated their children's employment. At one of the Fielden mills in Calderdale, labour recruitment turned on the role of a weaver's wife and her children.[19]

Working-class women were therefore closely involved in the exigencies of factory employment, and should be seen as potential protagonists in struggles over factory conditions. Apart from their own waged factory work, they were important gatekeepers between the family and employment, and their (largely silent) symbolic presence was invoked from ten-hours platforms; they must also have been important in sustaining the community networks that underpinned popular agitation.[20] But in the public discourses of factory agitation they were marginalised; while their waged work, crucial as it was to family survival, could also be seen as undermining the position of the idealised male breadwinner. Both gender and class were sites of interdependence, conflict and negotiation. Radical working-class perspectives on the factory question embodied shifting constructions of these conflicts and solidarities. The maintenance of perceived class interests was also the construction of a particular system of gender relations.

Workers envisaged factory regulation in terms of an equalisation of the balance between labour and capital, which would restore the independence and livelihood of working men. The property of men in their skilled labour entitled them to regular work under fair conditions and to a degree of moral independence and respect. This 'artisan ideal' seems to have extended beyond the ranks of artisans narrowly considered, to embrace mule-spinners, weavers, woolcombers and other textile workers.[21] Ideas of fairness could have different meanings. The property in labour and access to livelihood could be located at the level of the individual (skilled?) 'working man' – as was perhaps to become the dominant

---

[18] S. Moore, 'Women, industrialisation and protest in Bradford, West Yorkshire, 1780–1845', PhD, University of Essex, 1988, p. 85.
[19] 'Mytholmroyd Mill', Fielden Papers.
[20] Moore, 'Women, Industrialisation and protest', pp. 152–4.
[21] For the 'artisan ideal' see Prothero, *Artisans and Politics*; Rule, 'Property of skill'.

definition in the second half of the century[22] – or the household considered as a productive unit. This might also imply a community network of
producer interests, including areas of informal economy, articulated in
terms of customary reciprocal interests in 'the trade'.[23] These different
versions can to some extent be associated with the uneven development
of industrial sectors. In *The Poor Man's Advocate,* edited and mainly
written by John Doherty, the Manchester spinners' leader, reciprocity
and equal exchange are constructed in terms of the wage bargain, 'for if a
working man perform his contract to his employer, if he gives value for all
that he receives, there can be no obligation, much less any inferiority on
his part'.[24] In the woollen industry, fair employment could be seen in
more corporatist terms, related to the defence of domestic production
and a balance of interests threatened by disruption. Proprietors of
'company mills', who regarded their mill as 'no factory', but a facility servicing the domestic clothier, might articulate these views: 'the more you
shorten the . . . hours in the factories (I mean where power is applied) the
more you enable the industrious and highly valuable domestic clothier to
come nearer in competition with the opulent factory master'.[25]

These ideas of fair employment were linked to an alternative political
economy. This might be associated with a variety of political positions, as
the role of Richard Oastler testifies, but the links to popular radicalism were
of particular significance for working-class activism.[26] Short-time working
would even out economic fluctuations, strengthen the bargaining position
of adult male workers and raise wages in the longer run. There was a
connection between overwork and low pay. While individuals might raise
their earnings by working longer, 'you must for the *whole,* reason collectively
. . . over-production invariably sinks, not indeed the *intrinsic,* but the
exchangeable value of every article or commodity'.[27] This economic analysis
was linked to the radical claim to citizenship. The Huddersfield Political
Union argued in support of Sadler's Bill and 'against oppression in general':
'no individual, or any number of individuals, has a *right* (nor ever had, nor
ever will) to exercise a power over another, or any number of individuals,

[22] K. McClelland, 'Time to work, time to live: some aspects of work and the re-formation of class in Britain, 1850–1880', in Joyce (ed.), *Historical Meanings of Work*; and idem, 'Some thoughts on masculinity and the "representative artisan" in Britain, 1850–80', *Gender and History* 1 (1989).   [23] Cf. Berg, *Age of Manufactures*, chs. 6, 7.

[24] 'The justice of exposing tyrannical employers', prospectus for *The Poor Man's Advocate,* bound with copies in Goldsmiths' Library.

[25] Factory Comm., Supp. Report, employer questionnaires, C.1, pt ii, no. 77; see also nos. 78, 218, 279; cf. Select Committee 1832, qq. 431–586.

[26] See M. Berg, *The Machinery Question and the Making of Political Economy* (Cambridge, 1980), pt V; Weaver, 'Political ideology of short-time'.

[27] *The Justice, Humanity and Policy of Restricting the Hours of Children and Young Persons in the Mills and Factories of the United Kingdom* (1833), p. 71, speech by J. Hanson at Halifax.

which if exercised over themselves, they would consider, and call unjust . . .
social right either does or ought to emanate from the natural one'.[28]

Popular radicalism and alternative political economy therefore
attempted to empower the adult male worker as citizen, resisting the
impositions of arbitrary power in the workplace and the wider polity.
Legal protection of juvenile workers, or even of labour more generally,
was part of a just social contract between government and citizens.[29] The
claim to independence and citizenship implied the dependence of women
and juveniles. Factory agitation can be located in a developing 'working-
class public sphere', in which gender difference as well as class identity
were constructed.[30] Both the organisational forms and the public rhetoric
of the movement positioned women as symbolic dependants. It was men
who formed committees, made speeches, wrote placards and pamphlets,
lobbied potential sympathisers at local or parliamentary levels.

Women could be rhetorically addressed, as the mothers of innocent children and bearers of domestic virtue. *The Poor Man's Advocate* appealed to
'the mothers of children, we call upon the ladies of England', as well as 'the
mothers of those poor children themselves' to join the struggle against the
'proud oppressor'.[31] At meetings in the West Riding, the presence of 'here
and there, a mother clasping an infant to her breast, kissing it, and exclaim-
ing: "Factory slave thou shalt never be"' produced 'a dramatic interest,
remarkable, intense, and exciting'.[32] Such meetings represent a relatively
open and accessible form of activity, probably drawing on the practices of
popular Methodism, in which women's voices were audible, though never
from the platform. Those voices were mediated through a platform
rhetoric playing on the association of motherhood with 'nature' and
hinting at the threat of social breakdown and more active resistance.

And think you not that English Christian mothers feel as fondly for their young as
does the lioness? Ah, yes, they do, yet they have not the power of the lioness, but in
solitude and confinement are condemned to mourn over the helpless fate of their
offspring, and it is on that account they now take a part in our meeting, while we
are attempting that which the public order of society prevents them from doing –
publicly pleading the cause of their infant children.[33]

The possibilities of active resistance, in a situation where legal and
moral order had been undermined by the short-sighted greed of masters

---

[28] *A Few Arguments in Favour of Mr. Sadler's Bill . . . and Against Oppression in General, by a Member of the Huddersfield Political Union* (1833), pp. 4–5.
[29] D.Loftus, 'Natural workers', paper delivered at Women's History Network, Portsmouth, February 1995, explores the meanings of contract in this context.
[30] See Eley, 'Edward Thompson, social history and political culture'.
[31] *The Poor Man's Advocate*, 17 March 1832: one of many instances of ten-hours propaganda mimicking the language of anti-slavery, discussed further below, final section of
this chapter.   [32] 'Alfred', vol. I, p. 235.   [33] 'Alfred', *Factory Movement*, vol. I, p. 230.

working excessive hours, extended to the children themselves, as in Oastler's famous 'law or the needle' speech alluding to industrial sabotage; Joseph Firth, a Keighley operative, described his desire for personal revenge for ill-treatment in his childhood, 'but I have never yet had corporeal strength to do it, and now I am more anxious to combat him with reason and argument'.[34] The emphasis on 'reason and argument' is thus associated with the articulation of a masculine public voice.

As virtuous 'English Christian mothers' (or daughters), women had an important symbolic function in short-time propaganda, as well as, in reality, a crucial organising role in the mobilisation of community sentiment. As factory workers themselves, they might testify to their sufferings, but rarely gained the space to propose solutions. Three female operatives gave evidence to Sadler's Committee, compared to twenty-six adult and nine teenaged males; it was adult men who were invited to offer expositions of the economics of short-time working.[35] That women might nevertheless want to share in the radical search for an alternative political economy is indicated by a remarkable letter in *The Ten Hours Advocate* from 'Elizabeth', apparently a weaver at a mill near Todmorden. Presenting the ten-hours movement as 'this arduous and important struggle for the liberty of our sex, and the protection of our children', Elizabeth suggests that women's indifference to the struggle arose from 'the want of . . . education' and 'mental improvement' resulting from overwork, which had made them 'destitute of all knowledge respecting the *rule* which governs wages'.[36] Elizabeth positions herself as a worker concerned with wages, as well as a woman concerned with protecting children; and the language, which bears traces of Owenism, asserts a claim to arguments from radical political economy. But this was a rare (and possibly unique) instance of a factory woman making comments of a discursive nature on the issues involved. Women's views are otherwise recorded in more summary form, in replies to the questions of politicians, officials or journalists.[37] Elizabeth's intervention elicited a somewhat patronising response from the local short-time committee, praising her fund-raising efforts, but passing over the wider issue she had raised.[38]

Women, despite their obvious presence as waged factory workers and

[34] Driver, *Tory Radical*, p. 327; speech by J. Firth reprinted in *Justice, Humanity and Policy*, p. 75; S.O. Rose, 'Respectable men, disorderly others: the language of gender and the Lancashire weavers' strike of 1878 in Britain' *Gender & History* 5 (1993), discusses the connection between 'reason', restrained behaviour and masculinity.

[35] Select Committee 1832, *passim*.   [36] *The Ten Hours Advocate*, 26 Dec. 1846.

[37] See, e.g., Reports of Factory Inspectors: L. Horner, Dec. 1848, Appendix (all references to these reports in notes will be by inspector's name and date; for full citations see bibliography); J. Ginswick (ed.), *Labour and the Poor in England and Wales: Letters to the Morning Chronicle, 1849–1851* (London and Totowa, N.J., 1983), pp. 117–19.

[38] *The Ten Hours Advocate*, 9 Jan. 1847.

their less visible roles in organising the subsistence of working-class families and sustaining various protest movements, were publicly represented as beneficiaries of the desired reforms, rather than protagonists in the cause. By the same token factory agitation empowered working men as free citizens and manly protectors of their dependants, using 'reason and argument' to further these legitimate interests. But radical analyses constantly slipped into denouncing the threatened degradation of the male worker, forced into unequal bargains with capital and subjected to an oppressive and corrupt state. These contradictions are registered in a series of shifts in the referents of key terms like 'freedom', 'slavery', 'oppression' and 'protection'.

The demand for factory regulation envisaged the protection of specific categories of worker – children, teenagers below eighteen, subsequently adult women – from the rigours of an unregulated labour market. This was, however, linked to a wider conception of the protection of labour as property, threatened by destruction through monopolistic engrossment, intensification of work and over-production. The positioning of working-class men as free citizens established a link between these two levels of 'protection'. As the possessor of property in his own person and labour, the male worker was entitled to maintain his independence, to exercise control over his dependants (including control over their labour and incomes) in return for protecting them, and to expect the law to enable him to do this. The notion of labour as property could reconcile demands for regulation to protect adult men with their claims to free and independent status. The law should protect the *property* of adult men, but the *persons* of women and children.

De-skilling and tightened capitalist control in the workplace threatened to violate these rights, 'the act of stripping men of large portions of their property by violence'.[39] Consequently, 'our adult Operatives have generally no more choice than their children'.[40] This was represented as a threat to masculinity; spinners were obliged to 'go "piecing" for children's wages', and the adult man was 'deprived of his free agency as much as the child'.[41] But this lack of free agency had a particular significance when extended to adult men. Children should be protected because they were not free agents and occupied a subordinate position in the family, while the protection of labour in the broader sense would restore the free agency of adult men. Only 'power in his own hands of shortening the hours of labour' could sustain the worker's threatened rights.[42]

[39] 'Justice of exposing tyrannical employers', in *The Poor Man's Advocate*.
[40] *The Voice of the West Riding*, 13 July 1833.
[41] *McDouall's Chartist and Republican Journal* (1841; consecutively paginated), p. 115; [J. Leech], *Stubborn Facts from the Factories, by a Manchester Operative* (1844), p. 30.
[42] *McDouall's Journal*, p. 115.

The regulation of juvenile, and later of female, labour was one way of achieving this. The protection of these groups involved restriction and dependence, rather than the independent status in the marketplace and the polity, to which radical working men aspired. Active rebellion was the sign of masculinity.

> The father – worst and most wonderful of all – looks on and lives – not a man, but a dumb soul-bound thrall ... who, were there but a spark of life within the bonds-man's breast, dare as soon thrust his hand in the fire as thus pluck his neighbour's wife and babes from his bosom.[43]

There was thus a characteristic shifting, from the vulnerability of the juvenile 'factory slave' to the unequal bargaining-power of employers and adult male workers. Such shifts may of course be interpreted as tactical moves, in a campaign aimed at the *de facto* restriction of adult men's hours. It is certainly true that this was a fairly consistent and explicit aim of short-time committees. Public controversy was generally conducted on the assumption that factory hours for the whole work-force would neces-sarily be fixed by the restricted working day of juvenile workers (although, as was also to become apparent, this assumption of a uniform working day obscured considerable variability in working practices).[44] Strategic importance attached to teenaged workers; many of the 'children' invoked in ten-hours propaganda were actually in their teens. Such workers were becoming relatively more numerous than younger children, forming a large proportion of such key groups as cotton piecers, power-loom weavers and woollen cloth-finishers. As optimistically inclined economic historians point out, the employment of younger children was probably already diminishing by the 1830s – though this was an uneven process, most marked in Lancashire cotton – but such analyses can obscure the issue of teenaged labour.[45] The provisions of the 1833 Factory Act can be related to the changing labour requirements of some segments of textile employers. While the ten-hours movement demanded uniform restric-tion of all below the age of eighteen, the Factory Commission and the 1833 Act distinguished 'children' (aged twelve and below) from 'young persons' (thirteen to seventeen), a manoeuvre which to some extent wrong-footed the popular movement.[46]

---

[43] *The Truth-Teller,* 5 Aug. 1848; publ. at Stalybridge, copy in PRO, HO 45/2410B.

[44] This emerged in the battles over interpretation of the 1847 Ten Hours Act: see below, ch. 7. For public debate and economic and political opinion, see Robson, *On Higher than Commercial Grounds.*

[45] See, e.g., Nardinelli, *Child Labor,* pp. 105–15; official returns of numbers employed often obscure the issue, by lumping all females aged thirteen and over together, following the legal categories of the 1844 Act.

[46] For details of the relevant legislation see U.R.Q. Henriques, *Before the Welfare State: Social Administration in Early Industrial Britain* (London, 1979), chs. 4, 5; Hutchins and Harrison, *History of Factory Legislation*; Thomas, *Early Factory Legislation.*

Anxiety and anger about their children's welfare certainly added force to working-class short-time campaigns. Such feelings were more than a rationalisation of the patriarchal interests of male workers; indeed mothers may well have felt particularly acute anxieties about their children. It is important not to lose sight of the extreme pressure on working-class families, and perceived deteriorations in working and living conditions that underlay social protest. Some of this is graphically conveyed by witnesses at Sadler's Committee. One operative, a Leeds weaver, described his children as 'more like dogs dozing upon a warm hearthstone than like children'; and Joseph Firth from Keighley declared: 'The doctors may examine one man and may examine another man; but I would say, look . . . at the gentlemen's sons, and show me the proportion of the knock-knee'd and the deformed that there is among us.'[47] Another Keighley witness, an assistant overseer of the poor, explained how the system he was obliged to administer drove children to the mill on partial recovery from illness, even though it was quite apparent their health must once more break down.[48] There is also more systematic evidence of a crisis of physical deterioration in the 1830s, with a decline in the heights of males born in industrial regions at this period.[49] Factory employment as such was not necessarily a specific cause of this, but in the factory districts it was hard to separate the impact of factory expansion from frenetic cycles of boom-bust accumulation, economic insecurity and disruption of working lives. Rapid urbanisation, often separated out as a source of illness and death, was itself associated with factory concentration in the textile regions. To grasp the context of factory agitation it is necessary to try to imagine what it might be like to watch the foreseeable but, in the prevailing conditions, unavoidable breakdown in the health of a child.

The expression of these concerns was inseparable from a public language of patriarchal protection. Humane sympathy and stoical endurance, with the poet as detached but concerned observer, is the predominant tone of the various poetic treatments of the death of the factory child.[50] Amelioration was seen in terms both of regulating children's employment, which in a working-class context might itself be understood as the empowerment of adult male workers, and of improved job security and wages for adult men.

[47] Select Committee 1832, q. 963 (J. Drake, Leeds), q. 7005 (J. Firth, Keighley).
[48] Ibid., qq. 5518–30, 5541 (G. Sharpe).
[49] R. Floud, K. Wachter and A. Gregory, *Height, Health and History: Nutritional Status in the United Kingdom, 1750–1850* (Cambridge, 1990), pp. 205, 216, 304–5.
[50] See, e.g., 'Alfred', *Factory Movement*, vol. I, p. 239, vol. II, pp. 309–11; J.C. Prince, *The Death of the Factory Child* (1841), in Maidment (ed.), *Poorhouse Fugitives*, pp. 111–16; and cf. H. Cunningham, *Children of the Poor: Representations of Childhood since the Seventeenth Century* (Oxford, 1991).

Patriarchal protection of dependants also implied gender difference, and was implicitly or explicitly extended to adult women. The longer established concern with protecting children always had gender connotations, which may well have become implanted in the consciousness of working-class activists and their allies. Anxieties about childhood, seen in terms of innocence, danger and dependence, focused particularly on the female child, and implicitly on adult femininity as well. The rhetorical figure of the helpless and vulnerable child was often associated with femininity, just as de-skilling was seen as a threat to masculinity. In a polemic with Holland Hoole, a prominent Manchester manufacturer and opponent of the ten-hours bill, Oastler imagined Hoole's own children forced into the mill by the poor law; the child is given a feminine identity. '"Emma is of sufficient age, – she must go to the factory;" – and for this, he deducts – three shillings a-week; – *her* wages from *your* parish pay!!'[51]

Concerns about physical welfare were closely bound up with moral anxieties, expressed in the language of patriarchal protection. One preoccupation was the age at which children made their own bargains with employers. Eighteen was cited as the age when 'you were your own master' by an informant from Gomersal, whereas in Leeds 'I always bargained for wages ever since I began to work for wages.'[52] Loss of control over children and exposure to 'immorality' was a particularly acute fear with regard to teenage girls. One of Sadler's witnesses apparently broke down when asked about his daughters' conduct: 'impudence and immorality of every description appear to be their growing characteristics . . . a question that is calculated to harrow up the feelings of a parent'.[53] Sexual innuendo figured in protests against the 'inquisitorial' proceedings of the factory commissioners, with inspections of factory children likened to slave auctions: 'There are no crooked legs under the Petticoats – none at all – no ulcers under the stockings.'[54] Fears of seduction by employers or overlookers helped fix a connection between women's waged work outside the home and danger. Peter McDouall, the militant Chartist surgeon, gave a distinctly melodramatic account of rooms set aside at the mill, 'adorned with the appliances of luxury and the conveniences of vice'; this is represented as the theft of working-class young women, the 'most promising flowers of the workman's home', by implication belonging to their fathers or to suitable future husbands.[55]

---

[51] Oastler, *A Letter to Mr. Holland Hoole*, p. 29.
[52] Select Committee 1832, q. 1230, qq. 167–8.
[53] Ibid., q. 1173 (W. Kershaw, Gomersal).
[54] *The Commissioners' Vade Mecum Whilst Engaged in Collecting Evidence for the Factory Masters* (1832), pp. 6–7.
[55] *McDouall's Journal*, p. 155; cf., e.g, Saunders, 'Working-class movements', p. 21.

These accounts drew on popular melodrama and images of the wicked aristocratic seducer symbolising rapacious wealth and power.[56] Anxieties about 'temptation' and molestation (most such incidents probably in fact concerned male *workers*) were condensed and displaced on to an alien class. Patriarchal anxieties about girls and young women could be translated into class resentment and into a class-oriented radicalism that was itself deeply patriarchal in outlook.

By the early 1840s, these attitudes became linked to more specific demands for the regulation of adult women's work. This was a period of rapidly increasing female employment, associated especially with the growth of power-loom factories. Female factory weavers' earnings might at times overtake those of the reserve army of domestic weavers, or other trades under pressure, intensifying the crisis of working-class masculinity in textile communities.[57] Campaigns to extend legislation to adult women could be more or less directly and explicitly related to exclusionary strategies of male workers.[58] Debates about factory regulation provided important platforms for the articulation of the 'male breadwinner norm'.[59] This was sometimes expressed in terms of explicit calls for the exclusion of women from factory employment, for example by a West Riding delegation to Westminster in the depths of the 1842 recession.[60] More often, calls for exclusion formed part of a moralising platform rhetoric, common to Chartists, Tory paternalists and others. However this was tempered in working-class opinion by an awareness of economic pressures, and probably by a perception that women's factory work was not necessarily incompatible with 'respectability' in a working-class frame of reference. Challenged by Sir Robert Peel's case of 'a widow with two daughters' needing to support themselves, the 1842 delegation showed some sensitivity to the point, though they maintained their view.[61]

Apart from directly exclusionary policies, which figured in platform rhetoric more often than in formal programmes, demands for regulation could also be understood as leading to the diminished employment of

[56] Cf. Joyce, *Visions of the People*, p. 101.
[57] L. Davidoff, 'The family in Britain', in Thompson (ed.), *Cambridge Social History*, vol. II, pp. 96–8; for details of women weavers' earnings, C. Johnstone, 'The standard of living of worsted workers in Keighley during the nineteenth century', DPhil, University of York, 1976, pp. 71–2.
[58] For interpretations of protective legislation, see esp. John, *By the Sweat of their Brow*; S.O. Rose, *Limited Livelihoods: Gender and Class in Nineteenth-Century England* (London, 1992); Walby, *Patriarchy at Work*; Valverde, 'Giving the female a domestic turn'.
[59] W. Seccombe, 'Patriarchy stabilised: the construction of the male breadwinner wage norm in nineteenth-century England', *Social History* 11 (1986), pp. 53–76; cf. Evans, 'Separation of work and home?'; Moore, 'Women, industrialisation and protest'.
[60] *The Ten Hours Factory Question: Report Addressed to the Short-Time Committee of the West Riding* (1842), pp. 4–9, 23.   [61] Ibid., p. 5.

restricted categories of worker. This may well have had some relevance to specific sectors of employment, such as mule spinning at the time of the 1844 Act (the first to regulate adult women). By subjecting women of all ages to the same restrictions as juveniles, the Act removed the possibility of employing them as piecers for longer hours, and may thus have helped consolidate male control and the patrimonial spinner-piecer system. Some weavers may have entertained similar, but less realistic, hopes for restoring male employment, either by diminishing women's employment in power-loom weaving or by inhibiting the growth of power-loom factories themselves.

Restrictions on women may thus have aided a process of exclusion in some jobs, and this certainly figured in the rhetoric of short-time agitation, especially in the crisis of the early 1840s. But a longer term and less direct link between factory regulation and the pursuit of the male breadwinner ideal was probably more typical. Diminishing employment of women might figure as a generalised and indistinct *aspiration*, rather than a specific programme or strategy. Shorter hours formed part of a radical political economy, which would in the longer run raise the wages and job security of adult men and thus decrease the dependence of family budgets on the factory earnings of children, juveniles and women. *The Ten Hours Advocate* looked forward to 'the day ... when the husband will be enabled to provide for his wife and family, without sending the former to endure the drudgery of a cotton mill'.[62] But the expected arrival of that day was necessarily vague, open to interpretation by readers in diverse situations. Dependence on the unaided effort of the male breadwinner could be seen as a further stage in a long march of 'improvement', for which the ten-hours bill would be a necessary, but not sufficient condition.

In the immediate prospect, establishing adult men as the principal, but not necessarily sole, breadwinners seemed a more realistic goal. Given the importance of earnings by all employable family members, whether in the factory, at home or elsewhere, the patriarchal interests of adult men were more likely to be expressed in the hierarchy of pay and status within the workplace than in the exclusion of women from it. The earnings of factory-employed children and women were vital to family budgets, and short-time campaigns sought to ensure that such employment was under acceptable conditions and did not undermine the position of adult male labour. The ten-hours movement certainly did not envisage abolition of child labour, nor, for the most part, of female labour. The 'class politics' of short-time working could indeed form part of a patriarchal strategy by working-class men; but it was a strategy envisaged in terms of improvement in the bargaining-power of labour, and especially adult men's labour, rather than the direct exclusion of other categories.

[62] *The Ten Hours Advocate,* 24 Oct. 1846.

Demands for regulation could also, as is often suggested, be a tactic to shorten the hours of adult men.[63] Such tactical use of protected categories, which would seem to cut against the logic of exclusion, was certainly a consistent and abiding aim of factory agitation. It was, for example, quite explicitly claimed that men, too, needed 'more time for rest and for recreation', to maintain life, health and working strength; the ten-hours demand was justified by reference to the norm in many artisan trades.[64] Conventional arguments about the moral importance of feminine virtue could even, in another rhetorical shift, be claimed for men. '[T]he preservation of decency, if not of strict morality, in the male part of any population is an indispensable requisite to the preservation of female modesty . . . there never existed a society in which the men were profligate and the women virtuous.'[65]

But such explicit demands to shorten adult men's hours should not lead us to minimise the wider significance of the language of patriarchal protection adopted by male workers. This was more than the tactical and instrumental quoting of a dominant language; and, in any case, 'tactics have a way of becoming habits'.[66] Even where restriction was not seen as leading to diminished employment of restricted workers, the discourse of patriarchal protection formulated a pervasive set of assumptions about free labour, masculinity and independent and dependant statuses. Such assumptions were not always readily translated into legislative programmes. The relationship between platform rhetoric, the stated or hidden agendas of actors and eventual outcomes is rarely a straightforward one.[67] But assumptions about labour and masculinity nevertheless had real effects, in the cultural empowerment of adult men as workers, breadwinners and citizens.

Plantation slaves and factory slaves

These shifting constructs of freedom, dependence and protection made frequent reference to the concurrent, and more widely supported, agitation against slavery.

Contentious popular uses of 'slavery' as a term of denunciation played an important part in defining the factory question. This was of course

---

[63] Hutchins and Harrison, *History of Factory Legislation*, pp. 65–6, 109–10.

[64] *Bolton Chronicle*, 31 March 1849: *The Ten Hours Advocate*, 3 and 24 Oct. 1846.

[65] *The Ten Hours Advocate*, 24 Oct. 1846.

[66] A. Saxton, *The Indispensable Enemy: Labor and the Anti-Chinese Movement in California* (Berkeley, Calif., 1971), pp. 265–7, as quoted in D.R. Roediger, *The Wages of Whiteness: Race and the Making of the American Working Class* (London and New York, 1991), p. 180.

[67] The impact of legislation in practice is considered in Part 2 of this work; see also R. Gray, 'Factory legislation and the gendering of jobs in the north of England, 1830–1860', *Gender & History* 5, (1993).

related to the commanding position of anti-slavery in the humanitarian opinion which the ten-hours campaign was trying to mobilise. Both movements shared a common stock of imagery and metaphor, as well as divergent, at times tense, relationships with each other. Accusations and counter-accusations of an unduly selective philanthropic vision, and of diversionary tactics by vested interests, were related to deeper problems regarding the practical implications of humanitarian rhetorics.

Both anti-slavery and factory reform were themselves diverse movements. Anti-slavery was pushed from the gradualist approach of patrician Quaker and Evangelical reform to demands for immediate emancipation, associated with a wider provincial middle-class Dissenting constituency. On the other hand, factory reform, in the general sense of regulation of children's labour and the moralisation of the workplace, could appeal to liberal groups suspicious of the ten-hours campaigns of radical operatives.

The relationships between anti-slavery, factory reform and, subsequently, middle-class sympathy for Chartism have been variously treated in the recent historiography of anti-slavery. Historians of popular protest have emphasised the sharp polemical confrontations arising from the charges levelled by Cobbett, Oastler and many Chartists; while others, concerned to vindicate the anti-slavery movement's 'humane' credentials, have pointed to overlaps in support, and rightly emphasised the common heritage of anti-slavery and radicalism in philosophical rational humanism and religious Dissent. These differences may best be resolved, as David Turley has suggested, by attention to the internal differentiation of both movements, as well as to shifts over time in alignments and support.[68] For example, the Chartist sympathies expressed through Joseph Sturge's Complete Suffrage Union linked a peculiarly 'radical' strand of anti-slavery – or, more broadly, of middle-class Liberal Dissent – to peculiarly 'moderate' strands of Chartism. Both tendencies were rather isolated from their respective constituencies, especially in the crisis years of the early 1840s.

The polemical use of the terms 'factory slavery' or 'white slavery', to criticise the allegedly selective philanthropy of the liberal middle class, is well documented. Such comparisons between Caribbean slavery and the condition of the poor in Britain were already well established when

---

[68] Turley, *Culture of Anti-Slavery*; and see esp. S. Drescher, 'Cart whip and billy roller: anti-slavery and reform symbolism in industrializing Britain', *Journal of Social History* 15 (1981–2); P. Hollis, 'Anti-slavery and British working-class radicalism in the years of reform', in C. Bolt and S. Drescher (eds.), *Anti-Slavery, Religion and Reform: Essays in Memory of Roger Anstey* (Folkestone, 1980); C. Hall, *White, Male and Middle Class: Explorations in Feminism and History* (Cambridge, 1992), pt iii; R. Blackburn, *The Overthrow of Colonial Slavery, 1776–1848* (London, 1988), ch. 11.

Oastler penned his famous 'Yorkshire slavery' letters in September 1830; Sadler had been recorded talking about 'infant slavery in these accursed manufactures' nearly two years before this.[69] Imputations of special pleading and vested interest date back at least to the early 1820s, when Cobbett's assertion that the negro slave was better off than the English 'peasant' attracted several ripostes from Clarkson, J.J. Gurney and other anti-slavery luminaries.[70]

References to slavery quickly became established in the language and iconography of ten-hours agitation. Banners displayed the overlooker's strap, or the billy roller (a device used in slubbing, sometimes adopted to beat child workers), with slogans about 'white slavery', and 'the representation of a deformed man, inscribed – "Am I not a man and a brother?"'.[71] There are a number of significant transformations involved in the reworking of these slogans and symbols. The original 'am I not a man and a brother?', a Wedgwood ceramic medallion that was widely copied and adapted to function as a logo for the anti-slavery movement, shows a muscular, well-formed black man, in chains. This representation of the black labourer in terms of physical strength and suffering itself connotes the links between heavy plantation labour, unfreedom and blackness.[72] The black slave is a strong man, bearing the marks of oppression in the form of chains and the scars of whippings. The white factory worker's oppression is measured in under-nourishment, deformity and the destruction of the ability to labour. There is also a characteristic shifting, in this imagery, from the child as 'slave' to the adult man. The figure of the 'white slave' was ambiguously positioned: it implied the sharing of an oppressed condition, but it also marked difference, between black plantation slaves and white factory slaves, and between children and adult workers.

More was involved in the circulating of images of factory slavery than the simple rhetorical inversion of a fashionable cause for propaganda purposes. Claims that the British factory worker was in reality no freer than the plantation slave also drew on deep-rooted popular traditions of aversion to 'slavery'. In radical political tradition, the slave was the antithesis of the free citizen, and this could inform responses to work experience and economic insecurities, as well as to the oppressive state. Radical working-class opinion was not necessarily indifferent or hostile to slave emancipation, but might view with suspicion an organised anti-slavery

---

[69] Driver, *Tory Radical*, chs. 4, 5; Diary of Samuel Fenton, MS in Leeds Reference Library, 22 Jan. 1829.   [70] Turley, *Culture of Anti-Slavery*, pp. 36–7.

[71] 'Alfred', *Factory Movement*, vol. I, p. 254.

[72] Roediger, *Wages of Whiteness*, pp. 12–13, 21–3, 180; for the original plaque see, e.g., Blackburn, *Overthrow of Colonial Slavery*, p. 140.

movement whose main local protagonists were identified with entrepreneurial assaults on the worker's property in his labour. Suspicions and
resentments at the moral priority given to the slavery issue inevitably had
racial overtones. Aversion to slavery could be 'egotistical' rather than
'altruistic', and imply contempt for slaves (the tools of tyranny in classical
republicanism) as much as condemnation of their masters.[73] Protests at
the threatened enslavement of freeborn Englishmen shaped working-
class identities in terms of racial, as well as gender, difference. Continuing
struggle and negotiation over factory conditions was to rework and reinforce these identities.

It is also important to consider the local contexts of anti-slavery and
other agitations. Tensions may have been particularly acute in those manufacturing towns where employer groups, committed to aggressive entrepreneurial strategies and to Dissenting Liberalism, emerged as hard-line
opponents of the ten-hours campaign. Anti-slavery activists in the textile
towns sometimes expressed the suspicion that the ten-hours agitation was
a diversionary move by defenders of the planter interest, or more broadly
by a besieged Old Corruption – rather as, at a later moment, the 1847 Ten
Hours Act could be characterised as 'revenge' by the protectionist gentry.
In growing industrial towns anti-slavery, together with the triumph of
parliamentary reform, provided an impetus to the articulation of a
middle-class civic identity, through the adoption of such forms as the
public meeting and the celebratory banquet. On one such occasion, at
Bradford, the Rev. Benjamin Godwin (a Baptist, like many anti-slavery
advocates, and pastor to some of the town's rising new cohort of Liberal
entrepreneurs) attempted to negotiate the tensions.

At the table it was well known that though a greater part would be connected
with the factories of the town there would be gentlemen of different opinions on
the exciting and vexed question of the 10 hours bill. It would be difficult on such
an occasion altogether to ignore a question which was . . . so strongly agitating
Bradford as well as most other towns of the West Riding. I was therefore
strongly pressed to take up the subject in a toast or sentiment and to manage it
as delicately as I could without compromising my own views or irritating either
party.

Rising to the challenge with a carefully crafted speech, Godwin proposed
the toast 'the cause of humanity at home and abroad' and, 'after enlarging
for a few minutes on the application of the term *"family"* to the whole
human race' went on to allude both to colonial slavery and to 'the restriction of infant labour' as proper fields for legislative reform. Expanding on
the factory question, Godwin noted it was 'generally conceded that *some-*

[73] Blackburn, *Overthrow of Colonial Slavery*, pp. 36–63; Turley, *Culture of Anti-Slavery*, ch. 6.

thing must be done', but expressed reservations about the ten-hours bill, and especially about the tone of ten-hours propaganda: 'I cannot believe that the mills are little better than brothels, the overlookers worse than slave-drivers and the mill owners of this town at least more cold hearted and cruel and barbarous than slave proprietors, the buyers and sellers of human flesh and blood.'[74] Leading local advocates of anti-slavery could thus articulate resistance to the attempt to claim the ten-hours cause for a humanitarian consensus. This might well be combined with the view that 'something must be done' about factory regulation, but the content of that 'something' separated elements of middle-class Liberal Dissent from the popular demand for a ten-hour day. These sometimes tense relations were because of, rather than despite, the shared traditions and languages common to both movements. As Godwin's remarks indicate, responses to the ten-hours campaign suggest considerable sensitivity to popular denunciations of employer 'tyranny' and 'factory slavery'.

Both anti-slavery and factory reform appropriated a range of languages, including patrician reform, Benthamite rationalism, various strands of evangelicalism and popular radicalism. Within this framework, the 'borrowings' might be consciously adopted, or might arise from more deeply embedded images and metaphors. The adaptation of anti-slavery motifs to factory agitation has been widely noted, and briefly discussed above. The language of factory agitation could also, in turn, be applied to debates about plantation labour, especially in the post-emancipation struggles over the 'apprenticeship' imposed on the former slaves and the sugar duties. In a pamphlet against apprenticeship, the Reverend John Birt, a Manchester Baptist minister, echoed some of the characteristic themes of critiques of the factory system. Plantation apprentices were 'defrauded of their own time' and 'meanly and cruelly cribbed of their customary allowances'; pregnant women and nursing mothers were dragged 'to work for which they are utterly unfit'. These arguments are framed by reference to the steam-engine, 'which . . . is necessarily left to work according to its own construction and force'; human beings are degraded by such mechanical treatment, which failed to take account of 'the influence of the mind'.[75]

There is a similar cross-referencing in the writings of W.R. Greg, who intervened in these debates from a rather different point in the

[74] Rev. B. Godwin, 'Reminiscences' (written *c.* 1855; transcribed version in Bradford Reference Library), pp. 20–1; for Bradford, Koditschek, *Class Formation*; J. Reynolds, *The Great Paternalist: Titus Salt and the Growth of Nineteenth-Century Bradford* (London, 1983); for the public occasion as a political and cultural form, Morris, *Class, Sect and Party*, pp. 4–5, 174–6, 185–94.

[75] J. Birt, *Official Responsibility Affirmed and Enforced in a Letter to Sir George Grey . . .* (1837), pp. 5, 8.

spectrum of liberal opinion. Greg was linked to both factory and plantation interests, as a member of a major commercial and manufacturing dynasty at the centre of Manchester Unitarian intellectual circles, but also with family property in the West Indies; he was critically reviewed in the *Anti-Slavery Reporter* as a 'West Indian' (i.e. a member of the planter interest) in 'somewhat of a disguise'.[76] Concerned to restore the plantation economy on more acceptable and efficient lines, Greg suggested the model of the well-managed factory and the repertoire of industrial paternalism. The problems of the sugar agri-business reflected entrepreneurial shortcomings; the planters had 'struck out no new devices for exciting industry or economising labour'. The restoration of prosperity required active resident management, based on a mutual recognition of enlightened self-interest, 'to introduce without delay more economical modes of husbandry and manufacture, in order, so far as may be, to diminish their dependence upon manual labour', and to take steps to secure '*an ample and regular supply of continuous and combined labour*'.[77]

Critiques of slavery and the factory system drew on a common stock of assumptions and perspectives. The emphasis on religion, education and the disruption of proper family relations was one such organising theme. Rational economic incentives and a kindly paternalism would be substituted for the brutal sanctions of the plantation system. Emancipation, like factory legislation, could be represented as the 'protection' of innocent children from 'degradation to the level of the brute', requiring a necessary 'interference of the imperial legislature'.[78] There are also parallels in the construction of 'irresponsible' proprietorship, whether in factories or plantations. Duncan Rice has drawn attention to the fictional *topos* of the 'West Indian', a figure of uncertain origins and dubiously acquired wealth, burdened by a sinful hidden past to be expiated only by suffering and repentance, death or expulsion to the margins of civilised society.[79] This 'complex salvation/enslavement metaphor', as Rice calls it, extended beyond fictional texts to discourses of moral and social reform. For evangelicals, morally reprehensible conduct was never truly profitable, though God's providence might be so arranged as to require considerable

[76] *Anti-Slavery Reporter*, new ser., 27 Jan. 1841, pp. 22–3. For the Gregs, M.B. Rose, *The Gregs of Quarry Bank Mill* (Cambridge, 1986).

[77] [W.R. Greg], 'The sugar duties', *Westminster Review* 41, no. 2 (1844), pp. 490–1, 507–9.

[78] *Anti-Slavery Reporter*, 3, no. 2, 5 Oct. 1830, pp. 407–8, report of Leeds meeting, speeches of Rev. R.W. Hamilton and E. Baines; *Report of the Committee of the Manchester Society for the Furtherance of the Gradual Abolition of Slavery and the Amelioration of the Condition of Slaves in the British Colonies* (1827), pp. 6–7.

[79] C. Duncan Rice, 'Literary sources and the revolution in British attitudes to slavery', in Bolt and Drescher (eds.), *Anti-Slavery, Religion and Reform*, pp. 319–34.

intellectual labour in deciphering the connection between sin and its consequences.[80]

Adam Smith's rather incidental remarks about the inefficiency of slave labour thus acquired authoritative status as a demonstration of providence working through quasi-naturalistic laws of production and exchange. The 'cupidity' of the planters was short-sighted, even on its own economic ground; 'wages' would encourage productive labour more effectively than 'the whip'.[81] However, as Seymour Drescher has noted, major economic writers after Smith had little explicitly to say about slavery, and prognostications for a free labour economy were based on essentially moral assumptions.[82] Argument shifted between 'moral' and 'economic' ground. Emancipation in the legal sense could itself be seen as the prelude to 'that still more glorious emancipation, the abolition of ignorance'.[83]

Similar themes were present in the language of factory reform. Like anti-slavery, factory regulation was both a crusade against the 'Scotch philosophy' of amoral economic calculation, and the path to a more secure prosperity based on the solid foundations of restrained appetites and enlightened self-interest.[84] The 'irresponsible' employer, governed only by short-term financial gain, was an industrial equivalent to the literary figure of the 'West Indian'. Factory children, and later women, were positioned as victims of Mammon, to be rescued and redeemed through a crusade against 'ignorance', just as slaves were patiently to await emancipation at the hands of a benevolent imperial legislature.

The 'pleasures of benevolence', the claim to speak for inarticulate victims and the recruitment of the audience into this high moral purpose, were a characteristic form of address. Birt appealed to the British public as 'the vicarious functionaries of their [former slaves'] interests and of their sympathies'.[85] Oastler appealed to the conscience of 'a Briton and a Christian', and evoked the (largely silent) presence of working-class mothers as a symbol of claims to benevolent attention.[86] This rhetorical positioning in relation to a benevolent public was by no means confined to patrician philanthropists; on the contrary, it was perhaps most pronounced among those at the margins of the enlightened British public –

[80] See Hilton, *Age of Atonement*.
[81] Josiah Conder, *Wages or the Whip: An Essay on the Comparative Cost and Productiveness of Free and Slave Labour* (1833).
[82] Drescher, 'Cart whip and billy roller', p. 5; D. Eltis, 'Abolitionist perceptions of society after slavery', in J. Walvin (ed.), *Slavery and British Society, 1776–1846* (London and Basingstoke, 1982).   [83] *Monthly Repository*, new ser., no. lxxxiii (Jan. 1833), p. 447.
[84] 'Alfred', *Factory Movement*, vol. I, p. 144.
[85] Birt, *Official Responsibility Affirmed*, p. 6; cf. Hall, *White, Male and Middle Class*, pp. 212–13.   [86] 'Alfred', *Factory Movement*, vol. I, pp. 230–1.

provincial middle-class Dissent, including many women, and working-class men seeking empowerment as the protectors of their dependants. At the York county meeting: 'no such purpose had ever brought so many thousands of poor men to that city . . . a host upon whose faces were imprinted the deep lines of care, and yet the sure marks of tender affection for their helpless babes, their heart-sick wives, their degraded sisters and relations.'[87] The claim to speak for those unable to speak for themselves established the public presence of otherwise marginal groups.

The language of benevolent intervention, common to anti-slavery and campaigns for factory reform, could be contentiously claimed by various groups. This is especially marked with regard to the factory question, given the role of adult male operatives laying claim to citizenship. As has been argued above, working-class men were ambiguously positioned, demanding empowerment to protect their dependants, but also protection for their own property in labour and livelihood. They could also claim to be intimately connected with the sufferings of factory children, from their own earlier years and from what they saw in their families and communities. These 'humanitarian narratives' of factory labour had a parallel in the narratives of slavery circulated as part of abolitionist propaganda. In both sets of texts, 'reliance on detail' was taken as 'the sign of truth'.[88] But there may be significant differences between these narratives, in terms of the positioning of narrator and audience, the possibility of contention and dialogue between them. Narratives of factory labour were more open to qualification and refutation (as in the controversy over the status of some of Sadler's evidence, or over other testimonies of former factory children). The presence both of articulate working-class opinion and of employer interests inhibited any closure of narratives claiming to convey the 'truth' about the factory system. Slaves' narratives, by contrast, were more heavily mediated, while the West India interest, and certainly any outright defence of slavery, were more isolated than the employer interests involved in the factory debates.[89]

The convergences and divergences of anti-slavery and ten-hours campaigns helped shape the factory question in subsequent years. In the first place, contrasts between 'slavery' and 'freedom' – whether seen in legal, economic or moral terms – were the site of debates about acceptable and unacceptable forms of dependence and subordination. The earlier refuta-

[87] Ibid., p. 247; and cf. Cunninhgam, *Children of the Poor*, chs. 4, 9.
[88] T.W. Laquer, 'Bodies, details and the humanitarian narrative', in L. Hunt (ed.), *The New Cultural History* (Berkeley, Los Angeles and London, 1989), pp. 176–204.
[89] For slave narratives see *The History of Mary Prince, a West Indian Slave, Related by Herself*, ed. and intro. M. Ferguson (Michigan, 1987; original edn, 1831); for controversies surrounding accounts of factory labour, below, chs. 3, 5.

tions of Cobbett's assertions emphasised 'English freedom', drawing the contrast between an oppressive 'feudal' past and a free present; the integrity of the family, constantly violated under plantation slavery, was the mark of this enlightened liberty.[90] These notions of free English status were a double-edged weapon in debates about factory labour. Liberal justifications of industrial capitalism could represent the wage-contract as emancipation from deference and the constraints of a 'feudal' past. But such notions could also be appropriated to the defence of property in labour and customary working practices, which were represented as upholding the rights of 'freeborn Englishmen' against threatened 'enslavement'.

Ambiguities in the construction of 'free labour' also presented dilemmas for liberal opinion with respect to the post-slavery settlement envisaged for the Caribbean colonies. These tensions were to displace the anti-slavery consensus from the high ground it occupied in the 1830s and 40s – a shift marked in extreme, but nevertheless symptomatic, form by Carlyle's viciously racist tract on the 'negro question'.[91] It is worth noting that, for all his humane distaste for political economy and the cash nexus, Carlyle defined the supposed laziness of Afro-Caribbean people in terms of resistance to 'productive' labour within a capitalist cash-crop economy; living off the land was seen as an effortless existence, not truly labour at all. There is some common ground here with the liberal rationalism of Greg, who strikes an uncharacteristic note of hysteria about the problems of securing the required 'supply of continuous and combined labour'. Emancipation 'deprived the planter of that command of labour which is necessary to the cultivation of his estates'; it was as if 'the legislature in its wisdom were to deprive the cotton manufacturer of his *carding machines* or of his *steam* engines', or prohibit the use of harness for coaches: 'and for the future your horses must draw by suction or persuasion'.[92] In addition to the allusion to the factory, it is worth noting the metaphor of the harnessed horse; its adoption is certainly deliberate in a writer of Greg's accomplishments, and it says much about the nature of his 'liberalism'.

The link between slavery and command over labour was taken up in a rather different sense in some of the radical polemics against anti-slavery. The 'power of taking away the fruits of his labour' was the essence of

---

[90] James Kennedy, LLB, *An Address to the Inhabitants of Hull* ... (1823); Thomas Clarkson, *The Argument that the Colonial Slaves are Better Off than the British Peasantry Assessed* (1824).
[91] Hall, *White, Male and Middle Class*, ch. 10; [T. Carlyle], 'An occasional discourse on the negro question', *Frasers Magazine*, no. XLI (Jan. 1849).
[92] [Greg], 'Sugar duties', pp. 498–9.

slavery, and wage-slavery was thus no better than chattel-slavery.[93] Genuinely 'free' labour would be labour based on fair exchange, performed under economic and moral conditions acceptable to working men. The inherent ambiguities of free contract and its relationship to patriarchal subordinations of sex and age were to be the object of continued struggle and negotiation in the factory districts, and also in legislative and opinion-forming circles. Slavery and its connotations of racial difference formed an essential reference-point in these struggles, as the lowest rung in a hierarchy of constrained labour. The construction of this hierarchy in racial terms diverted the radical critique implied in the assimilation of wage-slaves to chattel-slaves. The phrase 'white slavery' is intended to carry a powerful charge of outrage and anomaly. In linking the condition of slaves to that of factory children – or even of labour more generally – ten-hours propagandists were also marking a difference. As the Reverend Hamilton of Leeds (an Independent, and the only one of his persuasion I have encountered on a ten-hours platform) declared:

I hate oppression whether at the Equator or at the Poles . . . I wish to have a character; and a character, mind me, made up of consistent acts; and I am not going to give all my attention and all my good wishes to the man of dark complexion, whilst I forget my fellow-white. (*applause*)[94]

The intimate, occasionally tense and polemical, relations between anti-slavery and ten-hours campaigns worked to construct a hierarchy of oppressions, of priority claims on the benevolence of a Christian nation. Comparisons between slaves and industrial workers were no doubt invidious and 'essentially meaningless'.[95] But they were thought to be of some significance in contests for the ear of a philanthropic public opinion. As Henry Whiteley concluded, the position of the slave was 'INFINITELY WORSE' than that of the factory child.[96] A West Riding Methodist and ten-hours activist, Whiteley had gone to Jamaica to take a post as a plantation book-keeper, claiming to have had no strong opinions about slavery, and thus to undertake the comparison from inescapable experience. His account was to circulate widely in the run-up to emancipation.

In the long debate about 'capitalism and slavery' this hierarchy of oppressions and moral imperatives deserves some attention. The posi-

[93] *The Destructive,* quoted in Hollis, 'Anti-slavery and radicalism', p. 301; and cf. the contemporaneous debates in the United States discussed in Roediger, *Wages of Whiteness,* pt ii.   [94] Speech of Rev. R.W. Hamilton, Leeds, in *Justice, Humanity and Policy,* pp. 51–2.
[95] B.W. Higman, 'Slavery and the development of demographic theory in the age of the industrial revolution', in Walvin (ed.), *Slavery and British Society,* p. 169.
[96] H. Whiteley, *Three Months in Jamaica in 1832* (1833), p. 22; see also Drescher, 'Cart whip and billy roller', pp. 11–12.

tioning of both slaves and factory children as victims to be rescued necessarily implied competing priorities, or at least a ranking exercise in the shopping-list of social and moral reforms. As Davis has suggested, anti-slavery probably had some relationship to the self-justification of emergent middle-class groups, and thus to the *ideological*, though not directly economic, needs of an expanding capitalism.[97] The simultaneous agitation over factory labour added a particular charge to this dimension of anti-slavery, especially in some of its characteristic constituencies in manufacturing towns. It is also true, but not necessarily incompatible with this, that anti-slavery arguments constructed freedom and 'free labour' in essentially moral rather than economic terms. The resulting ambiguities established a field of debate and negotiation concerning acceptable conditions of labour in an early industrial economy.

[97] D.B. Davis, *The Problem of Slavery in the Age of Revolution, 1770–1823* (Ithaca, N.Y., and London, 1975); and idem, 'Reflections on abolitionism and ideological hegemony', *American Historical Review*, 992, no. 4 (1987).

2 Humanitarian opinion and rhetorics of reform

Factory agitation was one important expression of a class-conscious working-class radicalism. At the same time, the language of patriarchal protection espoused by working-class activists provided a potential space for cross-class negotiation and the construction of alliances. The ten-hours campaign attracted substantial support within the propertied political nation, at both local and central levels, and a shared language of benevolent authority helped cement these alliances. This chapter briefly considers the nature of patrician advocacy of the ten-hours movement, and the question of paternalistic leadership.

The patriarchal concerns of many working-class activists could converge with the paternalist concerns of ruling-class philanthropy. Operatives themselves might share a language of 'paternalism', sometimes to a quite surprising extent, with propertied sympathisers. However this shared language could connote different meanings. On one hand, there was the image of the working-class male breadwinner exercising patriarchal responsibility and power; on the other hand, a cross-class paternalism, seeking to construct consensus around a moralised vision of the ideal family as model or metaphor for all social relations. The first image positions the working man as engaged in an arduous struggle, where necessary against the depradations of employers and the state; the second promises a more harmonious vision of social hierarchy.

The ambiguous functioning of gendered identities to construct a field of cross-class negotiation may explain the apparent enthusiasm of workers for a quite emphatically stated language of idealised paternalism. This was particularly marked in the West Riding, where it was often articulated by Methodist preachers.

I should be the last man in the world to relax the three-fold chord of *affection*, and *dependence*, and *obligation*, which should bind the employer and the persons employed together – no. Sir, I would rather twist it a *little* tighter. I would have every factory-master to consider himself as a *father* to his numerous family, and *command* and *forbid*, and *smile*, and *frown*, and *correct*, and *reward* as a father . . . Then reciprocal duty and affection would be delightfully profitable.[1]

Such endorsement of the claims of the paternalist master should be related to the context of the West Riding, with widespread factory employment of out-workers' children, towards whom this kindly paternal authority should therefore be exercised, *in loco parentis*. It is in striking contrast to John Doherty's contractual model of employment, rejecting the word 'master' as 'degrading to all but such as are anxious to be tyrants, or willing to be slaves'.[2]

It is tempting, but probably too simple, to see Doherty's as a 'Manchester' perspective, and contrast it to the less 'mature' factory system of the West Riding. However there is certainly no ground for regarding West Riding operatives as any less militant and radical than their Lancashire counterparts. And Lancashire figures like J.R. Stephens enunciated a similar idealised paternalism, though in a more directly critical relationship to the alleged behaviour of actual employers.[3] The figure of the benevolent 'good master' could function as a term of criticism; it carried utopian overtones of fair treatment and mutual regard, an ideal possibly rather far removed from the actual behaviour of most employers during the crisis years of the 1830s and 40s.[4]

The language of patriarchal protection and responsibility could also cut across classes. Accounts of factory reform have often emphasised the role of paternalistic leadership and a 'Tory–Radical alliance', embodied in personalities like Oastler or the political project of 'Young England', against middle-class entrepreneurial Liberalism.[5] What historians have labelled as 'paternalism' was indeed a widespread theme in early and mid-nineteenth-century public discourse, but it may be misleading to link it too closely to Toryism, the gentry or 'rural' values. There were also Whig and Liberal paternalisms (including the rhetoric of some large factory owners), and the figure of the gentleman radical 'friend of the people' had elements of pater-

---

[1] Speech by W. Dawson, in *The Justice, Humanity and Policy of Restricting the Hours of Children and Young Persons in the Mills and Factories of the United Kingdom* (1833), pp. 9–11.   [2] *The Poor Man's Advocate*, 3 March 1832.
[3] Cf. Joyce, *Work, Society and Politics*, pp. 57–60; local confrontations in Stephens' Ashton and Stalybridge are discussed in chs. 6 and 7, below.
[4] Joyce, *Visions of the People*, esp. pt ii, discusses the embedding of such notions in popular culture; and cf. M. Sonenscher, 'The *sans-culottes* of the Year II: rethinking the language of labour in revolutionary France', *Social History* 9 (1984).
[5] Ward, *Factory Movement*; for Oastler, see Driver, *Tory Radical*.

nalistic leadership.[6] Motifs of social responsibility, enlightened benevolence and reciprocal obligation cut across the established political spectrum. Evocations of an idealised family as a metaphor for social and moral
order could also, as already argued, have links to working-class radical ideologies of manly independence and patriarchal protection. Paternalism
can be seen as a theatre of negotiated power, and implicit contract between
governors and governed.[7] Paternalist languages could take on a populist
cast, especially where they related to the defence of local communities and
economies under pressure.

Paternalistic aspects of the ten-hours movement must be located, first
of all, in the context of local and regional constructions of a popular
'moral economy' also endorsed by fractions of the propertied classes. It is
important to bear in mind the diversity of the textile industries themselves, and of the propertied interests associated with them. Calls for
regulation could mobilise mercantile capitalists in domestic manufacture, finishing and merchanting. Such groups sought at times to maintain
a balance of power with mechanised spinners, or to inhibit the extension
of mechanised production.[8] Anxieties about unregulated competition
and make-or-break accumulation could be widely shared by entrepreneurs of all kinds, who might also, however, feel caught in a competitive
process that left little alternative. The language of social balance, orderly
expansion and distrust of speculation in distant markets articulated such
sentiments.[9] Appeals to rational benevolence, the moral and physical protection of children and the longer-run interests of the economic system
itself could also be framed in terms of enlightened self-interest.

Robert Heywood, a Bolton quilting 'manufacturer', operating as a
putter-out in this fancy branch of weaving, exemplifies these attitudes. A
Unitarian and leading local Liberal, Heywood gave fairly consistent
support to 'such humane and benevolent measures' as Sadler's Bill. This
enabled him to attack the Tory cotton spinner Bolling for his opposition

---

[6] Mandler, *Aristocratic Government*; J.W. Oakley, 'Utilitarian, paternalistic or both?': the
state in *England and the English*', *Prose Studies* 14, no. 1 (1991); D. Roberts, *Paternalism in
Early Victorian England* (London, 1979); J. Vernon, *Politics and the People: A Study in
English Political Culture*, c. *1815–1867* (Cambridge, 1993). For specifically industrial
paternalisms, see Joyce, *Work, Society and Politics*; A. Howe, *The Cotton Masters,
1830–1880* (Oxford, 1984), ch. 8. John Fielden, who played a central role in the successful Ten Hours Bill of 1847, manifests some features of the gentleman radical in an industrial setting: see Weaver, *Fielden*.
[7] E.P. Thompson's work on eighteenth-century society has been seminal here: see esp. his
Customs in Common (London, 1991).
[8] Foster, 'The first six factory acts'; R.G. Wilson, *Gentlemen Merchants* (Manchester,
1971).
[9] See J. Seed, 'Capital and class formation in early industrial England', *Social History* 18,
no. 1 (1993), pp. 26–8; Hilton, *Age of Atonement*.

to factory reform, but also offended Liberal allies such as 'the Messrs. Ashworths those staunch friends of freedom'.[10]

Attitudes similar to Heywood's could also be found among the millowners themselves, and not only those who fit the picture of the technically advanced and enlightened big employer. Employers as such are more fully considered in subsequent chapters (chapters 4 and 6, below). As will become apparent from that analysis, employer attitudes were by no means homogeneous, and such variables as technology and scale of production could have a different significance in different sectors and localities. The crucial distinction between support for some form of factory regulation and support for the ten-hours bill is also important in examining employer opinion. Outright and consistent support for the ten-hours movement was very much a minority position, though more widespread in the West Riding than in Lancashire. Its best-known exponents were John Fielden in Todmorden, the radical MP for Oldham from 1832, and John Wood, the Bradford Tory worsted spinner and ally of Oastler.[11]

The focus of the present discussion is not on employers as such, but on the broader spectrum of attitudes among the propertied and governing classes. At a regional level, support for a ten-hours bill, both among employers and other propertied elements, was probably most widespread in the West Riding, with its variegated combinations of out-work and factory labour, and established mercantile elites linked to the defence of the domestic clothier.[12] The fact that existing legislation did not apply outside cotton may also have provided an initial impetus for public concern, which became focused on the ten-hours bill, the main legislative proposal on offer at that early stage.[13] There is also some evidence that in the worsted industry, with its heavy dependence on young workers, regulation was associated with the desire to legitimise the employment of such labour.[14] In this regional context, Oastler attempted to construct a broad alliance in support of the ten-hours bill, comprising 'the landowner, the farmer, the *little* millowner, the domestic manufacturer, the little tradesman, the shopkeeper, the mechanic and the artisan'.[15]

A cross-section of local society was apprehensive at the prospect of

[10] Draft of letter to *Bolton Chronicle* [Dec. 1832?], Heywood Papers, Bolton Reference Library, MS ZHE 28/38; Walmsley to Heywood, Dec. 1849, ZHE 45/61; see also W.G. Brown, *Robert Heywood of Bolton, 1786–1868* (Wakefield, 1970); and on the Ashworths, R. Boyson, *The Ashworth Cotton Enterprise* (Oxford, 1970).

[11] 'Alfred', *Factory Movement*, vol. II, pp. 277–84; Weaver, *Fielden*.

[12] Gregory, *Regional Transformation*; Hudson, *Genesis of Industrial Capital*; Wilson, *Gentlemen Merchants*.

[13] Driver, *Tory Radical*, chs. 4–17, for a useful account of the manoeuvring in West Riding politics.

[14] See, e.g., Select Committee 18–2, qq. 3003–218 (evidence of J. Hall, Wood's overseer).

[15] 'Alfred', *Factory Movement*, vol. I, p. 144, quoting Oastler's open letter to Hobhouse.

further factory concentration, and saw its interests as identified with a balance between factory, out-work and artisan forms of production. Such attitudes extended from business leaders to professional men and the service economy. This is apparent among medical men (discussed in the following chapter), clergy and ministers. G.S. Bull was only the best-known and most flamboyant of several West Riding Anglican supporters of the movement; there was also substantial Methodist support. Speaking at Manchester, Bull emphasised the contrasting situation there, denouncing the reticence of his Lancashire colleagues: 'Do not the MINISTERS of this town feel that your system in factories obstructs them in their holy office and invades their province?'[16]

Attitudes to the factory question were also affected by religious and political affiliations. Ministers of 'old Dissent' (Independents/Congregationalists and Baptists) were rarely to be seen on ten-hours platforms. This may be partly because of their close links to those newly emergent entrepreneurs who were less open to arguments for regulation, but strong commitments to anti-slavery and suspicion of what they regarded as a diversionary movement also played some part. It is certainly possible, across all sectors of textiles, to find employers who could plausibly be identified with the cliché of the hard-faced Liberal Dissenting manufacturer. Speaking at Huddersfield, his home ground but also a town characterised by an identifiable employer grouping of this kind, Oastler castigated the indifference of local ministers, as Bull did at Manchester.[17]

The high-profile and aggressive Liberalism of some opponents of factory legislation, together with the responsiveness of Whig governments to manufacturing lobbies and economic orthodoxy, no doubt helped produce the alternative stereotype of gentry paternalism and the 'Tory–Radical alliance'. This is however in part a retrospective construct in order to serve Tory electoral purposes in later years. The flamboyant and widely celebrated personality of Richard Oastler, and his genuine popularity among the operatives, certainly contributed to the tradition of Tory paternalism in the industrial north. Oastler's Toryism was real enough, and he did try to use the factory question as one count in his partisan invective against the Whigs and the 'sleek, pious, holy and devout Dissenters'.[18] But he occupied a quite distinctive position, which was located to the context of the West Riding and helped to draw together local coalitions of support. Recent studies have emphasised the

[16] Ibid., vol. I, pp. 290–1; G.S. Bull, *The Duty of the Ministers of the Gospel to Plead the Cause of the Industrious and Injured Labourers of their Country* (1833).

[17] R. Oastler, *Speech at Huddersfield . . . June 18 1833* (1833).

[18] Driver, *Tory Radical*, p. 299.

contingent, locally variable and ephemeral basis of any Tory–Radical alliance.[19]

Oastler also contributed to the construction of Tory paternalism by his positioning as a simple English countryman, shocked to learn of the evils of the factory. The traveller seeing lonely mills lit up at night and encountering children on the way to work is one recurring image.[20] The honest squire or yeoman as moral touchstone is a rhetorical device, establishing an independent voice with resonances across a range of assumed audiences.[21] Oastler's own affiliations were in fact with commercial circles in the West Riding towns, as much as with agriculture; town and country, industry and agriculture were anyhow not that far distant from each other. There is something slightly disingenuous in the much-repeated story of Oastler's discovery of the factory question through a meeting with John Wood.[22]

Oastler was prepared to engage in colourful and direct polemics, which isolated him from the conventional pieties of patrician reform, and helped establish his popularity with working-class audiences. The languages of popular evangelicalism and gothic romanticism – a sensibility about childhood suffering seen in terms of the 'monstrous' – are important resources here. The story of what Driver calls 'Oastler's awakening', through his conversation with Wood, has all the motifs of evangelical conversion.[23] The conversation may have been as much to do with the tactical timing of a public campaign as with any sudden discovery of the problem. Oastler's explosive use of language sets him apart from other propertied 'friends of the poor'. Broken syntax conveys a sense of melodramatic confrontation far removed from the measured prose of most patrician reformers. Employers opposed to the ten-hours bill and their apologists could be denounced in disturbingly direct terms, often employing the melodramatic device of unmasking:

Now, Sir, with the most abhorrent disgust, I turn from your letter to yourself. I know not who you are, – what you are; I only know you as the author of *that* letter; – whether you are descended from patrician or plebeian blood, I care not . . . I *know* you are the writer of *that* letter, which stamps – for ever stamps – infamy on your name! – Hereafter, every thing cruel, disgusting, and abominable will be expressed thereby.[24]

[19] See works cited above, ch. 1 n. 6.
[20] See, e.g., R. Oastler, *Infant Slavery: Report of a Speech . . . at Preston, the 22nd of March 1833, with Extracts from his Speech at Bolton . . .* (1833), p. 14.
[21] Cf. R. Williams, *The Country and the City* (St Albans, 1975); Thompson, *Making of the English Working Class*, pp. 377–84, has some valuable comments on the nuances of 'paternalist' feeling.
[22] 'Alfred', *Factory Movement*, vol. I, pp. 95–7; Driver, *Tory Radical*, ch. 4.
[23] Driver, *Tory Radical*, ch. 4.   [24] R. Oastler, *A Letter to Mr. Holland Hoole* (1832).

The terrors of child labour are uncovered in the interstices of 'normal', avowedly Christian and philanthropic everyday existence; 'the tears of innocent victims' wet the 'the very streets which receive the droppings of an "Anti-Slavery Society"'.[25]

A concern with customary community norms and the criminalisation of offending employers also place Oastler close to the popular radical vision of an alternative political economy (indeed I have already quoted him in this context in the preceding chapter). A sketch of his 'life and opinions', eliciting support for the subscription to redeem him from the Fleet Prison and evidently seeking to appeal to a working-class radical public, emphasised the independent quality of Oastler's Toryism: 'We never yet found OASTLER tampering with the people. He has never coaxed them – never flattered them – never tried to mould them to any private or political purpose of his own.' He is represented as a prophetic or bardic figure; the 'broken and casual productions of Mr. OASTLER'S pen' were driven by a higher purpose, the pursuit of 'a sound and comprehensive scheme for the salvation of the country'.[26] Oastler, and to some extent Bull, adopted a course of itinerant agitation unusual among paternalistic reformers. His appeal was despite, rather than because of, his Toryism; while his paternalist language addressed working-class men defining themselves as protectors and providers.

This populist stance isolated Oastler from other Tory campaigners for the ten-hours bill, let alone a parliamentary leadership at least as sensitive as Whigs or Liberals to the dictates of 'orthodox' economic opinion and manufacturing lobbies. A sense of betrayal, of the 'abdication of the governors' runs through some of Oastler's polemics. Ashley, the major Tory parliamentary spokesman for the movement, evidently found Oastler an embarrassing ally:

Sorely tried as he was by his opponents, he was scarcely less tried by his supporters, and the labour of urging on some was often less than the labour of restraining others. One of the most irrepressible of the agitators was Mr. Richard Oastler – a worthy but eccentric man, wielding a large influence over the operatives – who kept up excitement to a white heat.[27]

Propertied advocates of factory reform generally adopted more measured tones. The 'Yorkshire nobleman' William Duncombe (subsequently Lord Feversham) employed the patrician evangelical language of divine providence and moral trial in his address to the great York county meeting (April 1832):

[25] 'Yorkshire slavery', *Leeds Mercury*, 16 Oct. 1830, quoted in Driver, *Tory Radical*, p. 43.
[26] *Sketch of the Life and Opinions of Richard Oastler* (1838), pp. 9, 13.
[27] E. Hodder, *The Seventh Earl of Shaftesbury*, 2 vols. (1886), vol. I, p. 214.

Not that I contemplate the possibility of being enabled, by any human law or enactment, to secure to all the various classes and interests of this empire an uninterrupted quantum of happiness; I believe it has been decreed otherwise . . . so has it been decreed in His inscrutable wisdom that we should experience a season of adversity as well as prosperity, that we may learn how to enjoy the one, and learn, also, how to appreciate the other.

It was nevertheless a 'bounden and indispensable duty' to attempt to mitigate the sufferings of 'the industrious and working classes', in the interests of 'the safety, honour, and welfare of the country'. Duncombe concluded his speech by quoting Gray's *Elegy*: 'Let not ambition mock their useful toil . . . '.[28] The labouring poor are humanised, but held at a distance, their utterances given coherent shape by the attentive gentlemanly listener, establishing their claim on active sympathy.

This patrician support, ranging from active advocacy to occasional platform appearances among the local notables, was linked in to parliamentary and metropolitan networks of opinion. Yorkshire ten-hours petitions were presented by Morpeth and Strickland, the county members in the last unreformed parliament: 'He had been convinced, from what had already occurred before the committee, that humanity demanded a speedy corrective of the evils to which the petition referred.'[29] At this stage, Sadler and his allies do seem to have attracted a fairly broad constituency of humanitarian concern. In the session of 1832, petitions in support of the Factory Bill had 112,863 signatures, coming in third in the league table of 'humanity and morality', after anti-slavery (over a million signatures) and sabbath observance (221,706). Welcoming this manifestation of humanitarian public opinion, the *Monthly Repository* expressed predictable enthusiasm for anti-slavery, 'a glorious monument for humanity', and endorsed the Factory Bill in rather more guarded terms: 'The subject is in some respects a difficult one; and it has been abominably entangled for party purposes; but the overworking of children is an atrocity that, whoever be the culprits, and wherever the burden may fall, must be put down; and will.'[30]

Many of these petitions were, predictably, from manufacturing towns, but there were also several from London (including 'gentlemen frequenting Gresham's Dining Room', 'medical gents. etc.', inhabitants of Clerkenwell and of Dean Street, Soho), and from St Albans, Dartford, Canterbury, Bury St. Edmunds, Brighton, Horsham, Ditchling (Sussex), among other places. Counter-petitions opposing Sadler were all, not

[28] W. Duncombe, quoted in 'Alfred', *Factory Movement*, vol. I, pp. 245–6.
[29] Ibid., vol. I, p. 320; for Morpeth, see Mandler, *Aristocratic Government*, and his article, 'Cain and Abel: two aristocrats and the early Victorian factory acts', *Historical Journal* 27 (1984).   [30] *Monthly Repository*, new ser., no. lxxxiii (Jan. 1833), pp. 441–2, 447.

surprisingly, from textile manufacturing towns.[31] The ten-hours petitions had been organised by the 'Society for Improving the Condition of Factory Children', which circulated a model petition in February 1832.[32] This body, rather distantly presided over by the Duke of Sussex (a slightly dissident royal and ornament of good causes), focused metropolitan support for Sadler, drawing on prominent medical men, a few MPs and monied Quaker philanthropy. The composition of the committee indicates significant overlaps with Quaker philanthropy, anti-slavery and prison reform, represented by figures like William Allen, as well as Tory Evangelicalism.[33] It is unclear how far petitioning in southern England was organised from above by these patrician elements, or drew on popular radical networks. At Horsham, political representation was dominated by the Whig Dukes of Norfolk, but the town was also a 'nest of radicalism', with 700 members of the National Union of the Working Classes adopting a proto-Chartist platform in July 1832; while Ditchling, also in Sussex, contained a large concentration of clockmakers and other artisans and tradesmen, perhaps fostering plebeian independency and radicalism.[34]

Metropolitan and southern English support for the ten-hours movement, like that in the manufacturing districts themselves, represents a spectrum of interests and opinions, not simply reducible to Tory paternalism. This was to be a continuing feature of the metropolitan political alliances which supported the movement. Ashley's role as parliamentary leader of the campaign has reinforced the image of Tory paternalism, but support was cross-party, and the Ten Hours Act of 1847 was eventually piloted through by the radical Fielden, a success adumbrated in the public 'conversion' of Macaulay and other prominent Whigs.[35] Ashley had to face the indifference of most backbenchers and the active hostility of a Peelite leadership. Much opinion in both parliamentary parties was indifferent or opportunistic, while party leaderships and governments were reluctant to challenge influential economic opinion or manufacturers' pressure-groups. This resistance to ten-hours

---

[31] *House of Commons Journal*, vol. 87 (1831–2), index entry 'factory petitions'.
[32] Society for Improving the Condition of Factory Children, circular, Feb. 1832, in *The Justice, Humanity, and Policy of Restricting the Hours of Children and Young Persons* (1833), pp. 6–7.
[33] *Justice, Humanity, and Policy*, pp. 6–7; 'Alfred', *Factory Movement*, vol. I, pp. 320–1; and cf. Turley, *Culture of Anti-Slavery*, ch. 5.
[34] Information from Ena Ainsworth, to whom I am grateful for sharing her extensive knowledge of Sussex in this period; W. Albery, *Parliamentary History of the Borough of Horsham* (London, 1927), pp. 255–65.
[35] Weaver, *Fielden*, ch. 8; and see W.C. Lubenow, *The Politics of Government Growth: Early Victorian Attitudes to State Intervention, 1833–1848* (Hamden, Conn., 1971), pp. 138–50; Robson, *On Higher than Commercial Grounds*.

legislation – though not necessarily to factory legislation as such – came to be more clearly formulated through the manoeuvres around Sadler's Bill, the 1832 Select Committee, the 'expert opinion' enunciated in the Factory Commission and the 1833 Act. Such pressures bore heavily on governments, while various pressure-groups and campaigns were associated with opposition and independent backbench opinion. The Whig incumbency for most of the 1830s may thus have reinforced the identification of factory reform with oppositional Tory values.

Evangelicalism is often associated with the 'Tory paternalism' of Ashley, Oastler, Sadler and others.[36] It is certainly true that evangelical language pervaded debates about factory regulation, as about other areas of social and moral reform. But, by the same token, there are several different strands of 'evangelical' opinion (I have tried to indicate this by capitalising references to the organised Anglican Evangelical movement specifically). In this broader sense, there was an appropriation of evangelical language across a social and political spectrum – not to mention the tendency of secular-minded historians to label any explicit religious reference within social debate as a manifestation of Evangelicalism. As Boyd Hilton has argued, Ashley, and still less Oastler, did not typify Evangelical opinion on social issues, which was itself diverse. Moderate patrician Evangelicalism was more influential, and more inclined to economic 'orthodoxy', than the pre-millennial strand represented by Ashley. In the moderate Evangelical perspective, the workings of markets could be read as manifestations of God's providence.[37] While Oastler's denunciatory prophetic language probably owed more to his Methodist upbringing, and indeed to secularised radical appropriations of aspects of popular Methodism, than to Clapham.

The moderate Anglican Evangelical *Christian Observer* did endorse Sadler's Bill, together with the Truck Acts, but placed this in the context of a carefully weighed argument about the protection of children: 'strictly speaking, they oppose a general principle upon which legislation should proceed, of not interfering between workman and master'.[38] The terms of the argument are, indeed, fairly close to those of the *Monthly Repository*, cutting across a theological spectrum from Evangelical Anglicans to rational Dissenters. In an article on 'the duty of studying political economy', the *Monthly Repository* criticised 'members of Parliament in the club-houses advocating petitions in favour of a fixed rate of wages', and singled out Sadler as 'a man who, by some means or other, has

[36] See, e.g., Driver, *Tory Radical*, ch. 2; Henriques, *Before the Welfare State*, p. 264.
[37] Hilton, *Age of Atonement*, pt ii.
[38] *The Christian Observer* 32 (1832), pp. 729–30, commenting on Bishop of Lichfield's charge to his clergy.

acquired a degree of influence to which his qualifications do not entitle him'.[39] As many commentators have remarked, the practical policy conclusions from Evangelical or Benthamite positions might be remarkably similar.[40] Both placed emphasis on rationality, temperate debate and carefully weighed intervention in order to produce the conditions of free agency among those who were not yet capable of rational economic and moral choices.

Such sentiments seem to have been orchestrated briefly in support of Sadler. But factory reform was to occupy a somewhat insecure place in the 'middle-class reform complex'.[41] While the need for some regulation of child labour established itself as part of the conventional wisdom of a concerned public – and effectively could scarcely be denied by any serious contributor to any of the subsequent debates – there was nothing self-evidently persuasive about the case for ten hours. Indeed the Act of 1833 was to stipulate eight for children. Questions of hours and other working practices entered a difficult and contested terrain of control in the workplace. Popular agitation, inspired by the doctrines of alternative political economy, and intemperate denunciations of 'tyrannical' masters threatened to elbow into the deliberations of patrician philanthropy. In the industrial north, employers, politicians and others were necessarily accustomed to confronting and negotiating such issues; outside that regional setting, it perhaps took the pre-millennial self-righteousness and patrician nerve of an Ashley to ride this particular tiger.

---

[39] *Monthly Repository*, new ser., no. lxi (Jan. 1832), pp. 24–5, 30.
[40] Hilton, *Age of Atonement*, pp. 215–18.   [41] Turley, *Culture of Anti-Slavery*, ch. 5.

3   Popular common sense, official enquiry and the state

The campaigns around Sadler's Bill were the beginning of a protracted struggle over factory legislation, expressed in popular protest, pressure-group campaigns, parliamentary lobbying and attempts to orchestrate wider public support. Legislative outcomes were the product of parliamentary and official manoeuvres, against a background of continuing agitation in the manufacturing districts themselves. The terms of public discussion, alternative ways of seeing the factory and its problems were as much at stake as specific legislative proposals. Manufacturing interest-groups were often anxious and defensive about the stigmatisation of the factory system as the site of social dangers, as well as about attacks on specific employers. The contested nature of social knowledge about the factory system formed a recurring sub-text to debates about factory regulation.[1]

Some of the main lines of debate were laid down in a series of parliamentary and official manoeuvres, during the closing session of the old parliamentary regime and the opening months of the new one. There seems to have been fairly broad support, in both parliaments, for Sadler's Bill (subsequently taken over by Ashley). Whig governing circles sought to negotiate their way round the issue, and to reconcile humanitarian concerns with anxieties and reservations about legislative intervention in labour markets.[2] Sadler's parliamentary opponents, arguing from the dangers of foreign competition, the threat of flights of capital and the desirability of child labour as the lesser evil to starvation, were somewhat embattled. Pressure for the Ten Hours Bill was deflected, initially by reference to a Select Committee ('Sadler's Committee', sat April to August 1832), then, in the new parliament, to a Royal Commission

---

[1] See esp. Carson, 'Conventionalization of early factory crime'; Idem, 'Symbolic and instrumental dimensions of early factory legislation', in R. Hood (ed.), *Crime, Criminology and Public Policy* (London, 1974).

[2] For Whig attitudes to economic and social issues, see Mandler, *Aristocratic Government*; P. Richards, 'State formation and class struggle, 1832–1848', in Corrigan (ed.), *Capitalism*, pp. 49–78.

(established April 1833). The Factory Act of 1833 was then quickly passed, broadly in line with the recommendations of a rather hasty, but skilful First Report from the Commission (dated 28 June 1833, available some days later; the crucial parliamentary vote was taken within days of publication, debate was completed within the month).[3] The 1833 Act stipulated a maximum of eight hours and compulsory schooling for 'children' (aged nine to twelve), together with a twelve-hour day for 'young persons' (aged thirteen to seventeen), and introduced an inspectorate and various registration and certification procedures. The 1833 Act also, importantly, applied outside the cotton industry, to all textile production using powered machinery, but excluding lacemaking and bleaching and dyeing and with modifications in silk. The inspection and registration provisions of the Act were to set the pattern for all subsequent regulation, though this outcome was by no means predetermined.[4]

The parliamentary *imprimatur* gave a special status to the evidence of both the Select Committee and the Factory Commission, and it was to be selectively quoted and extensively circulated in the ensuing years, functioning as part of a stock set of references cited in support of varied positions. At the time, these parliamentary and investigative manoeuvres were matters of bitter controversy. Select committees and royal commissions constituted competing models of social enquiry and legislative information. Sadler's Committee provided an extensive platform for local ten-hours alliances and their metropolitan supporters, ranging from factory operatives to medical men, clergy and propertied philanthropists. This presentation of a prepared case belonged within what might be termed an 'adversarial' model of legislative knowledge. The Factory Commission, part of an expanding and innovative use of this form of enquiry, was based on a model of expert investigation, which at times enabled government to short-circuit the balance of parliamentary opinion and corporate interest-groups.[5] That balance could certainly be a fine one; with regard to the factory question, the crucial government motion to establish a commission had only a bare majority.[6] Conceptions of law and its enforcement varied correspondingly. The claim to uphold a community consensus about 'fair' employment, which informed workers' demands for a ten-hours bill and the flamboyant populism of figures like Oastler and J.R.

[3] Select Committee 1832; Royal Commission on Employment of Children in Factories, First Report with Minutes of Evidence and Reports from District Commissioners, PP 1833 XX (hereafter cited as Factory Comm., First Report); and see Driver, *Tory Radical*, chs. 15–20;. Henriques, *Before the Welfare State*, ch. 4.

[4] See Thomas, *Early Factory Legislation*; Carson, 'Conventionalization of early factory crime'.

[5] H.M. Clokie and J.W. Robinson, *Royal Commissions of Inquiry* (Stamford, Calif., and London, 1937).   [6] Driver, *Tory Radical*, p. 221.

Stephens, confronted the administrative formalism of an expanding liberal state.

This chapter is concerned with these alternative conceptions, and their negotiation to set the terms of a continuing debate. It contrasts the perspective of community 'common sense', which underlay popular agitation, to the visions of regulation and surveillance elaborated by some professional men and functionaries of the official state. These differences were played out in the proceedings of Sadler's Committee and the Factory Commission, and their influence is also apparent in various medical contributions to the debate. The creation of an inspectorate after 1833 constituted a further arena for the articulation and renegotiation of official perspectives on industrial society.

Law, custom and community

In the framework of popular attitudes, legislation could be seen as symbolic endorsement of the 'common sense' of the working community. Groups within the community were struggling to elaborate forms of moral economy, and to impose them in practice – sometimes on workers driven to accept deteriorating terms of employment, as much as on employers. In this sense, the 'working community' should be seen as in process of construction. Law was a public enunciation of norms of natural justice, which would give a mandate to such efforts. Adopting 'the spirit of the laws' as the proper criterion, George Condy, a barrister and noted Manchester radical, argued that 'the law of reason, which coincides with the law of the realm, binds the state to interfere for the prevention of contracts which are detrimental to the public welfare'. Reason, natural law and legitimate authority in society would uphold English liberties and just and humane dealing, 'a spirit of rational kindness and sympathy for human wretchedness', as expressed in the Statute of Artificers.[7]

The demands of the short-time movement were often represented as 'common sense', especially when dismissed by the factory commissioners or others claiming authoritative social knowledge. The appeal to common sense had particular resonances, from eighteenth-century philosophy, and possibly from Paine's famous pamphlet of that title. Anyone endowed with normal reasoning and moral faculties, with 'common sense' in its philosophical as well as its more recent usage, must acknowledge the case for factory regulation. Conceptions of natural balance and order had a strategic place in this form of argument. The 'ordering economy of

---

[7] 'Alfred', *Factory Movement*, vol. I, p. 52; G. Condy, *An Argument for Placing Factory Children within the Pale of the Law* (1833), pp. 13, 16–17.

nature, and the principles of medical science' dictated some limitation of hours; twelve hours was evidently too long for children, and to require further proof of this 'implies the want of Common Sense or Honesty'.[8] Common sense likewise enjoined a more balanced and measured pattern of economic growth: 'Common Sense takes up the tables of this commerce, and shews us that it is nothing else than a process for making yarn and cloth for the other nations of the world, at prices far below the actual cost of production.'[9]

The same set of assumptions necessitated a 'simple and practicable' law, such as Ashley's Ten Hours Bill, to be enforced by local initiative and interpreted by a negotiated consensus of operatives, 'fair' employers and their allies; the demand was for a *law*, not a new apparatus of state intervention.[10] Such a law could be readily policed; a common working day would make infringement obvious to any passer by, especially if there was restriction on the hours during which the moving-power of the mill could be in motion. Even the common informer system, generally dismissed as ineffectual in Whiggish histories of protective legislation, might, in certain cases, empower worker representatives.[11] The working-class home and neighbourhood, and workplaces subject to regulation by trade custom backed by law, were proper sites for ensuring the well-being of children. Factory schools would remove parents' choice; the curriculum would be controlled by 'the choice of Lord Althorp's wise and well-paid inspectors'.[12] The uncoupling of children's hours from those of teenaged workers ('young persons') and the complicated relay system proposed by the factory commissioners was seen as a means of removing initiative from parents and other relatives, narrowing the space for flexible, negotiated interpretations of factory legislation.

The ten-hours movement and, equally, the factory commissioners and their associates, were concerned to manage the potential dangers of children's employment, rather than to bring about its abolition, or even its

---

[8] *The Commission for Perpetuating Factory Infanticide, Extracted from Frasers Magazine, June 1833* (1833), pp. 7–8; Driver, *Tory Radical*, p. 232, quoting protest against factory commissioners.   [9] Condy, *Argument*, p. 51.

[10] *The Factory Bill: Lord Ashley's Ten-Hours Bill and the Scheme of the Commissioners Compared* (n.d., but evidently 1833), p. 3; Sykes, 'Popular politics and trade unionism in south-east Lancashire', p. 92. On critical popular understandings of law and justice, see, e.g., R. McWilliam, 'The Tichborne case and the politics of "fair play", 1867–1886', in Biagini and Reid (eds.), *Currents of Radicalism*, esp. pp. 55–62; Thompson, *Customs in Common*.

[11] Foster, 'The first six factory acts', p. 5.

[12] *Proceedings of the Public Meeting held at Hebden Bridge ... August 24th 1833* (1833), p. 10, speech by Rev. G.S. Bull; for Bull, this may reflect suspicion of the Whig–Benthamite education lobby, but his language here has affinities to that of popular radicalism.

diminution. Such employment was regarded as a necessity, both for the maintenance of working-class family incomes and for the running of industry. For some philanthropists and government officials, the redemption of the factory child would come about through formal schooling on an approvèd pattern. For short-time activists, it required winning more time and space for both children and adults. 'Men, women, and children, are willing to work, and to work hard too'; the common ten-hour day would create acceptable minimum conditions for factory employment, allowing for schooling after work, and the restoration of the parental authority undermined by the factory system.[13]

The call for a ten-hours bill focused and symbolised concerns about the control of rapid industrial change. Such a law was seen as a mandate to enforce 'the spirit of the laws', which enjoined 'fair' employment practices. This was expressed in sharp local polemics and confrontations about the practices of particular employers. One such confrontation arose from a speaking tour of Calderdale by George Crabtree, 'an operative' with 'a friend' (Oastler), 'to ascertain as far as possible the minds of the inhabitants on the Ten Hour Bill, and to see the Workings of that System, which disgraces Britain and her sons'. Calderdale was an extensive district of small manufacturing towns and rural industrialisation, containing local concentrations of cotton, wool and worsted mills, as well as a scattered population of handloom weavers. Holding meetings to 'call the inhabitants together to ascertain their feelings', Crabtree collected detailed information about alleged abuses in mills, the attitudes of different employers and of the clergy. At Ripponden, despite obstruction by the local publican, 'the meeting terminated on the right side, after it was over the operatives told their tales of woe, fines, strapping, and oppressions'; while 'the Mothers wished the Ten Hours bill might pass, for their children were worked past their strength'. Cragg Dale, a picturesque valley running down to the Calder, was particularly mentioned as a site of hidden oppressions in remote mills.[14]

Crabtree's and Oastler's agitation in Calderdale was followed by a protracted battle of placards, in which the employers were attacked as 'tyrants and cowards', and in turn accused Oastler of 'receiving Corn law Rents

---

[13] *Factory Bill: Lord Ashley's Bill and the Scheme of the Commissioners*, pp. 7–10, 14–15. Cf. N.J. Smelser, *Social Change and the Industrial Revolution* (Chicago, 1959); Smelser may well be right to suggest that agitation was driven partly by concerns to sustain linkages between family and employment, although he argues this in a particular form that is less convincing and ignores the diversity of the textile industries.

[14] George Crabtree, *A Brief Description of a Tour through Calder Dale, being a Letter to Richard Oastler* (1833), pp. 3, 6; see also Thompson, *Making of the English Working Class*, pp. 381–2.

and a Corn law Salary'.[15] As the reference to the corn laws – and Oastler's own frequent allusions to the hypocrisy of entrepreneurial Dissent – suggest, there are sometimes hints of sectarian and party-political special pleading in such polemics. But the possible existence of ulterior interests should not obscure the wider confrontation of values in local communities faced with industrial change, in which Oastler could find himself allied with radical secularists and dissenters. The demand for a public hearing is a characteristic theme: '*Come out ye Tyrants; I accept your "Challenge"*', and I want to know your names.'[16] In what appear to be headings for a speech at this time, Oastler referred to 'Ashley's Bill' and 'Althorpe's Bill – Preamble', 'Free Agents', 'Caning', 'Bad Fathers' and 'Mr Fielden'; then to more detailed points about overwork and truck, concluding: 'Dick – tea 3/-6d ... wholesale warehouses at Rochdale say "Oh put it sideways it will do for Crag Dale masters to sell among their workpeople"!'[17]

Attempts to mobilise community pressure on employers were a widespread feature of factory agitation. An ephemeral Bradford publication (*The Bogart!!*, probably written by Bull) threatened:

I don't blame ye all alike; but I'll be after telling your Names however, if you don't alter your System; and *I'll haunt you every Week at every Corner of every Street, and Church and Chapel too, till you alter*, though I believe you will never do right, for long, without a little *Law* ... a Ten Hours Bill.[18]

Denunciations of 'hole in corner' lobbying by masters, and calls for an 'open court' were one theme in the protests that greeted the factory commissioners. Authoritative knowledge was based on the consensus of popular opinion, rather than on the commissioners' individualised enquiries.

I ask you my friends, for you understand the system –

1. Are straps used in factories? (*Here a multitude of voices cried out ... The Speaker was interrupted some time by loud cheers.*)
2. Are the children kicked and beaten shamefully? ... [etc.][19]

Speaking at Huddersfield, Oastler denounced the commissioners as 'a set of *Briefless* barristers and of *Feeless* doctors'. Referring to the case of Joseph Habergam, one of Sadler's witnesses repeatedly reexamined by factory commissioner Drinkwater, Oastler demanded an 'open court':

[15] *To the Factory Masters in Cragg Dale who have challenged Richard Oastler without publishing their Names* (July 1833); *An Appeal to the Public by the Factory Masters in Cragg Valley* (July 1833): Oastler coll. of broadsides, Goldsmiths' Library, University of London.
[16] *To the Factory Masters* ...
[17] Handwritten notes on reverse of copy of 1833 Factory Bill: Oastler broadsides.
[18] *The Bogart!!*, no. 1 (Dec. 1832): Oastler broadsides.
[19] C. Richardson, *Speech ... before the Short Time Committee and a Numerous Body of Delegates* ... (Leeds, 1833), p. 8.

'let us have the people to hear the cause between Addison [Habergam's former employer] and Habergam'. At a subsequent Huddersfield meeting, the commissioners, an unpopular MP and a local employer were burnt in effigy; Thomas Chalmers was passing through Huddersfield, and witnessed the scene from his hotel window: 'The spectacle I am sure is a depraving one, and fitted to prepare the actors for burning the originals.'[20] Such local confrontations, linking attempts to renegotiate working practices to popular politics and demands for legislation, recurred during the following two decades. As J.R. Stephens declared to an Ashton short-time meeting in 1836: 'I once asked . . . "Where are the masters?" I never will ask that question again. We don't want them now . . . now they shall be forced to ask us to come and speak to them.' Perhaps symbolically, this meeting was chaired by an operative, while 'many mill-owners were observed standing a short distance off'.[21] A local pamphlet attacking factory legislation complained that 'the four founders of the prosperity of this district, the Fathers of the Cotton Manufacture' were vilified from ten-hours platforms.[22]

Employers challenged by this kind of street politics may well have felt alarmed by the burnings in effigy and the meetings chaired by operatives. Several responses to the factory commissioners' questionnaire, including one Sowerby woollen manufacturer mentioned in Crabtree's account of Calderdale, alluded to unfounded allegations in meetings and placards.[23] The Commission report, and much subsequent parliamentary and official discourse, took the path of dissociating legislative measures from the intemperate language of popular agitation.

Sadler's Committee and the Factory Commission

Parliamentary and official enquiries intervened in, and inflected, local confrontations of the kind considered above. In this process, workers' and employers' understandings of factory regulation were variously represented, suppressed or redefined. This appears in particularly sharp relief

---

[20] R. Oastler, *Speech at Huddersfield . . . June 18 1833 (1833)*, pp. 5, 8; W. Hanna, *Memoirs of the Life and Writings of Thomas Chalmers* (1851), vol. III, p. 366, quoted Driver, *Tory Radical*, p. 236.   [21] *Manchester and Salford Advertiser*, 27 Aug. 1836.

[22] 'Philo Demos', *Appeal to Members of Parliament and the Working Classes &c.* (Stalybridge, 1836): Manchester Reference Library, tracts P1019, p. 30; there is another version under the alternative pseudonym 'MRCS', and the author may be George Cheetham, a Stalybridge surgeon (possibly related to the cotton-manufacturing Cheetham dynasty) whose certifying credentials were withdrawn by Leonard Horner: see below, n. 81.

[23] Factory Comm., Supp. Report, pt ii, employer questionnaires, C.1, no. 23 (W.H. Rawson, Sowerby); also, e.g., D.1, no. 223 (H. Ashworth, Turton, near Bolton), no. 237 (Fernley & Wilson, Stockport).

in the sequence from Sadler's 1832 Select Committee, to the Factory Commission, the 1833 Act and the subsequent development of factory inspection as an official source of social knowledge about the manufacturing districts.

Sadler's Committee provided a fairly extensive platform for the operative short-time movement and its philanthropic allies. Adult male working-class witnesses, recruited and briefed by the short-time committee network, were probably the recognised, and in some sense elected, representatives of their trades and communities. They were routinely asked to comment on general opinion in their localities:

Having had very extensive intercourse with them, do you believe that their views and feelings upon this subject have been taken up suddenly, or that they are likely . . . to be laid down again? – I think they so well understand the situation in which they are placed, that they are fully convinced that ten hours are quite sufficient, and will ultimately give them all the benefits of their labour, rather than any longer hours.[24]

The formal reiteration of testimony as to general opinion was evidently seen as having some pertinent claim on parliamentary attention.

Employer lobbies, the Factory Commission and much subsequent historiography have emphasised the biased selection and questioning of Sadler's witnesses, and the anecdotal and impressionistic nature of some of their statements. The recruitment of witnesses was carefully organised by the short-time committees, with a certain bias to the West Riding; this may be partly because of the role of Oastler and Sadler at this juncture, partly perhaps because the need for regulation outside cotton was one of the points at issue. And much of the questioning does draw on a stock of distinctly leading standard questions. However the presentation of carefully prepared cases, based on the representation of structured corporate interests, was a normal feature of the select committee procedure. In this instance it was caught up in the Reform Bill and the dying days of the old parliamentary system. Only the ten-hours movement put its case, possibly in a deliberate manoeuvre to push the Bill through under the exceptional parliamentary conditions of 1832. What also distinguished Sadler's campaign was the presence of an extensive and organised working-class opinion. Such a constituency perhaps depended on a greater measure of formal organisation to put its case – to select the best witnesses, prepare them for the proceedings at Westminster and meet their costs in getting there. As Oastler put it in a draft circular appealing for funds, 'the rich opponents of the Factory Bill' had obliged 'the poor operatives . . . of

---

[24] Select Committee 1832, q. 9123 (J. Hanson, Huddersfield); Driver, *Tory Radical*, appendix B, guidelines to short-time committees on selection and briefing of witnesses.

necessity to make out their children's case'.[25] Attacks on the validity of Sadler's proceedings were also, in the context of 1832, attacks on *any* structured representation of working-class opinion, on 'that class of men who entitle themselves, unfortunately with some truth, the delegates of the workpeople'.[26]

It should also be noted that the proceedings were by no means an easy ride for the witnesses. Although the Committee itself was certainly loaded with Sadler's allies, it did also include, for example, Poulett Thomson, Sir Robert Peel and Thomas Gisborne, all committed, in varying ways, to political economy and manufacturing interests. As well as the reiteration of stock questions (to which however those witnesses with direct experience of the factory system often gave considered and individual responses), there were some fairly sharp exchanges, particularly concerning economic arguments about the impact on output and wages.

Pressed in this way, the adult male working-class witnesses insisted on the validity of their own experience and observation. 'I have found this through life, that an increase of hours has caused a decline of wages', declared Stephen Binns, an overlooker at a Leeds flax mill; asked whether the operatives had considered the possible effect of shorter hours on wages, Binns replied: 'the labouring class are straightforward people; they are not political economists; they are determined to support the Ten Hours' Bill upon the score of humanity'.[27] Witnesses also developed economic arguments that a ten-hours bill would shorten hours for men, 'equalise labour' by evening out fluctuations in demand, strengthen the position of the domestic clothier and the small manufacturer, and raise wages.[28] There was thus a characteristic shifting between arguments that counterposed 'humanity' to political economy, and alternative versions of economic calculation justifying different policy conclusions. It was of course widely claimed, by the factory commissioners and other proponents of economic 'orthodoxy', that the regulation of children was instrumentally used, to further the protectionist interests of adult male workers. But the two were anyhow connected from the operatives' standpoint, though not necessarily that of their philanthropic allies. And there can be no doubt that the real concern, indeed anger, about children's welfare was more than a rehearsed script. If adult men wanted to work short-time, regulate output and increase their wages, it was partly in order to improve their children's life-chances.

[25] Handwritten circular, in 'Richard Oastler and the Factory Question', vol. of miscellanea in Goldsmiths' Library, B.831 fol.   [26]Factory Comm., First Report, p. 44.
[27] Select Committee 1832, qq. 4894, 4912 (S. Binns, Leeds).
[28] Ibid., e.g., qq. 559–83 (A. Whitehead, clothier, Holmfirth), 9124–38 (J. Hanson, Huddersfield).

Criticisms of existing conditions of child labour were also related to accounts of its intensification, rather than simply to isolated instances of cruelty and neglect; the use of the strap or other physical punishments was itself linked to the productivist pressure bearing on adults and children alike. Contrary to the bland image of the machine lightening toil, extended use of machinery was associated with an intensification of work. At one Leeds mill, 'lately they have put three children upon four children's work'; while at Marshall's flax mill, 'I have seen Mr. James and Mr. John Marshall go round the frames', trying to induce the 'girls' to mind extra spindles for 3d. a week more.[29] Factory children and young workers (Marshall's 'girls' were probably in fact teenagers and young adults) are here constructed as waged workers, forced into unequal exchanges of increased effort and productivity for inadequate payment, rather than simply victims of random cruelty. While such accounts are no doubt impressionistic, they do give more direct access to perceived changes in work-experience than the purportedly more systematic surveys of factory commissioners, inspectors and other authoritative official sources. Sadler's evidence relates particularly to the West Riding, where the uneven development of factory production had produced particular concentrations of child and juvenile labour (often rather younger than their counterparts in Lancashire cotton) in worsted mills and some sectors of wool.

Sadler's Committee was therefore staged as a public enunciation, for the benefit of the legislature, of what everyone in the localities already 'knew'. This is reflected in the suspicion and outrage that greeted the appointment of a royal commission to undertake still further enquiries. Sadler's evidence, it was claimed, was 'now admitted, by the intelligent part of the public, to be conclusive proof . . . that the factory system, as at present worked, does tend to deprave and degrade the labourers employed in it'.[30] Such claims justified protests against the factory commissioners; Sadler's witnesses had testified before a 'competent and orderly court', and any retrial, especially under the unprecedented forms of a royal commission, would be irregular. Public parliamentary hearings were analogous to a jury trial, while the Commission was a Star Chamber proceeding of dubious legality.[31] Royal commissions, and the work of figures like Edwin Chadwick, appear in Whiggish histories as milestones

---

[29] Ibid., q. 968 (J. Drake, weaver, Leeds), 4748 (S. Binns).
[30] 'Alfred', *Factory Movement*, vol. II, pp. 40–1, quoting protest of Manchester short-time committee.
[31] Ibid., p. 41; see also, *The Commission for Perpetuating Infanticide*; Geoffrey Crabtree, *Factory Commission: The Legality of its Appointment Questioned and the Illegality of its Proceedings Proved* (1833): the author is described as 'late barrister-at-law', and not to be confused with George Crabtree cited above, n. 14.

in the development of social reform, but they aroused considerable suspicion in the 1830s, as illegitimate extensions of executive power. This view was shared across a spectrum from popular radicals, to populist traditionalists and gentry and others who manifested an ancient suspicion of central government.[32] The appointment of commissions could certainly provide a quick-fix, to remove contentious issues from the parliamentary domain, while their models of enquiry into working-class activities were more akin to the investigating magistrate than to the social survey. These features are certainly to be seen in the Factory Commission. While working-class witnesses were examined under oath, employers were free to complete questionnaires as they saw fit 'in their own counting-houses'.[33] Like other commissions of the period, it was staffed by rising professional men and intellectuals, mostly of enlightened Whig or Benthamite inclinations, hired as consultants to government.

The authority of the Factory Commission was therefore contested; it was seen as an illegitimate manipulation of executive power, staffed by Whig jobbery, to reverse Sadler's findings, an 'attempt made by the Millocrats through their despicable tools the Commissioners, to misrepresent the motives and to vilify the character of the whole operative body'.[34] Aspects of the commissioners' proceedings, and of Chadwick's rapidly produced First Report, lent credence to this view. Such of Sadler's witnesses as could be made to testify were, like Joseph Habergam (a *cause célèbre* in the West Riding), subjected to reexamination, often with collateral testimony from other workers at the mills concerned. Considerable pressure must have been exerted, given the fairly solid support for the short-time movement boycott of the proceedings. This resistance led John Cowell, one of the commissioners for Lancashire, who sent frequent reports and complaints to Chadwick, to search out the 'Central Committee' of the operatives; he was predictably frustrated in this quest, but remained convinced of the existence of such a body: 'all we know is that it does, at present, control and govern the *general* conduct of the operatives'.[35]

A quasi-juridical, individualised model of proof was applied to workers' testimonies. In one such exchange, Charles Aberdeen, a Salford card-grinder (a notoriously unhealthy occupation) formerly employed at Holland Hoole's mill, was asked to explain his remark that he had 'seen

---

[32] See Clokie and Robinson, *Royal Commissions*.
[33] 'Alfred', *Factory Movement*, vol. II, p. 41.   [34] *The Voice of the West Riding*, 20 July 1833.
[35] Cowell to Chadwick, 6 May 1833, Chadwick Papers, 41 'Factory Commission'; and further letters from Cowell, ibid. The re-examinations of witnesses figured prominently in the evidence from district commissioners for Lancashire and the West Riding appended to the crucial First Report of the Commission.

men die daily for want of breath': 'I have seen men gasping in the card-room and carried out for want of breath'. The 'principal carder', a well-paid supervisory worker on a bonus scheme, refused to have the windows open, leading on occasion to 'a resistance, and . . . a scuffle, and bad language'. The questioning then switched to the heat in the room, about which Aberdeen had no complaint: 'Then it is only of the dust you complained? – Yes.' Aberdeen was also forced to qualify his statements about dismissals for refusing to work nights.[36]

This interview was conducted by E.C. Tufnell, Cowell's colleague for Lancashire, a cleric with leanings to political economy, and subsequently author of a well-known pamphlet on trade unions.[37] The organisation of Tufnell's interviews is interesting. The first series of examinations are grouped according to attitude to the ten-hours question. The minutes are not dated, unlike other minutes of evidence, and they may well have been ordered for effect. The sequence opens with 'witnesses in favour of the ten hours bill' and Aberdeen is placed first among these, therefore first in Tufnell's whole report. The proceedings begin with Aberdeen's refusal to take the oath, which is emphasised in a brief exploration of theological opinions: 'Truth is what I swear by, and wherever I meet her I embrace her . . . Can you tell me what God is? – God is incomprehensible. I am a moral character. When I was in London I lived in Mr. Carlile's shop, Fleet Street.' The interview ends on a similarly defiant note: 'If I was in solitary confinement I could write a history of my life, and I could show up the factory system then. It is a consolation to my mind, that I never put a bad example before children, either in word or action.'[38] Aberdeen's infidelism was to be cited polemically by W.R. Greg (himself a Unitarian, and thus scarcely a figure of unimpeachable religious orthodoxy), analysing the commissioners' findings for the Manchester Statistical Society.[39]

Tufnell's report also includes interviews with six other ten-hours supporters, followed by a similar number of 'witnesses against the ten hours bill'. These include an overlooker from Ashton's mill at Hyde (much cited as a 'model' establishment), the couple in charge of the apprentice house at the Gregs' Styal mill (another 'model' community) and various mule spinners from Aberdeen's former mill (called in to

---

[36] Factory Comm., First Report, Reports from District Commissioners, D.2, Lancashire, examinations by Mr Tufnell.
[37] See R. Johnson, 'Educating the educators: educational experts and the state, 1833–39', in Donajgrodzki (ed.), Social Control, pp. 84–5; E.C. Tufnell, The Character, Objects and Effects of Trades Unions (1834), which gives sustained attention to the Lancashire spinners, 'the secret source of nine-tenths of the clamour for the Ten-hours Factory Bill' (p. 29).   [38] Factory Comm., First Report, D.2, p. 1.
[39] [W.R. Greg], Analysis of the Evidence Taken before the Factory Commissioners . . . Read before the Manchester Statistical Society, March 1834 (1834).

refute his testimony); the last, and longest, word in this group is given to Robert Hyde Greg, whose statement is characteristic of submissions from leading liberal employers, supported by elaborate calculations about costs and returns on investment.[40] The third, and biggest group of interviews in the sequence are presented as 'disinterested witnesses on the ten hours bill', including various clergy, other professionals and local officials. The Rev. James Brooks, Unitarian minister at Hyde, was placed first among these 'disinterested' parties. His stance was that of the liberal professionalism represented by figures like James Kay, with close affinities to the outlook of some of the factory commissioners themselves, as well as to enlightened manufacturers. The factory was associated with improvement, shorter hours and expanded education were desirable, but legislation must take account of economic pressures. Brooks was 'decidedly of opinion' that factory workers 'are quite as sober and moral, as people employed in other trades'. He nevertheless thought the hours were too long, 'but I would not state to what extent they should be abridged'. The best means to ameliorate conditions for children was 'to raise the moral character of the parents' and expand education.[41]

This approach parallels the argument of Chadwick's main report. Despite the polemical concerns to refute Sadler, the Factory Commission was not simply apologism. Its report rather combined a qualified defence of the factory system with specific proposals for necessary regulation. The central thrust was to identify problems requiring intervention, but to dissociate this from radical critiques of the 'factory system' as such. This perspective is connected to that of the liberal intellectual circles grouped regionally in the Manchester Statistical Society   though a shared language could, as will become apparent from a closer look at employer attitudes in the next chapter, be combined with dissension over its practical implications.[42] As James Kay argued in his famous pamphlet on· *The Moral and Physical Condition of the Working Classes* (1832), the 'evils' he

---

[40] Factory Comm. First Report, D.2, pp. 2–44 (Greg's evidence is pp. 30–44, no other witness takes more than two pages).   [41] Ibid., D.2, p. 45.

[42] For the Manchester Statistical Society, T.S. Ashton, *Economic and Social Investigations in Manchester, 1833–1933* (London, 1934). For middle-class liberal culture generally, see V.A.C. Gatrell, 'Incorporation and the pursuit of liberal hegemony in Manchester 1790–1839', in D. Fraser (ed.), *Municipal Reform and the Industrial City* (Leicester and New York, 1982), pp. 16–60; Gunn, 'The Manchester middle class'; J. Seed, 'Unitarianism, political economy and the antinomies of liberal culture in Manchester, 1830–1850', *Social History* 7, no. 1 (1982). It should be noted that leading manufacturers belonging to Manchester intellectual circles might have firms located throughout the cotton region, e.g. the Ashtons (Hyde), Gregs (Cheshire, Bury and elsewhere), Ashworths (near Bolton); 'revisionist' accounts of Manchester as a commercial and service metropolis have themselves to be qualified in light of this metropolitan presence of out-of-town factory masters.

had identified, 'so far from being the necessary consequence of the manu-facturing system, have a remote or accidental origin, and might, by *judicious management* be entirely removed'.[43] The official expert knowledge claimed by Chadwick and his associates can be read as an elaboration of that proposition. Assumptions from political economy and the character-istic move of resorting to (often ill-digested) statistical information formed a set of organising assumptions.[44]

The identification of problems associated with unregulated child labour was framed by a comparison between factory and other employ-ments, and between larger and smaller factories, to the advantage of the large, technically rational factory managed on principles of enlightened self-interest. The benefits of a well-regulated factory system are illus-trated in lengthy quotations from the reports of the district commission-ers (especially from James Stuart, the commissioner for Scotland, who, whatever his shortcomings as a zealot for social reform, at any rate had a handy turn of phrase). On the other hand, 'where the harshest treatment of children has taken place, the greatest number of bad cases occur in the small obscure mills belonging to the smallest proprietors', and might well be the fault of 'violent and dissipated workmen'.[45] Chadwick also empha-sises the favourable comparison between factory work and other employ-ments for children, such as mining, domestic weaving, framework knitting and lace-running, foreshadowing the agenda of subsequent enquiries. Factory work was 'amongst the least laborious . . . and the least unwholesome' employments for children. The case for legislation rested partly on its greater feasibility where large numbers were concentrated in identifiable workplaces, 'buildings of peculiar construction, which cannot be mistaken for private dwellings', where timekeeping was subject to 'the regularity of military discipline'.[46] The very case for regulation helped establish the superiority of the factory as a regime of productive labour.

Medical men and industrial work

The process of official enquiry and debate gave particular status to the views of professional men, as informed and supposedly independent wit-

[43] J.P. Kay, *The Moral and Physical Condition of the Working Classes Employed in the Cotton Manufacture in Manchester* (1832), preface.
[44] See, e.g., P. Abrams, *The Origins of British Sociology, 1834–1914* (Chicago and London, 1968), pp. 3–23; Johnson, 'Educating the educators'; Mort, *Dangerous Sexualities*, pt i; for Chadwick, S.E. Finer, *The Life and Times of Sir Edwin Chadwick* (London, 1952).
[45] Factory Comm., First Report, p. 20; and cf. pp. 16–18. For Stuart, see U.R.Q. Henriques, 'An early factory inspector: James Stuart of Dunearn', *Scottish Historical Review* 50, no. 1 (1971).
[46] Factory Comm., First Report, p. 51.

nesses. The personnel of commissions and inspectorates, and their claims to official expertise, are considered in the final section of this chapter. The professional discourses of medical knowledge are also of some interest in this context.

Several key state servants had professional backgrounds in medicine, while a broader and rather more typical spectrum of medical men appeared as witnesses or as activists in reform pressure-groups at local level.[47] Arguments about 'health and morals' were central to critiques and defences of the factory system, and claims to authority based on medical professionalism figured in the language of debate. Like clergy and ministers, medical men constituted a geographically dispersed body of supposedly educated men, able to report back on regions otherwise remote from 'public' scrutiny. At the same time, notions of natural order, adaptation and the providential interdependence of the moral and the physical pervaded social debates. These assumptions could be deployed in support of differing arguments, and the role of medical men as 'expert' witnesses both paralleled and helped shape wider divisions in the middle class. Different styles of medical professionalism were also differently positioned in relation to the national and local state, and to the cultural networks of intellectual life.

Recent studies have emphasised the fragility of claims to professional status, internecine strife among medical men and the rather marginal position of many practitioners in the established middle-class society to which they aspired.[48] The medical profession was divided between physicians, surgeons and apothecaries, although the two latter were tending to merge to constitute the majority of ordinary practitioners in provincial towns. There was also a hierarchical division between a symbolic centre, represented by the metropolitan elites of the royal colleges, and provincial practitioners. Cutting across these formal hierarchical distinctions were competing intellectual networks and versions of medical knowledge. The profession was often seen as 'over-stocked', relative to the population of potentially lucrative patients; and market pressures added a certain edge to all these divisions.

Medical practice in expanding industrial centres could be represented as a strategic point from which to investigate 'the employments and the

---

[47] Mort, *Dangerous Sexualities*; I. Inkster, 'Marginal men: aspects of the social role of the medical community in Sheffield, 1790–1850', in J. Woodward and D. Richards (eds.), *Health Care and Popular Medicine in Nineteenth-Century England* (London, 1977); the following discussion draws on R. Gray, 'Medical men, industrial labour and the state in Britain, c1830–1850', *Social History* 16 (1991).

[48] Inkster, 'Marginal men'; see also esp. H. Marland, *Medicine and Society in Wakefield and Huddersfield, 1780–1870* (Cambridge, 1989); J.V. Pickstone, *Medicine and Industrial Society* (Manchester, 1985).

diversified moral and physical habits of society'.[49] The formation of local medical societies and anatomy schools provided platforms for claims to a knowledge not recognised by the metropolitan hierarchy. There were also, however, divisions within the local medical community, associated with patronage in prestigious institutions such as infirmaries, or alternative specialist hospitals and medical charities. Medical careers were to some extent dependent on the patronage of philanthropic local elites, and were liable to become embroiled in their politics.

Medical practitioners in manufacturing towns were delicately poised in relation to debates about factory reform or other social issues. On one hand, the *persona* of professionalism was as much concerned with enlightened philanthropy and public duty as with successful therapies (of which there were rather few); to appear on appropriate platforms and serve on appropriate committees was a way of getting known in the town and building up a successful practice. On the other hand, over-assertive and controversial public stances might alienate potential patrons and patients. It should therefore be noted that the following comments relate mostly to those practitioners actively engaged in public controversies over the ten-hours bill, and these individuals may well be atypical (they were certainly among the most prominent practitioners in the locality). Most medical men probably maintained a discreet silence.

Table 3.1 analyses identified practitioners publicly active as witnesses before enquiries, pamphleteers and speakers stating clearly defined views in controversies over the ten-hours bill.[50] The public stances of medical men can be related to divisions in the middle class (including employers themselves) in industrial towns. Supporters of the ten-hours bill had apparently stronger local connections and greater stability in local practice, especially in the West Riding towns, where Sadler's witnesses were

---

[49] *North of England Medical and Surgical Journal* (hereafter *North of England Jour.*) (1830–1, not published thereafter), preamble.

[50] Table 3.1 includes identified practitioners active as witnesses at enquiries, speakers at meetings, authors, etc., stating definite views for or against the proposed ten-hours bill; as for other groups involved, opposition to ten hours does *not* imply opposition to legislation as such. Career information relates to activities up to *c.* 1840; 'local medical connections' indicates apprenticeship in town of practice, close relative in local practice etc.; medical interests and publications are those other than expressed in interventions in the ten-hours debate. Sources used include: J.T. Anning, *The General Infirmary at Leeds* (London and Edinburgh, 1963), and 'The Leeds Public Dispensary', *Publications of the Thoresby Society* 16 (1974); J.H. Bell, 'Some fragments of local medical history', *Bradford Antiquary* 1 (1881–8); W.R. Lee, 'Robert Baker', *British Journal of Industrial Medicine* 21 (1964); Pickstone, *Medicine and Industrial Society*; M. Rose, 'The doctor and the industrial revolution', *Brit. Jour. Industrial Medicine* 28 (1971); A. Meiklejohn, intro. to reprint of C. Turner Thackrah, *The Effects of the Principal Arts, Trades and Professions . . . on Health and Longevity* (2nd edn, 1832; reprint, Edinburgh, 1957); references in local press, medical press, poll books, directories, etc.

Table 3.1 *Medical contributors to the ten-hours controversy: Lancashire and West Riding, c. 1830–40*

	Ten-hours supporters	Ten-hours opponents	Total
No. of practitioners	10	6	16
Status			
physicians	1	3	4
surgeons	9	3	12
Location of practice			
Manchester	—	2	2
Leeds	5	4	9
other	5	—	5
Years in continuous local practice			
<19	4	4	8
>20	6	2	8
Local medical connections traced	4	1	5
Posts held[a]			
infirmary	4	2	6
dispensary	3	2	5
specialist hospitals	—	2	2
medical school lecturer	2	3	5
parish surgeon	1	2	3
factory surgeon	1	1	2
none traced	3	1	4
Medical interests, publications, etc.[a]			
cholera, fever	1	4	5
statistics	1	2	3
midwifery, children	2	1	3
injuries, fractures	2	1	3
anatomy, physiology	1	1	2
phrenology	—	1	1
none traced	6	1	7
Politics			
Tory	4	—	4
Whig/Liberal	1	4	5
Radical/Chartist	2	—	2
none traced	3	2	5

Note: [a]The same individual can be counted under several headings in these categories.
Sources: see n. 50

often drawn from local medical 'dynasties', like William Hey, jnr (Leeds), and William Sharp, jnr (Bradford). Infirmary posts were probably the strongest indication of such local connections; it should also be noted that in Bolton and Bradford ten-hours supporters in dispensary appointments held posts in the most important medical institutions of towns without infirmaries. The medical support for Sadler in the West Riding towns parallels the attitude of entrenched local interests, with mercantile elites and a few manufacturers supporting the ten-hours campaign. Support seems to have been strongest in Bradford, where virtually all the local practitioners appended their names to a broadside supporting Sadler, thus cutting across their intra-professional, political and religious divisions. This is related to the high level of expressed employer support for some kind of factory regulation, and the rather less widespread support for ten hours (which nevertheless included some major local employers, notably Oastler's ally John Wood); the inchoate state of civic institutions and of middle-class culture and politics in the town may also have created more space for such medical initiatives.[51]

Leeds was marked by a polarisation in the middle class between an Anglican–Tory establishment, clustered around the old corporation, at one end of the spectrum, and its critics, at the other.[52] This is mirrored in medical alignments over the ten-hours movement. Supporters included several pillars of the Infirmary 'faculty', with family traditions in Leeds medicine and Tory connections. Debate on factory conditions tended to centre on flax spinning (generally regarded as the least healthy branch of textiles) rather than the local staple of wool. John Marshall, whose political stance as Liberal contender in the new borough no doubt helped stimulate polemical comment on his working practices, published a correspondence with Samuel Smith, surgeon at the Infirmary, following Smith's references at a public meeting to a girl he had treated from Marshall's mill: 'The situation which you fill in a great public charitable institution brings your medical opinion more particularly under public observation.' In reply Smith moderated his tone, and suggested the overlooker might be to blame, but stood his ground: 'I went with reluctance, having never in my life spoken in a popular assembly, but I believed, and still do, that I was performing a public duty.'[53] Another group of Leeds medical men, associated with the Liberal camp, were active in arguing against Sadler. They included James Williamson, the Infirmary physician (who was quoted in opposition to his colleague Smith over the health of

[51] *The Memorial of the Physicians and Surgeons of Bradford in Favour of the Ten-Hours Bill . . . July 13th 1832*, Balme Collection, Bradford Archives, box 27; and see below, ch. 4 for local variations in employer opinion.
[52] See Morris, *Class, Sect and Party*.   [53] *Leeds Mercury*, 21 Jan. 1832.

Marshall's mill workers), and Robert Baker, the parish and factory surgeon and future factory inspector. Baker had engaged in public polemics against the restrictive practices of the Infirmary 'faculty', and his refutation of the views of Smith in evidence to the Factory Commission may echo these intra-professional tensions.[54]

Most of the local medical support for the early ten-hours campaign therefore came from members of what might be termed medical establishments in the West Riding. Medical supporters also include two Lancashire practitioners identified with popular radicalism and Chartism, Peter McDouall (Ramsbottom, near Bury) and Matthew Fletcher (Bury). They related their radical politics to the deprivation and disease they saw around them, and also to a sense of insecurity and exclusion; the monopolising big millowner had even taken it upon himself 'to assume the duties of the apothecary'.[55]

Medical commentators opposing the ten-hours bill were concentrated in the regional centres of Manchester and Leeds. The division of opinion in Leeds has already been noted. Manchester medical men were notable absentees from the list of witnesses at Sadler's Committee or speakers at ten-hours meetings. This is particularly striking in view of the local medical involvement in campaigning for Peel's 1819 Factory Act, which indeed inaugurated a certain tradition of medical concern with industrial conditions.[56] Two former Manchester practitioners gave evidence for Sadler, but they had moved to London (and therefore are not included in table 3.1). The opinions of William Simmons, a leading Manchester medical man and witness at the 1819 Lords Committee, were cited by hearsay as authoritative support for the ten-hour day.[57] Some Manchester practitioners did also express support for a ten-hour day in a survey conducted by Bisset Hawkins for the Factory Commission, but this was in response to a questionnaire, and is sometimes hard to interpret.[58] The balance of opinion in Manchester had shifted since 1819, when there had been substantial support for Peel from mercantile interests in Manchester, analogous to that for Sadler among West Riding elites.[59] In

[54] Ibid., Royal Commission on Employment of Children in Factories, Second Report, PP 1833 XXI (hereafter cited as Factory Comm., Second Report), medical reports, C.3, pp. 8–12, 14–16; R. Baker, *Remarks on the Abuses in the Infirmary* ... (1827).
[55] *McDouall's Journal* (1841; 1 vol. only), p. 62; see also M. Dutton, 'Matthew Fletcher', BA honours dissertation, Manchester Polytechnic (1983), copy in Bury reference library; N. Kirk, 'In defence of class', *International Review of Social History* 32 (1987).
[56] See evidence reprinted in C. Wing, *Evils of the Factory System* (1837), pp. cxxvii–clxxviii; *Information concerning the State of Children Employed in Cotton Factories* (1818).
[57] Select Committee 1832, qq. 10630–705, 11137–82.
[58] Factory Comm., Supp. Report, D.3, Dr Hawkins' report.
[59] For Manchester in the earlier period, see R. Lloyd-Jones and M.J. Lewis, *Manchester in the Age of the Factory* (London, 1988).

the 1830s, Manchester medical men, including those active in a variety of other public causes, seem to have followed leading cotton manufacturers in balancing the desirability of shorter hours against the state of trade, and the perception that 'the *greatest temporal evil* which could happen to this community would be the *want of employment*'.[60]

Medical commentators opposing the ten-hours bill appear to be distinguished by their higher qualifications (four physicians and two surgeons), lower stability in local practice and ambition reflected in publication in a variety of fields. 'I look for publications arising from such talented individuals – It is in vain', Robert Baker commented tartly on the old guard of Infirmary surgeons.[61] Characteristic publication interests for men like Baker or, most famously, James Kay, were in medico-moral statistics, fever and cholera. Publications by ten-hours supporters, on the other hand, were more closely linked to the general run of ordinary practice (midwifery, injuries).

Supporters and opponents of the ten-hours bill therefore possessed particular kinds of cultural capital, underpinning their participation in public controversy. For ten-hours supporters this derived mostly from well-established local connections and links to local elites, as well as to the extra-local medical networks where they had gained their qualifications (strongly represented, as we shall see, among Sadler's metropolitan witnesses). Opponents of the ten-hours bill based their cultural confidence on education, links to intellectual networks and claims to challenge obsolete doctrines and practices.

All parties to the debate attempted to make use of these medical testimonies. Suitable medical opinion, especially that expressed in Sadler's evidence, was widely circulated by short-time committees.[62] Particular weight was attached to the views of medical witnesses associated with the royal colleges and London hospitals, 'composed of the most celebrated lecturers and instructors at the greatest medical schools'.[63] This reliance on London medical men followed a tradition established in the enquiries of 1816–19, when it reflected a (justified) suspicion that local practitioners would be suborned by employers hostile to intervention, as well as deference to the higher knowledge at the disposal of the metropolitan 'gentleman of science'.[64] The enquiries of that period also produced a list of alleged factory diseases which recurs in the debates of the 1830s, including deformities, leg ulcers, fever, scrofula (tuberculosis of the lymph glands, particularly affecting children) and general debility.

[60] Factory Comm., Supp. Report, D.3, p. 247 (J. Roberton).   [61] Baker, *Abuses*, p. 5.
[62] *Table of Medical Opinion and Testimony*, Bradford broadside, Balme Coll., box 27; 'Alfred', *Factory Movement*, vol. I, pp. 28–30, 49–53, 312–16; Wing, *Evils of the Factory System*.
[63] *Bolton Chronicle*, 2 Feb. 1833.   [64] Wing, *Evils of the Factory System*, p. cxxxii.

Sadler's witnesses included five practitioners from manufacturing towns, and no less than sixteen (including two who could claim Manchester experience) from London. However this mobilisation of metropolitan philanthropic opinion was a mixed blessing in the political conditions of the 1830s. Sadler's evidence was denounced as a 'string of medico-moral apothegms or axioms propounded by the chairman, and generally answered by a monosyllable'.[65] The questioning of London medical witnesses certainly tends to take this form. On the other hand, the propositions to which the eminent authorities were asked to assent had been derived from provincial medical evidence; witnesses were asked 'what your opinion would be, appealing to the general principles of your profession'.[66] Like the version of law and the constitution expounded from ten-hours platforms, views about the destructive effect of long hours were considered to be 'common sense', to which intellectual elites were to give symbolic endorsement.

This model of legislative knowledge was displaced by the Factory Commission, the 1833 Act and the inspectorate. These were informed by notions of regulation as the corrective of specific, manageable evils, collateral to the growth of a fundamentally rational and benign industrial system. Medical commentators like Kay helped shape this vision, though their ulterior schemes of medico-moral surveillance had little influence on the practical agendas of regulation. Those commentators I have labelled as opponents of the ten-hours bill should not, therefore, be regarded as Panglossian apologists for the factory system. Like some of the liberal employers to whom they were allied, they combined a defence of the factory system with an identification of those evils which required intervention, whether of a legislative or philanthropic nature. This is reflected in specific accounts of debility, disease and moral danger associated with factory work.

Specific diseases identified in medical commentaries are summarised in table 3.2.[67] As might be expected, the ten-hours supporters give a more extensive and more ominous list of morbid conditions attributed to factory employment. The most frequently mentioned problem, deformities, with important symbolic resonances in the whole debate on child labour, is not mentioned at all by opponents of the ten-hours bill. The

[65] *Barrow's Mirror of Parliament* (1833), vol. II, pp. 1194–5 (T. Gisbourne, MP for Derbyshire; the speaker had himself been a member of Sadler's Committee).
[66] Select Committee 1832, q. 10898 (T. Hodgkin, MD); London medical men are the last sequence of witnesses, following the provincial practitioners.
[67] Table 3.2 includes diseases mentioned in evidence, pamphlets, speeches, etc., by the medical practitioners in table 3.1. The concern is with the arguments as stated, not the accuracy of diagnosis, or the 'real' incidence of particular conditions, and I have adopted the terms used in the sources to identify diseases.

focus on deformities, varicose veins and leg ulcers relates to the destructive effect of the work itself, and undoubtedly reflects problems encountered by local practitioners. There is also a holistic notion of exhaustion,
debilitation and weakening of the constitution. As William Sharp of
Bradford put it: 'I think amongst the ill effects produced the injury to the
general health is of more consequence than any particular deformities; I
would not lay so much stress on the deformities as on the breaking up of
the constitution; the injury to the general health.'[68] One of the metropolitan authorities, John Farre, elaborated on the natural and providential
limits to labour; by exceeding these providential limits, man 'abridges his
life in the exact proportion in which he transgresses the laws of nature and
the Divine command'. Another London witness emphasised the dangers
of childhood and puberty, the importance of 'balancing the activities of
life' and 'due development'.[69]

Notions of natural limits, balance and 'due development' suggest links
between medical arguments and ideas of social and economic balance
used to criticise the accumulation of 'artificial' wealth.[70] Such ideas could
be appropriated across a political spectrum, from Tory traditionalists, to
Tory or Whig 'country party' oppositionists, to popular radicalism and
Chartism. McDouall's articles on the factory system rework medico-
moral and economic ideas of order, balance and the natural, and frame
them in an apocalyptic romantic imagery: 'The tender sufferer bends like
a rush to the power of disease, sinks into the grave . . . beneath the sweeping afflictions of the wandering plague.'[71]

Opponents of the ten-hours movement also acknowledged the debili-
tating effect of overwork. James Kay argued that 'every thing which
depresses the physical energies' produced 'predisposition to contagious
disease'.[72] It should be noted that Kay recognises 'extreme labour' as one
such threat to health, and indeed places considerable emphasis on the
exhaustion suffered by many factory operatives; the apologistic argument
that machine-minding involved little real effort received diminished
attention in the debates of the 1830s. These predisposing factors were
however seen as discrete, and manageable conditions. There was a
characteristic shift from the workplace to the urban environment, moral
habits, life-style and diet. The nervous exhaustion induced by prolonged
factory work was itself represented as leading to drink, dissipation,
domestic discomfort and inappropriate diet. The 'innutritious' diet of
cotton operatives might be adequate to those engaged in less demanding

[68] Select Committee 1832, q. 7114.   [69] Ibid., qq. 11532, 11371.
[70] See Berg, *Machinery Question*, chs. 11, 12; Hilton, *Age of Atonement*; Stedman Jones,
Languages of Class, pp. 114–23.   [71] *McDouall's Journal*, p. 61.
[72] Kay, *Moral and Physical Condition*, pp. 27–8.

Table 3.2 *Work-linked diseases mentioned by medical commentators*

	Ten-hours supporters	Ten-hours opponents	Total
No. of practitioners(as in table 3.1)	10	6	16
No. mentioning			
exhaustion, debility	5	2	7
weakened constitution	6	—	6
stomach, bowel disorders	5	4	9
cough, asthma, lung disease (not specified as consumption)	5	2	7
consumption	4	2	6
scrofula	4	—	4
fever	3	1	4
deformities	7	—	7
varicose veins, leg ulcers	3	—	3
pelvic deformities, childbirth problems	1	—	1
premature puberty	2	1	3
retarded puberty	2	—	2

Sources: see nn. 50, 67.

(but less productive) work; moral improvement and productive efficiency thus go hand in hand.[73]

Kay's writings are also notable for identifying factory workers' diseases linked to specific, isolable factors. Phthisis (consumption), which Kay argued *could* develop from 'those affections of the lungs . . . vulgarly denominated coughs', was commoner in card-rooms than in spinning-rooms and in coarse rather than fine spinning. 'In each succeeding step of these processes, the quantities of dust and filaments which escape diminish, until, at length, in some of the finest mills, they are, in the last stages, scarcely perceptible.'[74] This particular hierarchy was neatly symbolised in the layout of the standard cotton mill, with dirty raw cotton proceeding from the card-room on the bottom floor to 'at length' arrive, cleansed and prepared for spinning, on the upper floors. There is a corresponding hierarchy of pay, self-discipline, rational behaviour and personal health; the 'gastralgia', which Kay also identified as a condition afflicting cotton operatives, was less common among fine spinners, who were better paid, better fed, and 'generally a respectable and intelligent body of men'. This had been encouraged by 'several wise and benevolent regulations' introduced by leading employers.[75]

[73] Ibid., pp. 24–5.   [74] *North of England Jour.*, pp. 359–60.   [75] Ibid., pp. 225–6.

Liberal commentators on factory labour therefore combined a recognition of problems requiring intervention, whether by the state, medical philanthropy or 'wise and benevolent regulations' on the part of employers, with a defence of the factory system. The focus on specific and potentially manageable problems was linked to a comparative statistical approach. The assertion that factory children were at any rate as healthy as other poor children was a frequent theme in defences of the factory system, and this was taken up by medical commentators who emphasised the deficient state of statistics which might illuminate the question.[76] For Edwin Chadwick, the Factory Commission was the occasion to initiate a grand scheme of statistical investigation (later resumed in the Children's Employment Commission) but the results were partial and disappointing. The statistical approach was related to a shift of attention from the workplace to the urban environment and to 'the state of the child, preparatory to its being brought into the mill'.[77] Some commentators advocated 'a careful selection of children . . . and a periodical examination of their health by competent parties'.[78] The retention of factory surgeons was one mark of the enlightened millowner, such as the Gregs, John Wood of Bradford and the three Leeds employers retaining Robert Baker; their most important function seems to have been inspection of new recruits, no doubt in the interests of productive efficiency as well as the children's health. At the Gregs' Styal mill, poor law apprentices found to be unfit for work were in some cases ordered to be rested and fed, in others returned to sender.[79] Such posts were also of significance as part of the portfolio of fees and retainers from which medical men attempted to build careers. Expanding the role of the certifying surgeons established under the 1833 Act was one possible development, and there were attempts to do this. *The Lancet* gave occasional notice to the factory question, combining a high-flown moral rhetoric with the claims of medical men to staff any system of regulation.[80]

However this interest was intermittent; endorsing age certificates was just one of a range of routine fee-earning jobs for practitioners in manufacturing towns, and certifying surgeons did not constitute a cohesive reform pressure-group. At the same time, their vulnerability to pressure from employers, and from working-class families eager to get a child into

[76] Kay, *Moral and Physical*, pp. 18–19; Factory Comm., Second Report, C.3, pp. 11, 15.

[77] P. Gaskell, *Artisans and Machinery* (1836), p. 163.

[78] Factory Comm., Second Report, C.3, p. 11.

[79] Ibid., p. 14; Select Committee 1832, qq. 7053–5, 7108–9; Greg Papers, Manchester Archives, C2/4/2/2.

[80] *The Lancet*, editorials of 30 April 1836, 22 April 1843, 1 June 1850; and see S. Huzzard, 'The role of the certifying factory surgeon', MA, University of Manchester, 1976.

the mill, led to conflicts with the inspectors.[81] In the cholera epidemic of 1849, central authorities suddenly looked to certifying surgeons, issuing an extraordinary directive for the daily examination of 'the operatives'. The manifest impracticality of the instruction no doubt reflected its genesis in a moment of panic, and as panic subsided the factory came to be represented as a fortress against infectious disease, as well as against Chartist unrest.[82]

Surgeons were rather unreliable allies in the cause of factory reform, despite the high profile of some of their colleagues in generating its moral rhetoric. Calls for more systematic medical surveillance were significant in helping define a climate of opinion around the figure of the enlightened employer, rather than in affecting the actual process of state regulation. The health of towns, which had itself emerged as an issue in medical interventions in debates about the factory, was perhaps a more characteristic and continuing preoccupation for medical reformers. Medical opinion was most effective in generating a climate of concern, and pointing out the need for rational intervention (though not necessarily, or exclusively, intervention by the state), while eschewing partisan commitments to particular solutions.

If the destruction of health by long hours of work in insanitary conditions could be convincingly argued on medical grounds, the optimal length of working day was less self-evident. As James Williamson argued in his statement for the Factory Commission, 'as a physician I cannot assert that any uniform limitation of hours is essential to the physical health of children'.[83] Medical discourse was here caught up in a delicate negotiation with the claims of political economy, or, more crudely stated, 'whether it were better that a child should labour twelve hours a-day and be sufficiently fed, or ten hours a-day and be insufficiently fed'.[84] Liberal commentators such as Kay of course incorporated political economy as a central organising assumption, in a perspective of amelioration in which moral order, improved health and productive efficiency went together. As one of Kay's Manchester colleagues argued in an account of the 'medical topography' of the town, children of handloom weavers (whose problems were characteristically linked to the pressure of Irish immigration) could only escape the cycle of deprivation by finding more profitable employments, 'which, however, cannot reasonably be expected whilst the people

[81] G. Cheetham, The 'Inspector Inspected' in a Series of Four Letters relative to Mr. Leonard Horner (1839), and see above, n. 22; Thomas, Early Factory Legislation, pp. 124–33.

[82] Correspondence with factory inspectors, 21 Sept., 2 Oct. 1849, HO 87.2; for Chartism at this time, see esp. J. Saville, 1848: The British State and the Chartist Movement (Cambridge, 1987).   [83] Factory Comm., Second Report, C.3, p. 10.

[84] Barrow's Mirror of Parliament (1833), vol. II, pp. 1194–5, 3 April 1833.

continue to increase faster than the means of employing them'.[85] The laws of capital accumulation figured alongside physical geography, climate and other environmental factors in the medical topography of the town. Medical arguments could also propose natural and moral limits to political economy. As one of Sadler's London witnesses declared, political economy 'ought not to be suffered to trench on vital economy, because if it does, it is guilty of homicide'.[86] Childhood, female puberty and repro-duction were aspects of 'vital economy' particularly emphasised in medical critiques of the factory system. Ten-hours advocates could draw on a stock of medical knowledge in emphasising the peculiar dangers of adolescence, especially female adolescence, in response to the separation of children from young persons by the 1833 Act.[87]

Such anxieties about the boundaries of economic calculation, moral order and age and gender relations were pervasive features of public debate in the second quarter of the nineteenth century, variously treated in liberal, conservative or popular radical frameworks. In the context of factory reform, they undoubtedly reinforced hostile attitudes to the employment of women and rhetorical demands for their exclusion. However medico-moral concerns with work-linked threats to health and morals did not inaugurate any continuing tradition of medical surveil-lance. The central issue of the working day was not one on which medical expertise had much to say, apart from the obvious desirability of shorter hours, other things being equal. That was to be resolved in conflict, bar-gaining and negotiation involving workers, employers, politicians and state officials. The significance of medical debates lay in their contribu-tion to the languages of social debate, and a diffuse sense of social concern projected in the 'condition of England' debate. Discussions of factory labour, or later of children's employment in mines and elsewhere, marked out a difference, between the safe children of the middle classes and the endangered children of the poor. This difference at the same time functioned as a metaphor for anxieties middle-class people felt about themselves and their children. As one medical commentary on the Factory Commission report put it, 'unprincipled parents' had sold 'into bondage . . . children of an age at which those of the middling and upper classes of society are not permitted even to cross a street'.[88]

Concerns about 'premature puberty', sexual precocity and the 'animal propensities' of the working class also evoked cross-class anxi-eties about female adolescence, which might, in effect, extend to all

---

[85] *North of England Jour.*, p. 21.   [86] Select Committee 1832, q. 11547.
[87] See P. Jallard and J. Hooper (eds.), *Women from Birth to Death: The Female Life Cycle in Britain, 1830–1914* (Brighton, 1986).
[88] *Edinburgh Medical and Surgical Journal* 41 (1834), p. 200.

young unmarried women. The dangers of over-excitement and prolonged frenetic activity in crowded and over-heated rooms were apparent both in mills and in the 'high living, frequent balls, theatres, and places of public amusement . . . study of romantic and licentious works' indulged in by daughters of the wealthier classes. This linking of ballrooms and mills recurs in several medical texts of the 1830s.[89] There is a characteristic veering between the physical and the moral in these accounts. Peter Gaskell's *Artisans and Machinery* (1836) mentions the 'stimulus of a heated atmosphere', but this was effective only because the 'asbestos coating of moral decency' had developed cracks through the disruption of the family by industrial change. Often quoted (for example by Engels) as a critic of the factory system, Gaskell in fact argued on similar lines to Kay, basing a qualified defence of the factory on the inevitability of progress represented by steam-powered machinery, and the need to manage the negative consequences of such change.[90] The supposed causal link between environment and the age of puberty was in fact under question in a series of articles by John Roberton, surgeon to the Manchester lying-in charity. Writing as a liberal evangelical, Roberton welcomed the refutation of an environmental determinism which undermined hopes for a 'brighter day of moral and political renovation', in tropical countries abroad and among the working class in his own town.[91]

Medico-moral concerns provided an important stock of arguments in the continuing debate over factory regulation. But their impact on the practice of regulation was limited by intra-professional divisions which prevented the formulation of any single coherent 'professional' message. Juridical and administrative pragmatism and negotiation, informed by concerns with educational reform and class conciliation, were to be the predominant registers in the official language of factory regulation.

---

[89] Select Committee 1832, q. 10612; M. Ryan, *Manual of Midwifery* (4th edn, 1841), pp. 59–69; and cf. A. Combe, *The Principles of Physiology* (3rd edn, 1835), pp. 226–8; *McDouall's Jour.*, p. 51.

[90] Gaskell, *Artisans and Machinery*, pp. 108–11. For Gaskell see F. Engels, *The Condition of the Working Class in England*, ed. W.O. Henderson and W.H. Chaloner (Oxford, 1958), pp. xiii–xiv, footnote, 78, footnotes; J.G. Sharps, *Mrs Gaskell's Observation and Invention* (Fontwell, Sussex, 1970), p. 34, footnote. Gaskell was related by marriage to his namesakes, Elizabeth and William Gaskell, and also to the Ashtons of Hyde. I am grateful to Mr Sharps and to Professor C. Lansbury for their help with this point.

[91] *North of England Jour.*, p. 190; for a listing of Roberton's articles on this topic, see J.M. Tanner, *A History of Studies of Human Growth* (Cambridge, 1981), bibliography; I am indebted to Joan Mottram for this reference and discussion of her own work on Roberton.

Commissioners, inspectors and the agendas of reform

Medical commentators provided some of the rhetoric of factory reform, but did not give it any single clear or coherent direction. State functionaries, whose formation and *milieu* in some cases overlapped that of medical reformers, had a more integral and continued involvement in the process of regulation. The factory commissioners, and subsequently the inspectors, emerged as significant voices in debates about factory regulation. The factory question became, from one point of view, a classic debate in the construction of a selectively interventionist liberal state, a state actively concerned to 'construct its own absences';[92] overt interventions were justified as producing the conditions for rational and orderly behaviour among those not able, or not yet able, to act as free agents. Education and other forms of moral discipline were generally seen as central to this process. Factory reform was among the sites for elaborating such projects.

Various influences shaped state institutions and the moral and professional formation of their key personnel. There has been continuing debate about 'Benthamite', 'Evangelical' and 'paternalistic' influences, the relationship of aristocratic patronage to expertise and middle-class meritocracy, and the roles of reforming zealots and routinised pragmatists. Chadwick, some of his colleagues in the Factory Commission and at least one of the inspectors (Leonard Horner) might be seen as liberal reformers; and factory regulation certainly had a strategic significance in relation to the 'expert' programme of educational intervention. On the other hand, as Peter Bartrip has argued, the practical reach and efficacy of such projects of reform and surveillance were limited; the grandiose claims of a Chadwick have to be set in a context of Treasury parsimony, vested interest and jealously guarded boundaries between state and civil society.[93] The role of the factory inspectorate was initially conceived in rather broad and vague terms, as plenipotentiaries of a rational state. This aroused hostility from both workers and employers; closer definition, through case-law and responsibility to the Home Office, strengthened the inspectors' authority to exercise more restricted functions.[94]

The factory question was characterised by competing agendas of regulation, with pressure from organised workers and their allies as well as continued employer resistance to aspects of regulation. The role of state officials was consequently subject to renegotiation. This development

---

[92] Oakley, 'Utilitarian, paternalistic or both?', p. 28.
[93] P.W.J. Bartrip, 'British government inspection, 1832–1875: some observations', *Historical Journal* 25, no. 3 (1982).   [94] Field, 'Without the law?'.

illustrates both the capacity of key figures to appropriate social issues and to use them as platforms for their agendas of liberal reform, and the countervailing pressures and practical constraints that limited the practical reach of such schemes. The liberal project was nevertheless central to state formation, and factory reform was one of its key testing-grounds. It has to be understood, precisely, as a *project*, a set of guiding aspirations formulated by identifiable networks of influence and power, rather than as something firmly set in place and stamped on to an inert social formation. Exponents of the liberal project were often internally divided, on pragmatic as well as on ideological grounds, and these internal divisions were inflected by the external constraints of negotiation with organised social movements and pressure-groups.

The Factory Commission and the inspection process provided platforms for claims to authority based on expert enquiry into social conditions. Apart from their (often rather limited) impact on further legislation, these official documents were more widely circulated as part of an informed and enlightened opinion about industrial problems, and they carried with them the 'pleasures of benevolence' and the *frisson* of apprehended social dangers.[95] This intervention in the factory question was part of a wider construction of social knowledge, sponsored by or addressed to state agencies. Kay had argued the need for this in his 1832 pamphlet, claiming that select committees 'are never so minutely accurate as those results obtained from statistical investigation' and consequently 'frequently utterly fail . . . in convincing the public'.[96] The First Report of the Factory Commission was represented as 'a full exposition of the condition of the factories in the different districts of the kingdom'; and Chadwick subsequently claimed, in a begging letter to Senior, that his enquiries into the poor law and factories together comprised the most thorough such investigation 'since the Doomsday book'.[97] In reality, as critics did not fail to point out, there were considerable gaps and inconsistencies. The report itself was compiled in some haste, with a highly selective, sometimes tendentious, use of the district commissioners' findings. The subsequent publication of their detailed evidence together with medical reports and the questionnaires returned by employers may to some extent have lent authority to the undertaking; but it also provided evidence that could be used against Chadwick's conclusions.

[95] S.E. Finer, 'The transmission of Benthamite ideas, 1820–1850', in Sutherland (ed.), *Studies in the Growth of Nineteenth-Century Government*; Hall, *White, Male and Middle Class*, p. 213, for the 'pleasures of benevolence'; Mort, *Dangerous Sexualities*, alludes to the excitements of vicarious danger in the reading of such texts.

[96] Kay, *Moral and Physical Condition*, p. 5.

[97] Factory Comm., First Report, p. 7; draft of letter to Senior, Chadwick Papers, 1782.

The employer questionnaires are of some interest, as a rare example of information pertaining to identifiable individual enterprises, including their proprietors' opinions as well as structural variables. However, there are significant gaps, including Oldham and Ashton in Lancashire and Dewsbury in the West Riding (all of these are identifiable, coincidentally or not, as areas of particular industrial conflict), as well as a general tendency to under-enumeration.[98] Writing to Chadwick soon after arriving in Manchester, commissioner Cowell complained of the unforeseen dimensions of his task and the unsuitability of the questionnaire.[99] Some of the difficulties arose from inherent ambiguities, which also pervade subsequent official industrial censuses. It is not clear whether the enumeration was of mills or of firms, and different employers seem to have understood this differently. This is to some extent a reflection of the industrial structure itself, with the sub-letting of 'room and power' within mills, the shifting family partnerships of the typical firm and such specific forms as the 'company mill', jointly owned to service the woollen clothiers.[100] The large concerns often singled out for praise in official reports embodied a particular overlap of ownership, management and concentrated location (though such firms might in fact also employ large numbers of out-workers and acquire and dispose of additional assets on a more speculative basis). The frequent contrast between this and the obsolescent, marginal small producer, held responsible for the worst abuses, polarised a far more complex range of industrial structures and shifting and interlocking patterns of ownership and control.

Official enquiry therefore reinforced particular ways of seeing industrial problems. The characteristic emphases of Chadwick's report set the pattern for much subsequent official and parliamentary discourse about the factory question. The identification of problems requiring intervention was dissociated from any systemic critique of industrial capitalism, and indeed became linked to a vision of the well-regulated factory as the site of social and moral improvement, as well as the symbol of economic progress. This was framed by the 'statistical' move of comparison between large and small factories, and between factory and other employments. The revelations of such comparative enquiry helped sustain a more favourable view of the factory.

---

[98] Jenkins, 'The validity of the factory returns'. For discussion of attitudes from employer questionnaires, see below, chapter 4.
[99] Cowell to Chadwick, 5 May 1833, Chadwick Papers, 41.
[100] V.A.C Gatrell, 'Labour, power and the size of firms in Lancashire cotton', *Economic History Review* 30 (1977); R. Lloyd Jones and A.A. Le Roux, 'The size of firms in the cotton industry', *Economic History Review* 33 (1980); L. Davidoff and C. Hall, *Family Fortunes: Men and Women of the English Middle Class, 1780–1850* (London, 1987), pt ii; Hudson, *Genesis of Industrial Capital*, pp. 76–81.

The capacity of Chadwick and his associates to define a practical policy of intervention, addressed to the realities of the industrial situation, was more debatable. The projected relay system, with its vision of regulated labour combined with schooling, was of limited applicability. Even the leading manufacturers giving evidence to the central board saw many difficulties in the scheme. Among the employer questionnaires, only 20 out of 321 in Yorkshire and 22 out of 216 in Lancashire expressed any interest at all in the idea, while many others expressed strong hostility; in practice its adoption was to be very uneven and dependent on local conditions.[101] The effect of the 1833 Act, in so far as it was observed, was rather to accelerate a shift from child to teenaged labour. If the factory commissioners' outlook had affinities to that of large millowners, their specific proposals had a distinctly mixed reception. This was to be reinforced by the actual process of regulation; authority conflicts over the inspectors' powers brought them into collision with large as well as small employers, for example the celebrated confrontation between Leonard Horner and the Ashworths, noted exemplars of the enlightened manufacturer.[102] On the other hand, the 1833 Act was only at all viable because it incorporated a limit on young persons' hours, abandoning Chadwick's proposed deregulation of this group. The Act was undoubtedly a defeat for the ten-hours movement, and was so regarded by the movement itself. But it was by no means an unambiguous expression of the perceived interests of employers, nor even of the group of enlightened liberal millowners whose views were so assiduously foregrounded. The definition of a practical course of sustainable intervention followed further confrontation and negotiation.

Some of the shifts and redefinitions arising from this encounter between official expertise and the industrial north are illustrated in the career of Leonard Horner, the most famous of the factory inspectors and the one most closely linked to the intellectual world of liberal reform. While Horner's role has been much discussed, and may well have been inflated and mythologised, his career remains a revealing case.[103] A factory commissioner for the western district (on which he reported in fairly 'optimistic' terms), Horner was then appointed a factory inspector, and in this capacity was to be responsible for Lancashire from 1836 and

---

[101] Factory Comm., First Report, evidence taken before Central Board; Supp. Report, pt ii, employer questionnaires; M. Sanderson, 'Education and the factory in industrial Lancashire, 1780–1840', *Economic History Review* 20 (1967), p. 274.

[102] Boyson, *Ashworth Cotton Enterprise*, ch. 9. For further discussion of struggles over enforcement, see below, chapter 6.

[103] B. Martin, 'Leonard Horner: a portrait of an inspector of factories', *International Review of Social History* 14 (1969); cf. A.E. Peacock, 'The justices of the peace and the prosecution of the factory acts, 1833–1855', DPhil, University of York (1982), pp. 58–80.

throughout the crucial period of conflict over factory regulation that ensued. An Edinburgh Whig with impeccable credentials as an enlightened educationist, Horner believed he was among fellow-spirits on his arrival in the cotton metropolis. He was dined by leading liberal manufacturers, such as Henry McConnel, 'a most excellent man, and I am glad to say he is going to adopt that which I am urging so strongly upon the mill-owners, the employment of young children united with attendance at school'; the two men shared Scots origins, as well as commitments to rationalism and improvement, and Horner's network extended to the recruitment of a suitable teacher from the Edinburgh Sessional School.[104] Horner consistently urged employers to adopt the relay system, which would 'capture' a larger segment of the age-group for compulsory schooling, and clearly regarded the enlightened employer as a potential ally. As he argued in a celebrated exchange with Nassau Senior: 'The law was not passed for such mills as those of Messrs. Greg and Co. . . . Messrs. Ashworth . . . and Mr. Thomas Ashton . . . But there are very many mill-owners whose standard of morality is low, whose feelings are very obtuse, whose governing principle is to make money.'[105]

This vision of the enlightened big millowner was to be qualified, though never displaced, in subsequent experience. In many instances Horner continued to accept that 'the proprietor was not aware' of the offence, 'for I have the best authority for saying that he is a most benevolent good man'. In other cases, however, 'men of station and property . . . often occupying very large factories' were culpable, and these were scolded in schoolmasterly manner for setting a bad example: 'from the station of the proprietors, better things might have been expected'.[106] In addition to his commitments as an educationist, Horner retained a Whiggish concern with social conciliation and negotiated accommodation of interests based on mutual recognition of the obligations of 'station'. This concern to mitigate social tensions – if necessary by harsh words to employers – moved his official agenda towards the continued struggle over the length of the working day.

Horner may therefore fit the picture of the state servant as 'zealot'. His personal letters articulate the professional middle-class masculine identities, to which Frank Mort has drawn attention. Writing to his wife, Horner complained of the 'dull and mechanical and unvaried' nature of

---

[104] K.M. Lyell (ed.), *A Memoir of Leonard Horner*, 2 vds. (privately printed, 1890), vol. I, p. 329, Horner to his daughter Katherine, 7 Aug., 1836.

[105] Horner, in N.W. Senior, *Letters on the Factory Act* (1837), p. 34.

[106] Reports of Factory Inspectors: Horner, Jan. 1839, pp. 15–16, July 1839, p. 13: cf. W.G. Carson, 'The institutionalisation of ambiguity: the early factory acts', in G. Geis and E. Stotland (eds.), *White-Collar Crime* (Beverley Hills and London, 1980).

his duties, which necessitated visits to places like Oldham, 'about the most barbarous part of Lancashire . . . but whose fault is it that they are so? not their's, but that of the better classes around them who have neglected them'. Nevertheless: 'I recover my spirits by thinking that I am the instrument of making the lives of many innocent children less burthensome, and that by earnestness in my calling I may acquire that degree of credit, that my object of extending the protection to children more widely, will be attended to.'[107] His career also, however, illustrates the *ad hoc* and often fortuitous way in which such figures found official posts for themselves. The whole notion of the 'official career' has to be understood in the light of a considerable fluidity of occupational identities, and a conception of professionalism in terms of the independent educated gentleman performing a variety of stipendiary and voluntary roles.[108] Following an unhappy time as the first warden of University College, London (where he alienated the teaching staff by failing to guarantee their fee-based incomes, in marked contrast to his own assured £1,200 p.a.), Horner was appointed a factory commissioner, then an inspector, through the patronage network of the Edinburgh Whigs.[109] Factory inspection provided a platform for educational concerns, but it also embroiled the inspectors in the social politics of the manufacturing districts. Horner's zeal may have reflected some impatience about the time he was obliged to spend in Lancashire, rather than on his general cultural interests, especially his geological pursuits, to which he was a distinguished and *avant-garde* contributor, and which he himself may have considered his true vocation. Whatever its origins, this impatience led to high-handed interventions and to bad relations with his subordinates. It would certainly be misleading to take Horner's well-publicised activities as typifying the impact of liberal educationists on factory regulation. His style may well have been counter-productive, and, as Dr Peacock has suggested, more may have been achieved with less public confrontation by Horner's Yorkshire colleague, R. J. Saunders.[110] While these personality factors are clearly relevant, it remains true that anyone filling Horner's post would have found themselves involved in conflict.

Less is known about the other inspectors. One of them, Robert Baker,

---

[107] Lyell (ed.), *Horner*, vol. II, p. 14, letter to his wife, 18 June 1841; cf. Mort, *Dangerous Sexualities*. The reference to extending protection probably relates to the Children's Employment Commission, on which Horner was serving at the time.

[108] See Davidoff and Hall, *Family Fortunes*; T.W. Heyck, *The Transformation of Intellectual Life in Victorian England* (Beckenham, 1982), ch. 2.

[109] Martin, 'Horner', pp. 423–7. For the Edinburgh connection see A. Chitnis, *The Scottish Enlightenment and the Evolution of Victorian Society* (London, 1986); S. Collini *et al.*, *That Noble Science of Politics* (Cambridge, 1983), ch. 1; Johnson, 'Educating the educators', pp. 84–5.   [110] Peacock, 'Justices of the peace', pp. 58–80.

the Leeds parish surgeon, was among the medical commentators discussed above; appointed a superintendent (i.e. sub-inspector) and promoted to inspector after the period under discussion, he to some extent fits the pattern of the liberal reforming zealot. Another of the early inspectors was James Stuart, a Scottish Whig, but a less serious-minded and conscientious one than Horner.[111] Stuart, a lesser politician and hack writer fallen on hard times, owed his post to Brougham's patronage. He adopted a perspective of apologism for the employers, directing such prosecutions as he undertook at adult workers, or informally securing their dismissals; his relations with his official colleagues were consistently strained. As Ursula Henriques has suggested, more Stuarts and fewer Horners in key posts might have further exacerbated the social tensions of the 1830s and 40s.[112] Here again, differences of personality and individual zeal have to be set beside the differing contexts of the Scottish and Lancashire textile districts; the question to ask about Stuart is partly why he got away with it for so long. Scottish textiles were a relatively labour-intensive, low-wage sector, contracting into specialised products and markets in the face of competition from the north of England and other countries; the defeat of the Glasgow spinners in the 1830s probably also weakened possible pressures to enforce regulation on terms more acceptable to the operatives.[113]

However, the influence of liberal reform is to be seen not simply in the earnest endeavours of zealots, but equally in the scripts routinely spoken by their less thoughtful colleagues. Stuart's enthusiasm for the large employer as an agent of improvement and his understanding of law in terms of class discipline was not so far removed from the position of Chadwick. Paradoxically, though, his quarrels with his colleagues, and especially his reporting of Scottish employers' scepticism about relays, were also to be cited by ten-hours critics of the Commission.[114] Stuart's skills as a travel writer were readily pressed into service to provide graphic examples for Chadwick's report. He provided hyperbolic accounts of large concerns, like the famous Deanston mills (Perthshire). One such establishment (Bannerman's mills, Aberdeen) was described as: 'A splendid work, erected only a few years ago, the size over walls two hundred and thirty feet by fifty-three. There is here an ascending and descending

---

[111] Henriques, 'Early factory inspector'; Lee, 'Robert Baker'.

[112] Henriques, 'Early factory inspector', pp. 45–6.

[113] See T. Dickson (ed.), *Scottish Capitalism: Class, State and Nation from before the Union to the Present* (London, 1980), pp. 140–3, 164–8, 186–7, 198–9; Scottish manufacturers were prominent lobbyists in opposition to Sadler and Ashley, see Driver, *Tory Radical*, p. 218. I am indebted to John Foster for discussion of these issues.

[114] 'The cotton manufacture and the factory system', *Blackwoods Magazine* 40 (1836), p. 115; *Address to the Friends of Justice and Humanity in the West Riding of York* (1833), p. 7.

room, moved by steam; but what pleased me most . . . was to observe the sufficient space which each worker enjoys.' A contrasting case is provided in a racy description of a small mill at Bervie (Kincardineshire), visited the day after 'bacchanalian orgies' at a local fair, 'a moment not propitious for them'. This mill provided 'a fit asylum' to 'those engaged in vicious courses, to whom the regularity and excellent regulation in many respects of the Montrose establishments would of course be irksome'; even the owner's house (not normally a matter of comment in such enquiries) was filthy and uncomfortable and, worst of all, 'two or three young females' were found in the bothy, 'the eating and sleeping room of such a nest of profligates'.[115]

The repertoire of official enquiry played some part in redefining the agenda of factory regulation, and presenting it to a wider concerned opinion. But the coherence and practical reach of official responses should not be exaggerated. The role of inspectors was as much reactive as initiatory. New forms of official intervention and monitoring did nevertheless shift the terrain of debate, and popular short-time agitation itself responded to that shift. There was continuing suspicion of the inspectorate, and of the aspects of 'class legislation' embodied in the 1833 Act. These included the prosecution of adult workers, parents and others in the working-class community, especially as employers could and did shift liability on to such substitute offenders.[116] The trade- and community-based models of law and enforcement discussed earlier in this chapter continued to inform workers' understandings of factory regulation as an aspect of 'fair' employment. There was nevertheless a tactical shift towards pressure to enforce the existing law, together with continuing demands for a ten-hours bill. John Lawton, a former Manchester operative and short-time activist, claimed at a Select Committee on the working of the law (1840) that the appointment of 'shadow inspectors' from the short-time committees had led to a marked improvement in the efficacy of enforcement.[117] With the involvement of short-time committees in pressure to enforce the existing statute (albeit with a view to exposing its inadequacies), operatives' organisations were drawn on to a terrain of bargaining and negotiation, while still insisting on the demand for a uniform ten-hour day.

The 1840 Select Committee marked an important moment in this respect. Chaired by Ashley, its members included Fielden, Brotherton and Hindley, Lancashire MPs identified with textile interests, but also

[115] Factory Comm., First Report, pp. 16–17, 20.
[116] Carson, 'Institutionalisation of ambiguity'; and see below, chapter 6.
[117] Select Committee on the Act for the Regulation of Mills and Factories, PP 1840 X, qq. 8471–3 (hereafter cited as 'Select Committee 1840').

with the short-time movement and popular radical sympathies; R.H. Greg, likewise a Lancashire Liberal manufacturer, represented the other end of the spectrum of opinion on factory legislation. As its report noted, the Committee's terms of reference were limited to investigating 'the operation of the Act, . . . its defects, and . . . probable remedies', so as to fulfil 'the intention of the existing law'. The Act was placed in a rather bland perspective of consensual improvement:

> Your Committee must congratulate the House and the Country on the partial success of their efforts for the removal of many evils, which, down to the year 1833, had accompanied the employment of children and young persons in factories; much, unquestionably, yet remains to be done; the actual condition, nevertheless, of these young workers, contrasted with the state in which the first enquiry found them, is such as to give Your Committee considerable satisfaction for the past, and good hope for the future.[118]

Behind this bombastic optimism was a potentially controversial shift towards defining and strengthening the inspectors' powers of enforcement, registering parliamentary and administrative will to reduce the more blatant anomalies in enforcement practice (and sort out the differences between Stuart and his colleagues). Such measures would bring about 'the revival of a good understanding on all sides' and remove 'the several causes of heartburning and mutual distrust between the employer and the employed'.[119] But while the proceedings placed contending interests within an arena of parliamentary negotiation around limited terms of reference, they did also provide platforms for ulterior positions. Fielden questioned witnesses about the distances walked by piecers in a day's work, pursuing a controversy about the intensity of labour; while Ashley challenged employers on their moral obligations to the children they employed, which he implied extended beyond minimal compliance with the law: 'I speak to you as an honest man . . . whether you do or do not consider it to be a duty on your part to make yourself sure that the certificate [of age] speaks the truth?' Operative representatives like Lawton continued to advocate '10 hours a day, and a uniform working day for the whole', and to uphold a divergent popular model of enforcement. With a uniform day, the common informer could observe when the mill started and finished, in contrast to the 'inquisitorial' proceedings of the superintendents (the summary fining of workers, the burden of obtaining new certificates on shifting mills and the removal of the inspector's office from Manchester were particular grievances).[120]

---

[118] Ibid., Report.

[119] Ibid.; see also Field, 'Without the law?'; Thomas, *Early Factory Legislation*, ch. 12; Henriques, 'Early factory inspector', pp. 37–40.

[120] Select Committee 1840, qq. 38, 318–20, 350, 4425, 4879–85, 8384, 9224–44.

The 1840 Committee also provided a sounding-board for new initiatives, notably the accident clauses and the restriction of adult women, which were subsequently incorporated in the 1844 Act. These two issues were sometimes linked. As Ashley put it, in a leading question: 'Do not you think that little children are exposed to very great hazard, particularly female children with their flowing garments?'; the witness concerned (the superintendent for the Stockport area) duly obliged with a suitable instance from his experience.[121] In the extended interval between the Committee's report and the 1844 Act, the inspectors helped orchestrate opinion by highlighting suitable cases. Horner mentioned six accidents to women and girls, drawing attention to one where the victim was scalped 'while . . . dressing her long hair'. Subsequent discussion of safety regulations continued to emphasise particular risks to women, despite the fact that accident returns indicate a lower relative incidence for females compared to males in the relevant age-group.[122] Inspectors' reports of this period also drew attention to cases where prosecutions had failed because the 'girls' concerned were in fact eighteen or over, implying that this difficulty necessitated restrictions on all women.[123]

The factory question in the 1840s, like other aspects of the 'condition of England', was characterised by the construction of public debate in parliamentary and official enquiries, and their penumbra of informed opinion, to which a range of interests could feel they had some access, though by no means equality of access. This did not remove controversial, and often sharply polemical, divisions of opinion, but it did organise them into a more coherent debate, around a language of negotiation, a common reference to 'the prosperity of the trade, and the welfare of the nation'.[124] Operative short-time committees and their allies had some limited representation in this debate. But divisions in ruling-class opinion were more centrally represented. The 1840 Committee coincided with the Children's Employment Commission, in which the enlightened Whig Horner served alongside the Benthamite Southwood Smith and the Tory Evangelical Ashley. Campaigns about the health of towns and a variety of areas of 'reform' likewise elicited cooperation across this range of positions. Horner, the Whig conciliator, seems to have been concerned to bring these together; writing to Chadwick in June 1840, he expressed his concern to extend 'protection' (which doubtless implied compulsory schooling) to children employed outside the factories, suggesting a 'small

---

[121] Select Committee 1840, q. 2848.
[122] Reports of Factory Inspectors: Horner, July 1842, Jan. 1843; and see Gray, 'Factory legislation', pp. 70–3.
[123] Reports of Factory Inspectors: Horner, May 1844, p. 3; Saunders, July 1843, pp. 19–20, Jan. 1844, p. 25.   [124] Select Committee 1840, Report.

committee', which 'might get persons of opposite politics and sentiments to unite'.[125] If this unification of interests and opinions made some contribution to containing the Chartist threat, it is important to note that the redemption of endangered childhood provided the ground for cooperation.[126] It should also be remembered that the legislative outcome of these enquiries and debates was fairly modest (the restriction of women workers, in both the 1842 Mines Act and the 1844 Factory Act being one common theme in the measures that were passed). There was a greater impact on ruling-class morale and self-justification than on the purported objects of concern. The new alliances concerned with factory legislation, children's employment and the health of towns were, in part, alliances of the serious-minded official state and philanthropic opinion marginalised in the party political arena, a structure of feeling perhaps captured in Carlyle's denunciations of 'dilettantism'.[127]

The factory question became one item on a longer agenda of social reform. Enquiries into the weavers' distress, children's employment in mines and other non-factory occupations and the urban environment all served, explicitly or implicitly, to reinforce images of the factory as the site of rationality and improvement. The alternative image, of a malign 'factory system', extending beyond the gates of the factory itself, persisted in the language of Chartism and of Tory populists like Oastler and Stephens, but it was less central to parliamentary and official debates. At the same time, the operatives' key concern with the length of a standard working day formed part of an agenda of pragmatic negotiation for politicians, officials and some employers. This by no means neutralised conflict, especially at the level of divergent local interpretations, but it did establish a framework of bargaining, in which both official and popular perspectives were adapted and modified.

---

[125] Horner to Chadwick, 21 June 1840, Chadwick Papers, 1051; see also letters from Ashley, Chadwick Papers, 535, indicating cooperation on a range of issues, and Horner's letter cited above, n. 107. The Children's Employment Commission was appointed in October 1840.
[126] Cf. Cunningham, *Children of the Poor.*   [127] T. Carlyle, *Chartism* (1839).

4 The responsibilities of employers

One of the contributions of the factory question to the formation of industrial society was the crystallisation of employer interest-groups and opinions. Industrial employers themselves were actively engaged, together with workers, philanthropists, politicians and professional men, in seeking to define the terms of debate. Employers were by no means a unified or homogeneous group, but the debate on the factory was marked by organised expressions of opinion, which claimed to speak for manufacturing interests as a whole.

Employment practices were also the objects of critical scrutiny, which gave rise to defensive responses. Public scrutiny of 'good' or 'bad' conditions and the need for protection of child workers both exposed employers to criticism and foregrounded their role as the potential agents of improvement, whether or not this was thought to require the stimulus of legislation. This conception of the agency of the enlightened employer could often be linked to an aggressive economic liberalism, including strong opposition to the ten-hours campaign, if not always to other legislative measures. Organised expressions of employer opinion generally crystallised around this opposition, and sometimes carried it to the point of concerted resistance over the implementation of aspects of the factory acts (see below, chapter 6).

These stances would appear to correspond to the image of 'Manchester man'. That image has, however, been qualified in recent studies, and the attitudes of textile masters were varied and complex.[1] They were not a homogeneous or coherent group. Apart from variations in industrial structure, market conditions, work organisation and employment

---

[1] See esp. Davidoff and Hall, *Family Fortunes*; Gunn, 'The Manchester Middle Class'; S. Gunn, 'The "failure" of the Victorian middle class: a critique', in J. Wolff and J. Seed (eds.), *The Culture of Capital* (Manchester, 1988); Howe, *Cotton Masters*; Morris, *Class, Sect and Party*; V.A.C. Gatrell, 'Incorporation and the pursuit of liberal hegemony in Manchester, 1790–1839', in D. Fraser (ed.), *Municipal Reform and the Industrial City* (Leicester, 1982); Koditschek, *Class Formation*; and discussion of this in Seed, 'Capital and class formation'; Seed, 'Unitarianism'.

practices, there were political and cultural divisions; the claims of 'Manchester Liberalism' to speak for manufacturing as a whole, or even for Manchester itself, are open to question. There was always a significant Anglican and Tory presence and, within the liberal community, there were differences between the single-minded devotion to business activities of those struggling to survive and accumulate, and the broader outlook of more established manufacturing dynasties.

The 'market' and the proper sphere of economic calculation were themselves in part cultural constructs, whose meanings might vary between sectors and localities. Day-to-day business practice entailed moral values and assumptions: norms of 'fair dealing' and the importance of reputation and personal honour, the formal rules and customary practices of exchanges and marts, the male bourgeois sociability of the shared journey to work, the business lunch and the metropolitan club.[2] It was in such places that trade opinion would be formulated and orchestrated.[3] Large areas of activity might be governed by custom and habit until challenged by competitive pressures. Practices regarding prices, wages and working hours could be regulated in this way, and conditioned employer attitudes to legislation.

In this chapter I analyse employers' responses to the factory question, and then relate this to some broader issues of entrepreneurial middle-class culture and attitudes. I explore these issues by way of a discussion of religious discourses about economic life, and the nature of entrepreneurial liberal dissent. Finally, I shall consider debates about employers' rights and duties, which attracted the attention of publics concerned with the 'condition of England'. Some of the origins of a restated industrial paternalism may be identified in this context.

Employer opinion and public debate

The ten-hours campaigns of the early 1830s found textile manufacturers in a rather isolated and vulnerable position. There was substantial support within the political nation for protective legislation, and mounting popular pressure in the factory districts themselves. The initial defensive responses of employers and their allies drew on well-established lines of argument about the importance of the industry, the investment and employment dependent on it, the threat of foreign competition and

---

[2] Gunn, 'The Manchester Middle Class', pp. 162–6; Seed, 'Capital and class formation', pp. 27–8; and cf. E.J. Hobsbawm, *The Age of Extremes: The Short Twentieth Century, 1914–1991* (London, 1994), pp. 342–3.

[3] See, e.g., correspondence between John Fielden and his Manchester agent, Clegg, Fielden Papers, John Rylands University Library, Manchester.

apologetic assertions about the benign conditions enjoyed by factory children. Holland Hoole, in a pamphlet which attracted the formidable polemical powers of Oastler, described Whit processions of factory children 'well clad and often even elegantly dressed, in full health and beauty, a sight to gladden a monarch – not to be paralleled perhaps in the whole of the civilized world'.[4] Whig government circles showed some sensitivity to the defensive responses of manufacturing spokesmen. They out-manoeuvred Ashley in parliament and the ten-hours movement outside in the sequence of events leading to the 1833 Act.

More influential in the longer run were some of the arguments that emerged in the process of official enquiry, propounded by leading manufacturers and others with links to the intellectual *milieu* of rational dissent and liberal reform. Such arguments distanced themselves from crude apologism, in the context of a more strategic advocacy of the factory system as the potential agent of improvement. James Kay's assertion of the 'remote or accidental origin' of social evils, and the need for 'judicious management' was a keynote statement of this position.[5] Shorter hours were required to facilitate the favoured liberal programme of popular education, but measures had to take account of market conditions and the prospect of amelioration was linked to free trade. 'Evils' are recognised, but in a language far removed from that of factory slavery; in so far as regulation appeared appropriate, this was in order to discipline less responsible employers and the operatives themselves.

Within these broad assumptions there could be differences of view and emphasis. Some of the leading cotton masters, led by Henry Houldsworth, expressed support for judicious extension of restrictions, while implacably rejecting a ten-hour day (eight of the sixteen signatories of this memorial were among the twenty-two leading Manchester firms listed by Gatrell). Others, including such noted 'enlightened' employers as the Gregs, Ashworths and Ashtons, opposed any further restriction at all.[6] The latter group generally owned mills located outside Manchester, and produced coarser counts of yarn. This might suggest that, as has often been argued, there was greater resistance to regulation among 'country' millowners, engaged in coarse spinning.[7] However these notions (which are more fully examined below) provide only a partial

[4] H. Hoole, *A Letter to the Right Honourable Lord Viscount Althorp ... in Defence of the Cotton Factories of Lancashire* (1832), p. 10.

[5] Kay, *Moral and Physical Condition*, preface.

[6] Factory Comm., First Report, Central Board, evidence of Houldsworth, Ashworth, Greg, Ashton; cf. list of firms in Gatrell, 'Labour, power and the size of firms', p. 100.

[7] H.P. Marvel, 'Factory regulation: a reinterpretation of early English experience', *The Journal of Law and Economics* (1977).

explanation for differences in view. Both the groups mentioned were leading employers, prominent in Manchester-centred institutions and activities, regardless of the location of their factories; in particular, their association with the Manchester Statistical Society linked them to the intellectual networks of liberal reform.[8]

This discourse of liberal reform was often ambiguous about the respective functions of legislation and voluntary effort; it characteristically framed the analytical language of political economy in a moral rhetoric of impending crisis. These features are displayed in a powerful pamphlet by W. R. Greg, *An Enquiry into the State of the Manufacturing Population* (1831).[9] At that time the young, intellectually inclined and somewhat restless prospective heir to part of a cotton empire, Greg was associated with James Kay and the world of rational dissent. Published before Kay's *Moral and Physical Condition of the Working Classes* (1832), Greg's pamphlet argues along similar lines, but is, if anything, more outspoken. It concludes on an almost apocalyptic note, calling for:

> some cordial, faithful, vigorous, and united effort . . . on the part of the influential classes, to stem that torrent of suffering and corruption, which is fast sweeping away the comfort and the morals of so large a portion of our fellow countrymen; and which, if not checked, will soon send them forth into the world, desperate, reckless, ruined men.[10]

Like much of the literature of social and moral reform this call leaves fairly open the specific action to be taken; the appeal is to the 'influential classes', whether in a philanthropic or legislative capacity. Greg does, on the other hand, suggest that restricted hours are the precondition for effective educational intervention and, most controversially, he indicates ten hours as the desirable working day. Written at a point when the lines of opinion were perhaps still unclear, and qualified by the characteristic liberal move of linking amelioration to removal of 'the shackles and drawbacks to which the Cotton Manufacture is subjected', this apparent endorsement was to be sarcastically quoted from ten-hours platforms.[11]

In the context of hardening alignments on the factory question, Greg's pamphlet may indeed have been an embarrassment. As opinion polarised around the popular demand for a ten-hours bill, Greg's reference to this

---

[8] See Ashton, *Economic and Social Investigations in Manchester*; Seed, 'Unitarianism'.

[9] [W.R. Greg], *An Enquiry into the State of the Manufacturing Population and the Causes and Cures of the Evils Therein Existing* (1831); for the Gregs see Rose, *The Gregs*.

[10] [Greg], *Enquiry*, p. 39.

[11] Ibid., pp. 28–9; for use of Greg in ten-hours propaganda see 'Alfred', *Factory Movement*, vol. I, ch. 11; Oastler's annotated copy of [Greg], *Enquiry*, in Oastler Collection, Goldsmiths' Library, University of London; speech by Fielden, *The Ten Hours Advocate*, 21 Nov. 1846.

particular number must have become less acceptable in his own circle. Kay, arguing on rather similar lines in 1832, placed careful emphasis on 'the present state of trade' and dangers of 'commercial embarrassment'.[12] Greg himself retreated from the position of his 1831 pamphlet. In evidence to the Factory Commission he reported on his continental tour and the dangers of foreign competition; and answering the commissioners' questionnaire as proprietor of one of the family mills, he argued that the cotton trade was in 'too precarious a state to make any further restrictions safe'.[13] Greg was subsequently commissioned by the Statistical Society to prepare an analysis of the Commission's findings. The language of this report is as reassuring as that of 1831 had been disconcerting: 'the principal charges alleged against the factory system, are here most triumphantly refuted'.[14] The selective appropriation of Greg's arguments by more radical critics, and his own apparent *volte-face*, suggest a hardening of alignments in the struggle to defeat Sadler and Ashley. These shifts in emphasis also indicate that a variety of opinions and specific programmes might be debated within the broad framework of liberal reform. Opinion was by no means clear-cut, even among those articulate and vociferous millowners who were prepared to engage in public controversy. These men were overwhelmingly drawn from proprietors of big cotton firms, and were therefore not typical of the cotton industry, let alone other sectors of textiles involved in the struggle.

It is difficult to generalise about more 'average' employers, whose opinions remain at least as elusive as those of the 'average' worker. The questionnaire circulated by the factory commissioners does, however, afford some picture of a wider spectrum of employers (table 4.1). There are many difficulties with these returns, notably their geographical patchiness, and the responses cannot be treated as a representative sample.[15] The questions asked were also in some respects ambiguous, and any classification of the opinions expressed is bound to be arbitrary and impressionistic. The most relevant question asked about the 'probable effects' of further restriction, and responses vary in the extent to which they imply defined opinions.[16] There is a fairly high proportion of non-committal answers or non-responses. It is also essential to understand the

---

[12] Kay, *Moral and Physical Condition*, preface.
[13] Factory Comm., First Report, E.4, evidence of W.R. Greg; Factory Comm., Supp. Report pt ii, questionnaires from employers, D.1, no. 117.
[14] Manchester Statistical Society, *An Analysis of the Evidence Taken before the Factory Commission* (1834), p. 31.
[15] Jenkins, 'The validity of the factory returns'.
[16] Question 37 asks about 'the probable effects of a still further reduction of the working hours', and q. 79 invites 'further observations'; the alternative questionnaire used for most of the Yorkshire respondents (q. 27) simply asks for 'any remarks'.

Table 4.1 *Factory questionnaire, 1833, Cheshire, Lancashire, Yorkshire: employer support for further legislation*

	Supporting legislation	Total in returns	% supporting legislation
Cotton	39	260	15
Wool	20	147	14
Worsted	27	88	31
Manchester, Salford	18	92	20
Stockport, Hyde	7	55	13
Bolton	4	11	36
Wigan	3	11	27
Blackburn	2	10	20
Other Lancs./Cheshire	2	37	5
total[a]	36	216	17
Leeds	8	53	15
Huddersfield	8	50	16
Bradford	16	34	47
Halifax, Calderdale	6	45	13
Keighley	5	18	28
Other	10	121	8
Yorks.total[a]	53	321	16

Note: [a]Figures for localities also include flax, silk.
Source: Factory Comm., Supp. Report, pt ii.

distinction between the ten-hours' bill and legislation as such (which already existed in cotton). Some respondents direct their comments to the proposed ten-hours bill, while others discuss more acceptable forms of legislation; those appearing as opposed to further legislation may simply be particularly preoccupied with refuting the ten-hours campaign.

Table 4.1 gives a rough count of those respondents supporting further legislation, broken down by sector and locality. I have tried to identify those that regard legislation (of whatever kind) as positively desirable, excluding those prefaced by such remarks as 'if we must have a bill, then . . .'; the fairly frequent references to restrictions on the moving power among Lancashire respondents have not been counted, as they were in response to a semi-hypothetical question about how *any* law might be enforced.

Levels of support for further legislation are comparable for cotton and wool, but notably higher in worsted. It is important to bear in mind here that support for legislation in wool and worsted meant support for the introduction of any regulation whatever to these sectors, whereas cotton was already regulated, however ineffectually. This distribution of opinion may reflect the concentration of child labour in worsted mills, and the view that this required to be legitimised by some measure of regulation. Five worsted employers (6 per cent of those in the returns or 18 per cent of those supporting legislation) specifically supported the ten-hours bill, a small minority but nonetheless a bigger one than in other sectors.

There are also important variations between localities. In the cotton region, the highest proportions favouring legislation appear to be in Manchester, where employer opinion was probably most developed, Bolton, Blackburn and Wigan. The lower proportions elsewhere ('other') and the intermediate position in the Stockport and Hyde district lend some support to the thesis of less enthusiasm for regulation among 'country spinners'. In the West Riding, and indeed in all three counties combined, the highest level of support for legislation (and also for ten hours) is in Bradford, which had emerged as the centre of mechanised worsted spinning. In Halifax and Calderdale, an area of mixed industrial composition, there is less support for legislation, with similar proportions in favour among cotton (two out of seventeen returns), wool (one out of eight) and worsted (three out of seventeen) employers; strongly expressed opposition (rather than simple non-response) is also comparable in all three sectors, approximately twice or three times as frequent as support. This may reflect competitive pressures affecting all branches of textiles in the locality, with the rise of Bradford in worsted, and the difficulties of small mills producing cotton water twist (strong yarns for warps, spun on water-frames) or coarse woollens. Here, the picture of resistance to regulation in water-powered country mills may again be of some relevance.

The language used by employers, whether they favoured or opposed legislation, also provides some contrasts between sectors and regions. Replies from the cotton districts seem more standardised. They generally argue, whatever the conclusions reached, from the competitive position of the industry and the problem of cyclical fluctuation. Opponents of further restriction, like Henry Ashworth, anticipated 'the extension of rival manufactories abroad' resulting from 'a considerably diminished rate of profit, a material increase in the cost of the article produced'. The inevitable consequence would be 'diminished wages and want of employment'. Supporters of legislation, on the other hand, saw it as of paramount importance to frame an act judiciously so as to avoid 'any reduction of the profits of the master beyond what will encourage the outlay of capital fast enough to give employment to the workpeople'.[17] Most Lancashire responses tended to be variations on these themes (which were also set out at length in the submissions of employer witnesses in the commissioners' reports).[18]

Woollen and worsted manufacturers' responses seem less standardised and elaborated than in cotton, suggesting a more inchoate state of opinion. Among opponents of legislation there is less emphasis on foreign competition and more on the absolute rights of property 'in this country where freedom is tolerated', and the need for the poor to labour diligently.[19] As a pamphlet by one anonymous worsted master put it, 'man' had to labour 'wherever Providence has cast his lot'; moreover 'PROVIDENCE' (sic) required children to earn their keep (a remark Oastler annotated 'miserable stuff!!').[20] Supporters of legislation argued simply that 'restrictive hours would be beneficial', 'legislative enactment [is] the only way to protect children'.[21] Customary notions of trade regulation and economic and social balance seem to have influenced the responses of some West Riding employers. As one small worsted spinner in Calderdale argued, restriction was 'what every reasonable man will agree to, except the large mill-owner', and would enable the smaller concerns to survive; while the proprietors of mills servicing the small woollen clothiers could express a vision of a balanced domestic economy: 'let the steam engine (which cannot feel) do the chief part of the labour that is required to be done; and let human beings, especially children, be spared, *but not starved* in this land of plenty'.[22]

There are thus significant sectoral and local differences in expressed employer attitudes, apparent both in the views expressed and in the language used to convey those views. While some of the impetus of factory agitation came from the West Riding, it was Lancashire cotton that dominated employer responses, the official mediation of manufacturing interests and much subsequent debate – and historical interpretation. This 'Lancashire' perspective tended to associate longer hours, worse conditions and opposition to all regulation with small, water-powered 'country' mills. There is, as noted above, some evidence to support this view. But it also requires qualification, especially with regard to the differing experience of the West Riding, where regulation could be proposed as the *defence* of the small mill against the monopolising tendencies of the large steam-powered concern. Arguments about 'town' and 'country' mills,

[17] Factory Comm., Supp. Report, D. 1, no. 223, 174.   [18] See above, n. 6.
[19] Factory Comm., Supp. Report, C. 1, no. 142.
[20] *A Letter to Sir John Cam Hobhouse ... on the Factories Bill* (1832), pp. 12, 16.
[21] Factory Comm., Supp. Report, C. 1, nos.45, 52.
[22] Ibid., C. 1, nos. 271, 279.

and about large and small units of production, thus have to be qualified in specific contexts. Even in cotton the differences are more complex than single variables, such as steam- or water-power or grades of yarn.

Arguments about the greater burden on water mills of factory regulation generally point to the peculiarly intensive use of child labour in such enterprises, partly for technological reasons, and partly because of the shortage of older workers in rural locations, in addition to the problems of irregular working occasioned by drought or flood.[23] But the association of water mills and child labour requires some qualification. In cotton, these mills were generally engaged in the frame spinning of coarse yarns for warps ('water twist'), where the water-frame had definite advantages in the production of yarn of the required consistency and strength.[24] This process employed a high proportion of juvenile and female workers on the spinning-frames, in contrast to the spinner-piecer system of mule spinning. The majority of the work-force in both types of mill, however, were engaged in various preparatory processes, rather than in the final spinning; many juvenile and female workers were engaged in carding, roving, etc.

In mule spinning, the requirement for older and more responsible juvenile workers on bigger and faster machines may have encouraged support for factory reform among some manufacturers. But there appear to be variations in the proportion of child labour independent of the technique employed. Manchester, Ashton, Bolton, Blackburn and Oldham were all centres of mule spinning (and Ashton, Blackburn and Oldham were producing similar counts of yarn), but employed varying proportions of children.[25] This seems to be reflected in responses to the factory commissioners' question about the need for children below twelve. Four out of ten Blackburn respondents considered these children necessary, compared with twenty-one out of seventy-three (28 per cent) in Manchester, and three out of fifteen in Bolton. The alleged need for children was variously based on their cheapness, nimbleness, desirability of early training or the demands of adult operatives to give openings for their children. Children were employed in a variety of processes. Apart from piecing and scavenging, they might undertake any task that did not demand adult strength or reach. Their employment cannot simply be associated with particular technologies, such as the water-frame.[26]

The conventional distinction between urban and rural mills was similarly variable in its significance. Such typologies generally condense

[23] Marvel, 'Factory regulation', pp. 388–90, 401–2.
[24] J. Montgomery, The Theory and Practice of Cotton Spinning (1833), pp. 158–9.
[25] See below, table 6.1.
[26] Information from questionnaires, Factory Comm., Supp. Report, D.1 Lancashire.

together a range of variables, implicitly placing all mills on a continuum from large, successful and technically 'rational' Manchester fine spinners, to technically obsolescent coarse-spinning water mills at the other extreme. There is no clear or consistent way of defining 'town' or 'country' mills, either in the numerous contemporary sources employing such distinctions, or in the recent scholarly literature.[27] The 'country spinner', whose competitive pressure 'enlightened' employers adduced as a constraint on their freedom of action, remains a somewhat shadowy figure. For leading Manchester spinners, he might be anyone anywhere more than a mile or two from the Manchester Exchange; for substantial and established firms elsewhere he might be any interloper entering 'their' markets; he might even be the *alter ego* of the respected big manufacturer, dumping stock in unaccustomed markets to ease a liquidity crisis.[28] Places like Stalybridge (a rapidly expanding industrial frontier in the 1830s and 40s) no doubt represented the 'country' in a Manchester perspective; but they had their own rural industrial hinterlands, along the county borders towards Glossop and Saddleworth. The figure of the undercutting country manufacturer represented the threat of uncontrolled competition, pushed to a symbolic periphery. There clearly were differences between town-centre mills and those in more dispersed locations, and some responses from rural mills do indicate strong opposition to legislation for the reasons generally adduced as characterising the position of the rural mill. But other respondents, particularly in the West Riding, do not fit this picture, and the use of this distinction to construct a demonology of undercutting competition and unacceptable managerial practices must be treated with some scepticism.

The West Riding was characterised by rather different relationships between merchanting and manufacture, large- and small-scale enterprises, town and country and water- and steam-power. The largest concentrations of child labour were in worsted spinning, which adopted a form of spinning-frame, often in steam-powered mills. Here employers emphasised the need for child piecers, on similar grounds to those Lancashire masters who took this view; while this perceived requirement might sometimes lead to support for legislation, the proposed minimum

---

[27] See M. Huberman, 'The economic origins of paternalism: Lancashire cotton spinning in the first half of the nineteenth century', *Social History* 12 (1987); M. Rose, P. Taylor and M. Winstanley , 'The economic origins of paternalism: some objections', *Social History* 14 (1989).

[28] See, e.g., McConnel & Kennedy, letter to Joseph Brotherton, in C.H. Lee, *A Cotton Enterprise: The History of McConnel and Kennedy* (Manchester, 1972), pp. 129–30; Factory Comm., Supp. Report, D.1, no. 174 (H.Houldsworth); *Blackburn Gazette*, 2 Dec. 1835 (complaint about Glossop undermining 'town manufacturers', reprinted from *Stockport Advertiser*).

age for entry was one area of concern for the manufacturers' lobby.[29] In wool, there was a complex pattern of variation, with a lower overall proportion of children, but higher levels in specific localities. This was related to the diversity of processes and types of mill. Children were employed in those mills incorporating the slubbing and spinning processes, especially in the Dewsbury heavy woollen area.[30] The mechanised finishing processes employed teenaged lads; this is perhaps reflected in a Huddersfield manufacturers' memorial requesting a cut-off age of sixteen rather than eighteen for entry into 'adult' work.[31]

There is therefore some broad association between particular sectors, processes and technologies and the age composition of the work-force. But the pattern of variation is a complex one. Labour supply may be more significant than particular technologies in explaining age composition and employer attitudes; jobs might be designed with children in mind, where conditions favoured their employment.[32] Relevant factors here include demographic regimes, the structure of adult employment and survival strategies adopted by working-class families. There may for example be some association between high levels of child employment in factories, and regions of handloom weaving or other out-working or artisan trades under pressure. This pattern would link the West Riding woollen and worsted districts to the Lancashire 'weaving' district.[33] This might produce mixed employment patterns with different household members working in different sectors, whether in the factory or elsewhere. Firms establishing more heavily capitalised enterprises in such regions (like the Fieldens or the combined firms developing in Blackburn) adopted strategies shaped by this local labour market, in some cases embracing factory regulation.[34] Handloom weaving likewise persisted, though for different reasons, around Bolton, which specialised in fancy goods; here, as in Blackburn and Bradford, support for regulation may to some extent have reflected the 'merchant-manufacturer' outlook of some leading employers.

Finally, it is necessary to consider changing market conditions. The structural differences so far discussed are at best static snapshots of a process of industrial restructuring, which coincided with and

---

[29] Factory Comm., Supp. Report, C.1, pt i Yorkshire, also pt ii additional questionnaire issued in Yorkshire; Driver, *Tory Radical*, pp. 547–50.
[30] Factory Comm., Supp. Report, C.1, pts i and ii.
[31] D.F.E. Sykes, *History of Huddersfield and its Vicinity* (1898), pp. 321–3.
[32] Moore, 'Women, industrialisation and protest', p. 67.
[33] Farnie, *Cotton Industry*, pp. 295–301; Joyce, *Work, Society and Politics*, pp. 57–64.
[34] See D. Walsh, 'Working class political integration and the Conservative Party: a study of class relations and party political development in the north-west, 1800–1870', PhD, University of Salford, 1991, pp. 458–62, 465 (Blackburn); Weaver, *John Fielden*.

conditioned struggles over factory regulation. The 1830s and 40s saw important changes in products and markets in textiles. In cotton, there was a relative contraction of fine spinning (but with leading firms consolidating their hold on this more limited market), expansion of a broad band of variegated medium-fine to medium-coarse counts, and shifts in export markets to colonial and semi-colonial regions, notably India. Specialisation in new types of fabrics and/or yarns was one aspect of the process. The generic term fustians, for example, covered 'stout cloths . . . of infinite variety', and shirtings and calicoes were similarly diverse.[35] Strategies of specialisation were however liable to be undermined by the violent fluctuations which punctuated the restructuring process; contraction in one sector could place pressure on others, as firms attempted to find alternative outlets.[36] The growth of the medium ranges, with some possibility of switching products within these ranges, may be particularly significant in this context. There was continuing insecurity, as manufacturers remained uncertain whether newly expanding markets offered more than immediate speculative gains.[37] Employers might regard short-time working as a way to control this environment, but they were also likely to regard the prospect of achieving this as somewhat utopian, however desirable.

There were also shifts in products and markets in the woollen industry, including the consolidation of Huddersfield as a fancy woollen centre; but this was in the context of a less rapid process of factory concentration and a lower level of export commitment than in cotton. Arguments about regulating output and the steady expansion of home markets may have found a readier response than in cotton. In worsteds, the proliferation of mechanised spinning mills, especially in Bradford, was accompanied by the uneven growth of power-loom weaving and the mechanisation of combing; a few leading combined firms found market niches in new types and styles of cloth.[38] Changes in merchanting and credit, short-circuiting the clothier-merchant chain and accelerating turnover, were a feature of the period in both wool and worsted.[39] The consequent tensions meant

[35] Farnie, *Cotton Industry*, ch. 3; L.G. Sandberg, 'Movements in the quality of British textile exports, 1815–1913', *Journal of Economic History* 28, no. 1 (1968); 'Explanation of the principal terms used in the cotton manufacture', Factory Comm., Supp. Report, pt.i, PP 1834 (167) XIX, D.2 Lancashire, Appendix, p. 190; T. Bazley, 'Cotton as an element of industry', in *Lectures on the Results of the Great Exhibition*, 2nd ser. (1852).

[36] M.M. Huberman, 'Auction or contract? The cotton-spinning labour market in Lancashire, 1822–52', PhD thesis, University of Toronto, 1984, pp. 84–92.

[37] See, e.g., letter from H. Ashworth to Chadwick, 17 May 1836, Chadwick Papers (expressing scepticism about prosperity based on Eastern markets).

[38] J.James, *History of the Worsted Manufacture in England* (1857); Koditschek, *Class Formation*; Reynolds, *The Great Paternalist*; E.M. Sigsworth, *Black Dyke Mills* (Liverpool, 1958).   [39] Hudson, *Genesis of Industrial Capital*, chs. 7, 8.

that the struggle over factory regulation was in part a struggle between different types of entrepreneur committed to different working and marketing practices, a transformation of the small producer similar to that described by Clive Behagg in the Birmingham trades.[40]

Structural conditions no doubt predisposed employers to particular attitudes. But the relevant conditions were too complex to be reduced to single variables such as power-source, technology, product or plant size, or to some condensation together of these into a unitary spectrum. There are varied local configurations of these factors, and associated entrepreneurial cultures and accumulation strategies.

Employers of all types were pulled in conflicting directions: between market opportunities and the search for stability, commitment to trade custom and fear of undercutting competitors, the policing of unfair competition and reluctance to accept outside intervention. It was local configurations, and associated cultural assumptions, that determined the balance struck between these conflicting pressures. Industrial employers were both agents and potential victims of the competitive process. Their attempts to negotiate this situation have to be understood in the wider setting of middle-class life and culture.

Morals in the marketplace

Versions of economic individualism were proverbially linked to the identity of a 'northern', industrial middle class. This is of course a historical cliché, but, like most clichés, it contains an element of truth; early Victorian textile manufacturers, or certain segments of them, were perhaps the closest living approximations to stereotypes of bourgeois economic man. But this remains a partial and one-sided view of middle-class culture. As Davidoff and Hall have suggested, rational accumulation and the pursuit of wealth were often in tension with religious values, the search for stability and the cultivation of domesticity. Economic life was itself inflected with the importance of family connection, and the characteristic aspiration was the maintenance of an expected standard – though this was, in reality, an increasing standard in many cases – and its reproduction in the next generation through inheritance, suitable marriages, settlements and career openings.[41] On the other hand, the achievement of stability might dictate a commitment to accumulation and growth, in the Hobbesian logic of competitive capitalism, while economic horizons might expand, as particular cohorts of business owners grew visibly richer. Nor should the desire for augmented wealth, and its attendant power and

[40] Behagg, *Politics and Production*.   [41] Davidoff and Hall, *Family Fortunes*.

status, be discounted as a motive for some individuals, whatever the ends to which wealth, power and status were thought to be a means.

Competitive pressures were particularly marked in the textile industries, where rapid structural change could undermine the search for stability, or for agreed ground-rules considered desirable even at the level of purely economic calculation.[42] An economic arena subject to fluctuation and change posed dilemmas of conduct, with no guide to the proper course but that of individual reason and conscience. At the same time, public attention was being focused on conditions of factory labour, and the largely uncharted ground of the rights and duties of employers in new types of work situation.

Religion provided one place to address and negotiate these dilemmas.[43] Like the medico-moral discourses considered in the last chapter, religious discourse incorporated assumptions about the importance of commerce and its connection with civilisation, but at the same time brooded over the dysfunctions and dangers of a rapidly expanding market economy.[44] The following discussion considers the ways in which sermons and tracts negotiated the unease – at times, the terror – of a commercial and industrial middle class faced with an apparently uncontrollable process of competitive accumulation and market fluctuation.

The links between political economy and Evangelicalism – in its moderate, 'Clapham' form – have been persuasively analysed in Boyd Hilton's important study of *The Age of Atonement*.[45] In Hilton's account of 'Christian economics', the market was a sphere of moral probation, a test of prudence, restraint and fortitude. Its crises and breakdowns were to be read as providential warnings about speculative greed and other moral shortcomings. Bankruptcies, like those experienced in the 1825–6 financial crash, were positive checks on capital, equivalent to the famous Malthusian checks on the increase of the labouring poor. In this perspective, *laissez-faire* and free trade were underpinned by a vision of economic equilibrium and restabilised social hierarchy, disciplined by market forces, rather than a more expansive and optimistic vision of growth. This, Hilton suggests, is linked to the rentier and financial interests of 'gentlemanly capitalism', to a southern and metropolitan patriciate, closely connected to the world of the Clapham Evangelicals and the intellectual establishment. Policy debates were more strongly influenced by this mind-set than by provincial-based industrial capital.

---

[42] Koditschek, *Class Formation*, esp. the comments on Davidoff and Hall on pp. 210 n. 27, 222–3 n. 68.
[43] On the role of religion see esp. Davidoff and Hall, *Family Fortunes*; Morris, *Class, Sect and Party*.   [44] See Hilton, *Age of Atonement*.
[45] See Ibid., to which this discussion is much indebted.

The influence of this outlook has already been touched on, in the context of metropolitan elite responses to Sadler's ten-hours campaign. Here, the focus is on the mediation of such ideas among the provincial manufacturing middle class. Hilton describes industrialists as belonging to a 'lesser' middle class 'as likely to be Nonconformist as Anglican in religion'.[46] This is qualified by Maxine Berg, who draws attention to the influence of 'Ricardian', growth-oriented economics, within ideologies of improvement which foregrounded the advance of industrial productivity.[47] This may to some extent be a matter of interpretation and emphasis, within a series of overlapping paradigms and models. Divine providence itself could be read in different ways, from rationalist emphasis on links between virtue and happiness to pre-millennial signs and warnings. The pervasive evangelical sense of sin may reflect a pessimistic outlook on the insecurities of life, but it may also reflect a sense of responsibility to act in the right way so as to diminish those insecurities.

Providential readings of economic problems also influenced Dissenters in industrial towns. Attempts to negotiate the dilemmas of survival in a market economy gave rise to a religious literature about the duties of the Christian in trade and commerce, with common themes and some denominational differences in emphasis. This is discussed below with particular reference to the Independent or Congregationalist tradition. Congregationalism was by no means the sole or predominant religious affiliation among textile employers, but it is arguable that it is particularly significant for its links to a more assertive economic and political liberalism among new cohorts of industrial leaders emerging in the 1830s and 40s.[48]

Anglicans probably account for the largest single grouping among textile masters as a whole (especially as those with no recorded affiliations must often have been nominal Anglicans). The second quarter of the century saw a considerable Anglican resurgence in the textile districts, partly financed by major employers.[49] The predominant social concerns of Anglican preaching seem to have been with mutual obligation within a hierarchical order, the prerogatives of the Church, the threats of Romanism, Dissent and infidelity and the duties of charity incumbent on the wealthy.[50] Hugh Stowell, the Evangelical vicar of Salford, was an

---

[46] Ibid., postscript to paperback edn, p. 386.
[47] M. Berg, 'Progress and providence in early nineteenth-century political economy', *Social History* 15 (1990).   [48] See esp. Koditschek, *Class Formation*, pt ii.
[49] Howe, *Cotton Masters*, pp. 61–5.
[50] Ibid.; and see, e.g., J.A. Atkinson, *A Memoir of the Rev. Canon Slade* (1892); J.W. Whittaker, DD, *Sermon Preached at the Parish Church, Blackburn, on Sunday August 4th 1839* (1839).

important contributor to the literature on the Christian businessman, enjoining just and moderate conduct and the importance of serious religious motives; in the Chartist crisis of 1848 Stowell criticised wage-cuts and the notion of labour as 'a marketable article . . . [S]uch is not the language in which we ought to speak of *the sweat of the brow of our fellow men*'. He then balanced this with appeals to the working class drawn from a well-worn loyalist repertoire.[51] Stowell was unusually outspoken, especially in the direct criticisms of wage-cuts, but his sermons can readily be placed in the context of calls for class conciliation and mutual understanding in the later 1840s, as well as of his specific populist protestant loyalist concerns.

Among Dissenters, Unitarians account for the largest single non-Anglican category in Howe's cohort of cotton masters.[52] They were a particularly wealthy and influential group; their strategic role in liberal culture and projects of reform is a familiar theme in the social and cultural history of the period. Theologically, Unitarianism constituted an alternative pole to evangelicalism in its various forms. Unitarian preaching emphasised links between virtue and happiness, the possibility and desirability of improvement, the philanthropic duties of wealth and the restoration of mutual sympathy within a hierarchic, but open and dynamic society.[53] This vision could accommodate a range of shifts and developments, including the articulation of a reworked industrial paternalism and, eventually, factory regulation as part of a wider social settlement. During the 1830s and 40s, however, the emphasis was on voluntary initiative and the enlightened benevolence of propertied elites; industrial paternalism was the alternative to state regulation, not its complement.

Congregationalism was associated with a rather different style of religious Dissent among textile masters. Its importance lies, not in any numerical preponderance, but in its integral connection with an identifiable sub-culture in key cohorts of millowners. Typically, they were 'new' entrepreneurs struggling to establish themselves in the 1820s or 1830s and, in some cases, rising to prominence as the bearers of industrial wealth in the following decades. Notable examples were proprietors of expanding cotton firms in the Ashton and Stalybridge area (Mason, Cheetham, Reyner, Buckley), the Nonconformist segment of the

---

[51] H. Stowell, *A Model for Men of Business: Lectures on the Character of Nehemiah* (1854); *A Plea for the Working Man: Do Not Lower his Wages* (1848), esp. p. 6; *No Revolution: A Word to the People of England* (1848).   [52] Howe, *Cotton Masters*, pp. 62, 69.
[53] J. Seed, 'Theologies of power: Unitarianism and the social relations of religious discourse, 1800–1850', in R.J. Morris (ed.), *Class, Power and Social Structure in Nineteenth-Century Towns* (Leicester, 1986).

Blackburn employers (Pilkington, Eccles, Shorrock) and a new generation of leading figures in the Bradford and Halifax areas (Salt, Crossley).
Often migrants starting new businesses, their wealth was initially precarious and, with important exceptions, it remained modest by the standards
of Unitarian, and some Anglican, cotton lords.[54] However that wealth was
substantial, visible and visibly expanding in boom years; its possessors
emerged as leading figures in their districts, beginning to fill public offices
as magistrates, mayors and MPs. They also (as will become apparent in
subsequent chapters) followed a particular trajectory which merits attention, from hard-faced economic liberalism to public gestures of industrial
paternalism and endorsement of factory regulation.

This cohort of employers occupied key positions in regional networks
of liberal dissent, closely identified with the expansion of Congregationalism – though that expansion certainly cannot be reduced to this or
any other single social group. The culture of voluntaryism, and the flexibility of the congregational form, were perhaps particularly appropriate
for aspirant and mobile individuals within communities which were
themselves rapidly expanding. The role of the ministry is also of some significance here. Ministers and clergy of all persuasions were themselves an
important segment of the middle class. In the major Dissenting
denominations, there were moves towards 'professionalism' and a broadened intellectual formation, adapted to the 'variety in the mental
constitution of different classes of hearers'.[55] The congregation's choice
of its minister (in most cases, a right restricted to adult men) could be
represented as the choice of a teacher and guide, whose position had to
rest on free consent; by the same token, the minister laid claim to a professional authority, based on this consent, won by his learning, piety and
powers of persuasion.[56] In practice, there might be considerable tensions
around such claims, but in some key congregations there was a symbiotic
relationship between new wealth extending its cultural horizons and ministers formed in a broadened and modernised intellectual culture.[57]

The relocation of the old Blackburn Academy, refounded in
Manchester as Lancashire Independent College, was an important

[54] Howe, *Cotton Masters*, pp. 67–8; Joyce, *Work, Society and Politics*, ch. 1; Koditschek, *Class Formation*, pt ii.
[55] 'Our colleges and ministry', *Eclectic Review*, new ser. II (1842), p. 10; see also E. Miall, *The British Churches in relation to the British People* (1849), pp. 252–4; K.D. Brown, *A Social History of the Nonconformist Ministry of England and Wales, 1800–1930* (Oxford, 1988), pp. 65–6.
[56] J.A. James, *The Principles of Dissenters* (1834), as reprinted in G. Parsons (ed.), *Religion in Victorian Britain, vol. III Sources* (Manchester, 1988), pp. 132–4; cf. Davidoff and Hall, *Family Fortunes*, pp. 130–4.
[57] Koditschek, *Class Formation*, pp. 271–2; J. Guinness Rogers, *Autobiography* (1903), ch. 6, for examples from Bradford and Ashton.

moment in the drive to produce an 'educated ministry'. As Robert Vaughan, one of the college's early luminaries (and a controversial figure there) argued, Congregationalism went together with the advance of 'popular intelligence': 'This is the spirit of our system, and if so, where is the department of human knowledge with which it may not be expected to sympathise and intermeddle?'[58] The founding deed of the college specified a range of disciplines, in addition to theology and bible studies, for those students 'not otherwise sufficiently instructed', including philosophy, rhetoric, natural philosophy, history, English literature and anything else the committee thought appropriate.[59] Whether directly or indirectly, political economy would have figured in this kind of intellectual formation. Guinness Rogers (an early student at the college, and subsequently minister at Albion Chapel, Ashton, a central site in the networks of Lancashire Nonconformity) recalled the lively atmosphere and the 'singularly able and intelligent men of business' among the trustees; attendance at Anti-Corn Law League lectures at this time was 'one of the influences that educated my political thought'.[60]

Dissent could be seen as linked to commerce, industry, social and moral progress, a message with particular resonances in the textile districts. As Edward Miall argued: 'Trade, then – employing it in the broadest sense of which it is susceptible – is not only not antagonistic in its own nature to the main object of Christianity, but is eminently auxiliary to it . . . Trade multiplies our relations with our fellow-men.'[61] Miall edited *The Nonconformist*, a journal established with financial support from some of the Dissenting textile manufacturers to represent a highly politicised strand of radical voluntaryism. In its pages, the voluntary principle was justified in a language of enterprise, efficient machinery and the optimal allocation of scarce resources (including the limited numbers of serious Christians, who were most effective when gathered into voluntary churches).[62] This identification with economic progress was probably more strongly accented than in the Anglican Evangelical tradition; but, like their Anglican counterparts, evangelical Dissenters qualified this enthusiasm with warnings about over-absorption in worldly business, speculative greed and other perils. The expansion of commerce was to be

---

[58] R. Vaughan, *Congregationalism or the Polity of Independent Churches* (1842), p. 17; see also J. Harris, *The Importance of an Educated Ministry: A Discourse Preached Preparatory to the Opening of the Lancashire Independent College* (1843).

[59] J. Thompson, *Lancashire Independent College, 1843–1893* (1893), p. 42.

[60] Rogers, *Autobiography*, p. 85.   [61] Miall, *British Churches*, pp. 295–6.

[62] *The Nonconformist*, 21, 28 Sept. 1842, pp. 632, 64; 22 March 1843, p. 177; Miall, *British Churches*, p. 232; A. Miall, *Life of Edward Miall* (1884), pp. 41–6; Rogers, *Autobiography*, p. 69.

welcomed for its *moral* benefits, and these were inevitably attended by moral dangers.

The economic crisis of 1825–6 seems to have focused these concerns, among Dissenters in the manufacturing north as well as Hilton's metropolitan rentier Anglican Evangelicals.[63] In one pamphlet of 1825, Jacob Kirkman Foster, minister of the Huntingdonian chapel in Rochdale, addressed 'persons engaged in business' on the advantages and dangers of commerce, taking his text from Mark viii. 36–7 ('what shall it profit a man . . .'). Trade 'calls forth a thousand inventions, awakening the dormant energies, and bringing the mind into an infinite variety of exercises'; it enabled the relief of want, endowing 'our favoured nation' with a divine mission 'to distribute heavenly benefactions to all the people of the world'; and, in a characteristically 'northern' note, trade encouraged moral independence among the humble but respectable and industrious. But there are also 'demoralising' effects, above all worldly absorption and thoughtlessness about eternal salvation; measures such as the moral control of factory workers by a voluntary 'combination' of leading employers may mitigate these dangers, but it is the 'depravity of the heart' that is at the root of social evils.[64]

Jonathan Sutcliffe of Ashton (Guinness Rogers' predecessor) interpreted the financial crash as a special providence, 'a message from Heaven' which he was called to convey to his flock. The 'secondary causes' of distress, such specifically economic factors as speculative lending, machinery and so on, were not the province of the preacher, who had rather to address 'loftier themes'. 'If God's uplifted hand be not regarded, we may certainly expect severer punishment. He can direct the whole course of nature against us.'[65] Greater 'moderation' in the pursuit of wealth, increased support for Sunday Schools and a more 'Christian spirit' between 'masters and men' would be hopeful signs of increasing righteousness in the community.

Special providence continued to be invoked in relation to epidemics, natural disasters and events like the Irish famine. The prayer 'for a time of pestilence' in *The Altar of the Household* (1853), a Nonconformist compilation for family worship, prays that 'all classes of society be awakened to a sense of their duty to one another' and denounces the false pride of worldly success: 'our commerce and greatness, in the hour Thou dost

[63] Hilton, *Age of Atonement*, pp. 118–35.
[64] J.K. Foster, *A Discourse on the Moral Influence of Trade* (1825); see also review of this pamphlet in *Evangelical Magazine*, new ser. 4 (1826), p. 64, and article 'uncertain riches', pp. 56–8.
[65] J. Sutcliffe, *The Design of the Divine Chastisements Considered in relation to the Present Disturbed State of the Country* (1826), pp. 5, 10, 28–9.

blow upon them, shall wither, and the whirlwind shall take them away as stubble'.[66] Evangelical beliefs about sudden divine visitations, sin and repentance could thus allude to anxieties about social and economic relations. The trade cycle itself was increasingly likely to be seen as a manifestation of 'general providence', predictable occurrences of law-governed regularity – in which, however, moral as well as purely economic factors played some part. This is apparent in a series of sermons by Jonathan Glyde, minister at Horton Lane, Bradford (like Ashton, a key point in the cultural geography of liberal dissent). During the worsted boom which followed the recession and Chartist disturbances of 1847–8, Glyde delivered a sermon on 'prosperity, secular and spiritual'. Taking his text from Ecclesiastes (vii. 13–14), Glyde emphasised the rationality of providence, refuting as 'pagan superstition' the idea that God would arbitrarily punish the prosperous. Although such superstitions are attributed to 'the ancients', there may also be a reference to popular beliefs and prophetic denunciations, perhaps associated with radical forms of Methodism, or simply to the *Schadenfreude* which sometimes greeted events like mill fires.[67] Prosperity and adversity were 'disciplines which He employs' to bring our 'free wills to filial obedience'. Both have their particular dangers; adversity led to forgetfulness of God through material anxiety and overwork, prosperity carried the danger of 'unrestrained, unreflecting enjoyment'. The appropriate message for times of returning prosperity was attention to 'acts of justice and charity'. Justice required the prompt discharge of debts and care for 'friends'; charity should be increasingly directed to the spiritual and cultural needs of the poor, now that their food and clothing was a less pressing problem.[68]

In this scheme, justice is presented as a matter principally of relations within the propertied class; the working class appear as objects of charity rather than as claimants for justice. A funeral sermon for James Garnett, represented as a model employer, gave occasion to address problems of class relations more directly. 'Masters, listen to your workpeople – hear their reasonings, and reason with them. Workmen, put a generous confidence in your masters, desire to do right. Work out the social problem in true love and mutual forbearance.'[69] This is balanced by a sermon on 'the rich and the poor', inspired by the death of 'our poor brother Robert Sutcliffe', an unemployed woolcomber in the congregation. Unable to

---

[66] J. Harris (ed.), *The Altar of the Household* (1853), p. 743; Hilton, *Age of Atonement*, pp. 108–14, 133.

[67] J. Glyde, *Prosperity, Secular and Spiritual: Two Sermons Preached in Horton Lane Chapel in July 1850* (1850), p. 6.   [68] Ibid., pp. 6–9, 12–13.

[69] G.W. Conder (ed.), *Memoirs and Remains of the Late Rev. Jonathan Glyde* (1858), p. 135, and see also Glyde's prayer for the town of Bradford, ibid., p. 238.

work through disability, Sutcliffe existed with aid from the congregation (restricted, Glyde is careful to explain, to 'a proper liberality') and the earnings of his children: 'like a wise man he became a woman, was the mother of his children, kept all things clean and bright, and though in feeble health, made them a comfortable home'.[70] Beyond its surface reference to problems of working-class life, this striking comment may suggest the need, in all classes, for a redefined Christian manliness, a feminised personality and greater domestic commitment. At the same time, the very necessity for role reversal in a poor family evokes the distance between classes; while Sutcliffe's wisdom in being prepared to change in this way could be an implied comment on other unemployed men in domestic industries, often seen as clinging to obsolete notions of their status at the expense of their children.

The discovery of moral qualities and wisdom in the poor is at any rate part of an appeal for cross-class dialogue, characteristic of the moment of the late 1840s and early 50s (though the text is undated in the reprinted version, it belongs unmistakably to that period). 'Let us sit down, as it were, by the Comber's grave, where it is very probable the pressure of our social system has prematurely laid him. Let us sit down, rich and poor together, and listen to Moses and Jesus.'[71] A fictional comber is then made to speak for the poor and enumerates their grievances: the treatment of men as 'machines', wage-cuts, unchristian contempt and distance between the classes, the hypocrisy of organised religion. A 'master' replies, castigating the immorality and improvidence of the poor.[72] Such appeals for listening and dialogue were a widespread theme in the 'social' literature of the years around the mid-century. Delivered to a congregation including several newly prosperous merchants and manufacturers, it may have been audacious, but probably still acceptable, social criticism. The device of fictional dialogue distances conflict, while the focus on woolcombers as standing for the 'poor' (not, Glyde insists, synonymous with the working class, many of whom have enough to live decently) directs attention to a group of declining hand-workers, rather than to factory work. The appearance of even-handed listening and mediation is somewhat contrived; James Garnett is held out as a model for his class, but not made to stand for it, as the comber is for the 'poor'.

The 'educated' Dissenting ministry of the mid-nineteenth century were at least as attentive as their Anglican colleagues to the message of social critics from the literary intelligentsia. *The Nonconformist*, reviewing a collection of sermons on *Religion and Business* (1853), mentioned the influence of Carlyle, Maurice and Kingsley: 'If the Dissenting pulpit has

[70] Ibid., pp. 336–7.   [71] Ibid., pp. 337–8.   [72] Ibid., pp. 340 et seq.

not dropped behind the march of opinion it has done little to guide it.'[73] In his *British Churches in relation to the British People*, Miall described trade as 'eminently auxiliary' to Christianity; the 'spirit of trade' could nevertheless be one force undermining religion unless 'made subordinate to a dominant spiritual purpose'. 'Ours is the rush of railway life . . . The march of trade is like the irresistible career of a locomotive – and even those who most delight in rapid movement are compelled to ask themselves at times, "Can such speed as this be safe".'[74] This particular image would undoubtedly have called to mind the speculation and fraud that accompanied the railway boom, as well as the possible dangers of high-speed travel. The 1850s saw a cluster of tracts (and no doubt many more ephemeral sermons) on the duties of Christians in business, including the Anglican Hugh Stowell's much-cited *Lectures on the Character of Nehemiah* (1854) and a number of Nonconformist treatments of the same theme. In *The Altar of the Household* a reading from Nehemiah is explained in terms of his forbearance in giving up his own 'legal' claims in order to expose 'illegal' exactions, through 'the force of public opinion'; and the accompanying prayer calls for a 'life of active benevolence . . . Let no thought of injustice ever stain our minds.'[75] A prizewinning essay on *Mammon* by John Harris, a prominent London divine and editor of *The Altar of the Household*, deplored excessive competition, from which even the liberal professions were suffering, 'excess of covetousness' and conspicuous consumption which wasted the capital invested in luxury trades, as well as inducing consumerist greed; divine retribution was still active and, if deferred, would be all the more severe: 'whatever is morally wrong cannot be politically right'.[76]

The 'stewardship of wealth' encapsulated some of these concerns about the Christianisation of business life. As *The Altar of the Household* explained the parable of the talents: 'Intellectual capacity is a talent – time is a talent – property is a talent, and then, our religious privileges bear the same character. God retains his property in them; He lends them to us for a season; and he requires us to use them for His glory and for our good.'[77] The practical implications of this teaching most often related to acts of philanthropy, including the developing repertoire of 'industrial paternalism'.[78] How far religious promptings modified the practice of business or industrial relations is necessarily ambiguous. Calls to restrain the pace of business

[73] *The Nonconformist*, 8 June 1853, pp. 464–5.
[74] Miall, *British Churches*, pp. 298, 303.
[75] Harris (ed.), *Altar of the Household*, p. 557, reading from Nehemiah v. 6–18.
[76] J. Harris, *Mammon, or Covetousness the Sin of the Christian Church* (1856), pp. 86, 180–1, 205.   [77] Harris (ed.), *Altar of the Household*, p. 123.
[78] See esp. Howe, *Cotton Masters*, ch. 8.

expansion may have struck a chord among businessmen themselves and their families, as well as ministers and others in the wider middle class; but the chances of opting for a quieter life were limited. Not all, and probably not many, middle-class men were in a position to chose to act like the 'tradesman' in one edifying anecdote, who abandons family prayers under pressure of work, and is then recalled to his duty by a pious letter from a former apprentice, even though it means contracting his enterprise.[79]

On the other hand, the conduct of substantial enterprises was itself seen as entailing responsibilities to others, and the stewardship of wealth could imply the increase of that wealth as a duty to God and to society as well as to oneself. 'If the Lord shall aid us in this place the poor shall taste of it', Martha Crossley is supposed to have declared to her sons when they were building up their famous carpet-manufacturing concern at Halifax (one of innumerable examples of the reported influence of a pious evangelical mother).[80] In the light of this injunction, ensuring the success of the business might itself become a primary duty to the poor (as employers often argued in controversies about factory regulation). Condemnations of financial speculation, 'covetousness' and conspicuous consumption could likewise legitimise accumulation within the 'productive' economy. Jonathan Glyde advocated 'attention to business, well directed, well sustained energy, due proportion between the amount of capital and the amount of business', rather than 'wild speculations, desperate effort, collapse, panic, stagnation, ruin', and praised James Garnett as an exemplar of this gradual and deliberate growth; this gradualism was also the practical advice of informed commentators on the textile trades.[81]

Such strictures were in any case inherently ambiguous, and their practical interpretation was necessarily a matter for the individual protestant conscience. If the excesses of cut-throat competition were to be deplored, the competitive principle remained 'necessary to the activity and healthy condition of the social economy'.[82] 'Speculation' could be hard to distinguish from the risks inherent in investing talents rather than burying them; it might also be necessary to gamble in order to survive at times of pressure.[83] And a somewhat hazy line separated frivolous luxury from the 'comfort' and 'decency' which formed part of the civilising process, and

---

[79] *Evangelical Magazine* new ser. 20 (Sept. 1842), p. 425.
[80] As quoted in Joyce, *Work, Society and Politics*, p. 142.
[81] Glyde, *Prosperity*, p. 10; Conder (ed.), *Memoirs of Jonathan Glyde*, p. 135; and cf. the comments of James Kennedy as reported in B.M. Ratcliffe and W.H. Chaloner (eds.), *A French Sociologist Looks at Britain: Gustave d'Eichthal and British Society in 1828* (Manchester, 1977), pp. 98–9.   [82] Harris, *Mammon*, p. 84.
[83] Koditschek, *Class Formation*, pp. 207–8.

might extend even to the honest poor. Thomas Chalmers, the great Scottish Evangelical economist, himself linked improvidence to 'a low and grovelling taste among the people'.[84] Increased levels of comfort and the elevation and diversification of popular desires were often represented as the moral mission of mechanised textile production.[85]

A variety of concerns might be encoded in this literature on Christianity and commerce. Fair dealing among men of property, and justice to creditors and friends, were probably more significant than the treatment of workers. There was also a preoccupation with the moral dangers facing young men (often in their teens) setting out as commercial clerks away from home.[86] Criticisms of the frenetic pace of business life might relate to tensions surrounding the absence of husbands from home and the negotiation of relationships in entrepreneurial families. Glyde's praise for the moral wisdom of the poor comber may be partly a challenge to the middle-class men in his congregation; and the routine of family prayers had the advantage of encouraging the regular presence of the head of household.[87] Evangelical discourses about over-absorption in worldly business might be a way of talking about matters nowadays dealt with, under a different set of codes, as 'stress' and 'nervous exhaustion'.[88]

Religious literature was aimed at a wide and diverse public – though largely a middle-class one – for whom the large-scale employment of wage-labour was not a typical experience. Employment relations were often assimilated to a model of the patriarchal household, which encompassed servants and apprentices, and gave injunctions to treat them justly and attend to their welfare and morals. In this context, sermon literature from the industrial north is of particular interest. Here it is possible to trace a shifting language. Jacob Foster in 1825 referred to 'servants and . . . the more laborious classes in society', Jonathan Sutcliffe at the same period to 'masters and men'. In Jonathan Glyde's mid-century sermons, the language shifts from 'masters and workpeople' – which then becomes 'workmen', an interesting elision in view of the gender composition of worsted mills – and 'rich and poor', with the poor differentiated from the working classes more generally.[89] These shifts register the difficulties of adapting models of paternalism centred on the household (which had

---

[84] Hilton, *Age of Atonement*, p. 81.
[85] Bazley, 'Cotton as an element of industry'; W. Felkin, *History of the Machine-Wrought Hosiery and Lace Manufactures* (1867), p. 559.
[86] See, e.g., Harris (ed.), *Altar of the Household*, p. 733, prayer 'for a child leaving home'; J.B. Owen, *Business without Christianity* (1856), published version of lecture to Manchester YMCA.
[87] Conder, *Memoirs of Jonathan Glyde*, pp. 336–7; Harris (ed.), *Altar of the Household*, p. viii.
[88] See, e.g., sermon 'the worth of life', in Conder, *Memoirs of Jonathan Glyde*, pp. 270–2.
[89] Foster, *Discourse*, p. 24; Sutcliffe, *Divine Chastisements*, p. 35; Conder, *Memoirs of Jonathan Glyde*, pp. 135, 333 *et seq.*

probably always represented an ideal rather than a reality) to the growth of factory employment, and of a working class whose laudable 'independence' could too easily degenerate into 'rudeness'.[90]

Religious discourses could thus represent some of the dilemmas of an intensely competitive market economy. These dilemmas were felt in northern Dissenting entrepreneurial circles, as well as in those of the patrician Anglican Evangelicals. Dissenting evangelicals, like their Anglican counterparts, combined a broad endorsement of the market system with nagging unease, and occasional terror, at some of its actual manifestations. However the practical implications of such unease were often ambiguous, or they were left to the individual consciences of serious Christians. Even criticisms of rapid accumulation and intense competition were framed by a respect for the laws of the market, and deference to the judgment of the employer as their mediator. While the duties of Christian philanthropy and of moral influence over dependent employees were themselves posited on a successful course of capital accumulation.

Paternalism, contract and the enlightened employer

Doctrines of the stewardship of wealth therefore provided both a justification for capitalist accumulation, and a potential criticism of some of its less benign manifestations. But anxiety about the morally and socially destructive impact of unregulated economic expansion rarely led to enthusiasm for state intervention, and still less for the forms of regulation demanded by radical operatives. Emphasis in official enquiries and pamphlet literature on the enlightened benevolence of leading manufacturers contributed to continuing debates about the role of industrial employers, as a relatively new category of property-holders responsible for the governance of their subordinates. A more self-confident rhetoric of 'paternalism' emerged in the 1850s. In so far as this rhetoric reflected a wider social settlement, the acceptance of a standard working day formed one of its necessary foundations. In this respect state regulation underpinned the image of paternalism, deference and reciprocity in industrial settings. However, the relationship between employer initiatives and the state was fraught with tensions and ambiguities. The workings of what has been labelled as 'paternalism', and the possible meanings enacted in its ritual performances, are more fully explored below (chapter 8). In the present context, it is relevant to make some brief comments on how commentators viewed the rights and duties of employers in the tenser and more polarised atmosphere of the second quarter of the century.

[90] Foster, *Discourse*, p. 25.

'Paternalism' is a blanket term, in some ways a misleading one.[91] What historians and sociologists have labelled as paternalism might be referred to in the language of Victorian social debate by a variety of terms: the 'humane', 'just' and 'benevolent' master, 'mutual sympathy' and 'respect' across class barriers, 'honest' and 'manly' dialogue. Paternalist claims, and their apparent validation through gratifying displays of worker loyalty figured in images of a restabilised, 'post-Chartist' industrial world around the mid-nineteenth century. Much of this was foreshadowed in the management practice and moralising rhetoric of the preceding decades. The practices involved were not, in themselves, new, though the scale of some workplaces probably entailed a greater degree of formalisation, while two decades of public debate (from c. 1830) encouraged employers to publicise their benevolence.

As John Seed has pointed out, paternalism was an integral part of the social experience of the propertied middle class before it became a special strategy of industrial relations.[92] Paternalism in this sense was bound up with powers of patronage exercised by the propertied, and extended to 'servants' (in the varied senses of that elastic term), tenants, small tradespeople and shopkeepers, even lesser members of the middle class itself. Responsibility for moral, as well as material, welfare, and discriminations based on reputation and connection, formed part of such relations. The well-ordered family was one imaginary reference-point, a fantasy of benign hierarchy, which provided an alternative or complement to market relations. Commentators on the responsibilities of employers generally assimilated together the 'manufacturer, landowner, shop-keeper, chief of artisans, or [employer] in any other capacity ... the head of every household ... all who are in authority'.[93] Notions of governing class duty and 'paternal and protective' government also informed the debate, and might be used to justify protective legislation.[94] The duties of employers were thus constructed by reference to the family on one hand, the state on the other.

[91] For the debate on paternalism see esp. H.I. Dutton and J.E. King, 'The limits of paternalism: the cotton tyrants of north Lancashire, 1836–1854', Social History 7 (1982); Joyce, Work, Society and Politics; R. Price, 'The labour process and labour history', Social History 8 (1983), and exchange between Joyce and Price in Social History 9 (1984); Roberts, Paternalism. See also the pioneering comparative work of R. Bendix, Work and Authority in Industry: Ideologies of Management in the Course of Industrialization (Harper Torchbook edn, New York and Evanston, 1963); M. Burawoy, The Politics of Production: Factory Regimes under Capitalism and Socialism (London, 1985) is an important recent exercise in comparative theorisation.   [92] Seed, 'Theologies of power', p. 145.

[93] E.A. Helps (ed.), Correspondence of Sir Arthur Helps, K.C.B., D.C.L. (London and New York, 1917), reprint of pamphlet on Chartism (1848), p. 65; Helps, a Whig literary figure, minor politician and courtier, was a prominent commentator on employers' duties.

[94] See Mandler, Aristocratic Government; Oakley, 'Utilitarian, paternalistic or both?'.

Factory masters could adopt this repertoire, often with a strong evangelical tone. Mill rules of 1834 (Hirst, Bramley & Co., Leeds), apparently collected by the factory inspector, as an exemplar of 'a well regulated mill', are accompanied by lengthy addresses. There is a special word to the 'Burlers and other Females': 'We are fearful that many of you seldom reflect upon the duties required from you, in your several relations of daughters, sisters, wives or mothers, and of the strict account which will one day have to be given, of the manner in which you have discharged the duties of these several stations.' The men, on the other hand, are addressed as potential junior partners in the moral management of child labour, in place of corporal punishment: '[A] man, by endeavouring to control his passions and to attain a higher degree of moderation, will be assisted in becoming a better Christian – a kinder father – a more affectionate husband.'[95] The Manchester spinner David Holt, publicised as a benevolent employer, likewise emphasised the moral control of the workforce, especially given the dangers of its 'contamination' in a big town; Holt's familistic imagery ('they should be regarded as part of my own family') was reciprocated in an address on his retirement (in 1835) referring to his 'kind and paternal affection' and 'fatherly solicitude'.[96]

Concerns with moral discipline and more humane management were often formulated in religious terms, and, as we have seen, might be enjoined from the pulpit. Underlying this were providential assumptions that moral order and economic prosperity went hand in hand, at least in the long run. In the shorter run, however, there might be difficulties in balancing the two, especially at times of pressure (whether recession, or labour shortage and other forms of 'overheating' in boom periods). Few employers can have felt entirely confident of their ability to follow the Reverend Foster's advice to sack dissolute characters forthwith, whatever their usefulness as skilled workers.[97] Unstable employment, migrant populations and urban anonymity and an insurgent working class rendered projects of moral control problematic. At the same time, external criticism and scrutiny of employment practices were being brought to bear. It was in this context that the claims of employers were debated and reworked, to provide some of the themes of the paternalistic rhetoric characteristic of the mid-century.

Developments in the industrial north, from Luddism to Chartism, focused attention on specifically 'industrial' problems. There was a degree of partisan polemic in the unfolding of this discussion. Patrician

[95] Mill rules, in papers on factory inspection, HO 45.1120.
[96] *Incidents in the Life of David Holt, Written by Himself* (1843), pp. 5–8.
[97] Foster, *Discourse*, p. 26.

commentators, especially those identified with agricultural protection (itself under attack as an irresponsible use of power and privilege), stigmatised the factory as the source of moral disorder and social disintegration; while liberal millowners and allied groups identified aristocratic misgovernment as the chief obstacle to social harmony and moral order. The strikes and disturbances of 1842 brought these differences into sharp focus. Interestingly enough, much of the comment concentrated on the textile districts, perhaps because of the longstanding debate about the factory system there, though the strikes themselves also affected the potteries, the Black Country and other industrial areas. The Anglican Evangelical *Christian Observer* gave extensive, but somewhat impressionistic, coverage to the events. Noting (accurately) that Stalybridge, where the movement in the textile districts began, had a preponderance of Dissenters among its leading employers, the article went on to describe Henry Ashworth as 'joint partner in the extensive house of Ashworth and Greg, manufacturers at Stalybridge', and to hold this duo responsible for the deficient state of education there.[98] Greg and Ashworth were of course well known as leading manufacturers (though not in partnership, and not in Stalybridge) and as liberal polemicists.

From the liberal camp – though a somewhat more radical part of it than that represented by Greg or Ashworth – *The Nonconformist* paid considerable attention to the events. Committed to a mobilisation of the 'people' against privilege, and aiming to draw in working-class support (including that of some Chartists), its columns presented the strikes as an understandable manifestation of discontent, but an ultimately futile and destructive one, arising from the 'alienation of mind from the middle classes', deliberately fomented by 'the whig and tory press'. 'These are the desperate heavings of the people to throw off the intolerable weight of oppression which serves to crush them. They indicate deep-seated disease, and we fear they will do little else but increase it.'[99]

But, if there was partisan polarisation in the attribution of blame, there were also shared concerns, centred especially on the need for more effective schooling, although the form this was to take, its control and management, the proper role of the state and related issues were deeply divisive. Carlyle, and other figures of the literary intelligentsia less immediately attached to political parties or religious denominations, had a strategic role in this regard. Their impact was registered, though not uncritically, in the liberal culture of northern industrial towns. W.R. Greg (who represented a less populist and radical version of Liberalism than Miall's

---

[98] *Christian Observer* 41 (Sept., Nov. 1842), pp. 572–5, 699–702.
[99] *The Nonconformist*, 17 Aug. 1842, p. 560.

Nonconformist) positioned himself on the higher ground of the condition of England debate staked out by Carlyle and others. Whereas the 'wrongs and sorrows of the distant negro awakened the ungovernable sympathy of the generous and charitable zealots of the land', the condition of the 'poorer classes . . . form topics of inquiry in the sight of which all party questions . . . sink into comparative insignificance'.[100] Like other liberal commentators, Greg treated the disturbances as understandable but ineffectual and ill-advised, a symptom of deeper problems, rather than a solution; free trade and popular education would give more constructive expression to working-class aspirations. He emphasises the claim of enlightened employers (like himself and his brother) to social leadership:

Government should know that there exists in most parts of England, but especially in the populous commercial districts, a large, powerful, and increasing body of men – apart from the working classes – friends and employers of the working classes . . . They are men of wealth, energy and education; systematic and severe thinkers; prompt, daring and decisive actors.

These entrepreneurial saviours regarded the petty preoccupations of parliamentary politics 'as the small dust of the balance', but would 'toil night and day, summer and winter, and will spend thousands, if need be' in the cause of popular education and free trade.[101]

This somewhat hyperbolic account of employers' commitment to popular education reflected both the convergence of different strands of opinion around the need for more effective schooling, and continued debate about obstacles to its achievement. The factory inspectors' reports identified the well-managed mill as the site of educational and other improvement. Saunders, the inspector for the West Riding, noted the difficulties of education in scattered rural woollen mills, and advocated enhanced employer authority: '[T]he more direct control and superintendence which this . . . gives to the occupiers of the mill, the greater becomes the interest he feels in all employed in it, and the more effectually can he detect and punish irregularities of all kinds.'[102] Saunders pointed to the 'company mill', with its absence of clear-cut individual ownership or management, as the site of the worst problems. The inspectors also noted the sectarian divisions which impeded school provision, as well as the 'inefficiency' of many factory schools; such deficiencies, Horner argued, were 'generally neither the fault of the parent nor of the

---

[100] [W.R. Greg], 'The outbreak of August in the manufacturing districts', *Westminster Review* 38 (1842), pp. 395, 406.
[101] Ibid., pp. 406–7.
[102] Report on the Effects of the Educational Provisions of the Factory Act, PP 1839 XLII, pp. 26, 42.

mill-owner'.[103] The responsibility without power laid on employers for factory education (especially in scattered locations, without adequate schools accessible or the numbers employed to support them) was one of their grievances against factory legislation. The agenda of factory regulation could thus lead in to that of national educational schemes, and the protagonism of enlightened employers in campaigning for this, as well as providing Sunday or day schools on a voluntary basis. Emphasis on the role of the enlightened employer helped fix a connection between technical progress, capital accumulation and improvement, but it could also have a critical edge, in setting up a standard of best practice to which large employers might be expected to conform, as part of the duties of their station.

Claims to enlightened benevolence were rarely uncontested. They often reflected partisan or sectarian rivalries. The reputation of the 'just and benevolent employer' was a staple of electoral polemic.[104] The passing of the Ten Hours Act in 1847 led to a number of factory festivities and loyal addresses to employers, of the kind that became part of a familiar repertoire of industrial paternalism. The role of those exceptional employers, like John Fielden, identified with the ten-hours campaign was particularly celebrated.[105]

Popular demands and expectations thus entered into the construction of the benevolent employer. Criticism of management practices at particular mills was, as I have shown, a feature of local campaigns for factory reform, and one which, not surprisingly, elicited defensive reactions from employers. The Gregs, widely cited as enlightened manufacturers, were at some pains to warn Doherty and the Short-Time Committee off from publicising an incident concerning a runaway mill-girl (perhaps significantly, this was in 1835 when some millowners were experiencing labour shortages), and ten years later short-time delegates were again seen off from Quarry Bank Mill.[106]

The clustering of commentary on industrial relations that marked the Chartist crisis of 1848 and its aftermath incorporated popular notions of fair employment and equal and manly dialogue between employers and workers (often with a particular inflection towards the 'northern' virtues of plain speaking). J.R. Stephens at Ashton used the device of fictionalised dialogue and the restoration of mutual sympathy over 'a smoke and a jug of homebrewed' as a vehicle for his polemic.[107] '[K]ind treatment and

---

[103] Ibid., p. 6; cf. Howe, *Cotton Masters*, pp. 215–29; Sanderson, 'Education and the factory'.   [104] Vernon, *Politics and the People*.
[105] 'Alfred' *Factory Movement*, vol. II, pp. 286–9.
[106] Greg Papers, Manchester Archives, C5/8/22, 34.
[107] *Ashton Chronicle*, 9 Dec. 1848.

gentlemanly manners from their employers' was placed next to 'equitable wages' in a list of the working man's legitimate demands given by the London-based *Working Man's Friend*, one of several magazines of the years around 1850 espousing a Smilesian radicalism and a characteristic didactic tone. The employer 'who seemed to be a perfect gentleman in the parlour' became 'a rough, rude trooper or barbarian, the moment he entered the presence of his workpeople'; the 'despised operatives' could indeed teach such employers how to behave.[108] This sense of (masculine) moral equality was obviously in some tension with a language of paternalist authority, but it might also to some extent be negotiated in the implied reciprocities of fair employment.

The emphasis on moral equality was also characteristic of liberal employers' discourse, often in defensive response to ten-hours campaigns and the polemics of figures like Stephens. Free contract was the basis of moral independence, and this was linked to future advance through free trade, popular education and, perhaps, political citizenship. But the boundaries of the contractual relationship were inherently problematic. Patrician and metropolitan commentators sought to generalise the obligations of employers on what might be termed a 'territorial' model of *noblesse oblige*.[109] W.R. Greg insisted on the separation of employment from philanthropy within the community. The latter was undertaken as 'neighbour' (albeit a neighbour endowed with wealth, power and, Greg would claim, superior understanding) rather than as employer.[110] Carlyle is acknowledged as 'the most brilliant and influential writer of the day', but nevertheless criticised for attempting to revive the archaic forms of a less enlightened feudal past. In the modern world, 'the first duty which the great employer . . . owes to those who work for him is to make his business succeed'; such business errors as under-capitalised expansion are a dereliction of this duty.[111] In this argument, the workplace appears as a bounded space, governed by contractual relations, the source of the wealth on which philanthropy depends; any other employer initiatives depend on the economic soundness of the enterprise. Outside intervention, whether by the state, popular agitation or simply by metropolitan *literati* constructing a more open-ended model of employer responsibility, is to be resisted.

There were inherent ambiguities in the liberal vision of employer

---

[108] *The Working Man's Friend and Family Instructor*, vol. I (1850), pp. 35–6.
[109] See, e.g., [Sir Arthur Helps], *The Claims of Labour* (1844).
[110] W.R. Greg, 'The relation between employers and employed', reprinted in his *Essays in Political and Social Science*, 2 vols. (1853), vol. II; I have benefited from perceptive readings of these and related texts in unpublished work by Donna Loftus.
[111] Ibid., pp. 268–72, 282–3.

leadership based on individualism, mutual self-interest and citizenship. Gender and age divisions in the labour-force fitted awkwardly with models of authority derived from the employment contract. Paternalism itself could imply the 'infantilisation' of working-class men, with consequent difficulties for appeals to moral independence and self-respect.[112] This might be resolved, to the satisfaction of liberal commentators, through notions of wise parenthood as the fostering of moral growth by a carefully phased extension of freedom and responsibility – a theme that resonates across the discourse of the British governing class, from the appropriate organisation of boarding-schools to the governance of empire.[113] But the debate about contract and the extra-contractual duties of employers has remarkably little to say about the employment of juveniles and women, who lay outside the liberal discourse of potential citizenship. 'What is the object which we all of us ought to have in view, so soon as the care bestowed by the parent upon the child has ceased, and the approach of manhood tells us that we are become free agents?'[114]

Commentaries on the duties of employers thus became focused on adult male juridical free agents, who were also, of course, seen as the main protagonists of the Chartist challenge that provided the context of these debates. Yet the issue of factory regulation, with its focus on the protection of categories regarded as dependent and unfree, had also contributed to the proliferation of social commentary, and remained the unspoken premise of attempts to engage the reasonable working man in a free and frank discussion. Remedying the deficiencies of education was the key, both to the protection of the unfree and to the future fitness of working-class men for responsible free agency. Liberal reform projects looked to the incorporation of the rational and respectable working man, as a junior partner in the causes of popular education and the moral control of women, young people and children in the workplace and community.

The boundaries of the labour contract were partly about the allocation of responsibilities in this imagined partnership. Contractual relations in industry were by no means straightforward, and factory regulation became entangled in these complexities. The treatment of juvenile workers might be held to be the responsibility of the adult men in charge of them, and often (as with mule spinners and their piecers) hiring them. Employers' disclaiming of direct responsibility for juvenile workers hired in this way undermined the image of enlightened benevolence; while the shifting of legal responsibility for infringements was one continuing griev-

---

[112] C. Gallagher, *The Industrial Reformation of English Fiction: Social Discourse and Narrative Form, 1832–1867* (Chicago, 1985), pp. 127–8.
[113] Greg, 'Employers and employed', p. 300, quotation from Helps.
[114] [D. Power], *On the Responsibilities of Employers* (1849), pp. 26–7.

ance about factory act enforcement.[115] At the same time, the public debate on factory regulation, and the wider discussion of the duties of employers, tended to push towards the absolute responsibility of the employer for work-practices and abuses, in a moral if not in a legal sense. Adult male workers, on the other hand, might resent the legal manoeuvres by which employers shifted responsibility, but wish to retain the autonomy and control represented by the direct hiring and supervision of their assistants. The nature of industrial employment was thus contradictory for both sides; and both, to some extent, probably wanted the best of both worlds.

Conclusion

The public attention fastened on social conditions in the manufacturing districts led to various attempts to reformulate models of the authority of property, which tended to vest responsibility and leadership in industrial employers. This was implied in images of the 'well-regulated' factory circulated in the official enquiries of the 1830s. Political economy seems to have been incorporated in the practical ideology of leading employers, especially in cotton; enlightened benevolence was thus linked to technical rationality and accumulation, and frequently cited to justify resistance to regulation. Commitment to economic individualism and accumulation was, however, tempered by anxieties about the consequences of unregulated expansion, and tensions between economic calculation and moralised views of social relations, often expressed through metaphors of the idealised family. Religious discourse expressed and negotiated some of these conflicts, though it could not resolve them.

Liberal models of employer leadership based on individualism, self-help and prospective citizenship had a real appeal. But this was limited, during the 1830s and 40s, by its association with resistance to factory legislation and to other aspects of popular understandings of fair employment. Acceptance by hitherto intransigent liberal employers of the standard working day, and to some extent of collective bargaining, was a necessary precondition of the 'social settlement' established in the textile districts after c. 1850.

Issues emerging from this experience furnished material for a wider discussion of employers' responsibilities and the 'claims of labour'. This placed new emphasis on the industrial employer as an agent of moral and social improvement, a construct which had both critical and legitimising

---

[115] Lloyd-Jones and Lewis, *Manchester in the Age of the Factory*, ch. 5; Carson, 'Institutionalisation of ambiguity'; for further discussion, see below, ch. 6.

functions. Outside commentators adapted generalised models of the duties of station, whereas employers were careful to attempt to define the boundaries of their responsibility, and to draw attention to their primary function as agents of the accumulation process. It was the effective discharge of this function that was held to make possible philanthropy, shorter working hours and other improvements.

What these discussions signal is that free contract is a relative rather than absolute concept, with a necessary moral, legal and cultural context. Much of the debate was about the drawing of boundaries, between economic and moral realms, free agency and mutual dependence, contractual obligations and paternalistic responsibilities, and these boundaries could only be provisional ones. The ambiguities of notions of contract, free agency and dependence, and images of the factory and the factory district as sites of improvement or moral danger and decline, also appeared in a wider range of cultural forms and media. These processes of representation form the subject-matter of the following chapter.

5   The factory imagined

The debates considered in the preceding chapters achieved a wide circulation. Their significance for the making of an industrial society is to be sought in these cultural resonances, as well as the more direct outcomes in terms of factory regulation and the renegotiation of employment relations. The process of regulation, and its associated narratives of progressive improvement and a stabilised factory system, are taken up in Part 2 of this book. The present chapter concludes Part 1, with some account of the circulation of social imagery and languages related to the debates on factory reform. The proper mode of representing industrial realities was indeed part of what was at issue.

The production of social imagery was conditioned by changing cultural forms and conventions of representation. New techniques of graphic illustration, as well as improved letterpress printing, and new reading publics, encouraged a number of experiments in periodical publication during the 1830s and especially the 1840s.[1] These were often hampered by uncertain and unstable modes of address, and mis-identifications of the potential audience. The best-known survivors, *Punch* and the *Illustrated London News*, marked a more clear-cut separation of traditions of caricature (somewhat toned down compared to its antecedents) and blandly 'optimistic' documentary illustration, respectively. Fiction also underwent changing forms of publication (including outlets in some of the new magazines), subject-matter and styles. The so-called 'industrial' or 'social' novel of the 1840s and 1850s laid claim to a higher moral seriousness, in depicting questions of import to an enlightened public.[2]

---

[1] C. Fox, *Graphic Journalism in England during the 1830s and 1840s* (New York and London, 1988); J.R. Harvey, *Victorian Novelists and their Illustrators* (London, 1970).

[2] On the industrial novel, see esp. Gallagher, *Industrial Reformation*; J.P. Kestner, *Protest and Reform: The British Social Narrative by Women, 1827–1867* (London, 1985); R. Williams, *Culture and Society, 1780–1950* (London, 1958), part I, ch. 5. On Victorian literary culture more generally, A. Blake, *Reading Victorian Fiction* (Basingstoke, 1989); T. Lovell, *Consuming Fictions* (London and New York, 1987).

This chapter explores the representation of industrial issues in these various media and literary forms, and it touches on associated debates about appropriate registers and conventions – problems signalled in familiar assertions about 'realism'. I discuss a selection of texts, including examples of industrial topography and documentary journalism, more radical critiques of the factory system and various fictional works. These all, in varied ways, treat themes familiar from the preceding chapters; but all also actively construct definitions of industrial society. My approach is inevitably selective, particularly in its treatment of the novel. This focuses on texts generally treated as unsuccessful precursors of the mature industrial novel. They are however of interest for their fairly direct addressing of current controversies. I then make some comments on the writing of Elizabeth Gaskell and Charlotte Brontë, two writers located in the industrial north. The metropolitan reception of their work established such communities and their members as topics about which serious fiction might be written.

Topographies of the factory system

Themes and imagery from the social debates of the 1830s and 1840s had a wider circulation in edited and sometimes garbled forms. Official enquiries and related literature were extensively treated, often with lengthy quotations, in the heavyweight periodicals, and, in briefer versions, in a range of journals, newspapers, pamphlets and placards.[3] This permeation of social enquiry could produce a sensationalist identification of the factory districts with 'misery and vice' comparable to that associated with certain dangerous quarters of the capital.[4] However there was also a recognition of efforts to 'cleanse these Augean stables' and of the improvability of the factory population, the possibility of 'making the factory and its neighbourhood a scene of happiness and refinement'.[5] The recognition of the problem was also the recognition of its possible amelioration, and of the reader as part of an enlightened public aware of such issues.

This message of reassurance was certainly the predominant theme of the *Illustrated London News,* whose occasional references to the industrial

---

[3] S.E. Finer, 'The transmission of Benthamite ideas, 1820–1850', in Sutherland (ed.), *Studies in the Growth of Nineteenth-Century Government*; C. Fox, 'The development of social reportage in English periodical illustration', *Past & Present* 74 (1977).

[4] *Pictorial Times,* 2 Sept. 1843, p. 30.

[5] Ibid.; *Chambers Edinburgh Journal* (hereafter *Chambers Jour.*), no. 541, 11 June 1842, p. 163 (commenting on [S. Greg], *Two Letters to Leonard Horner, Esq. on the Capabilities of the Factory System* (1841).

north included such events as a royal visit to Gardner and Bazley's Barrow Bridge Mills, near Bolton, the Bolton Operatives' Bazaar, the opening of Salt's new mill at Saltaire and works outings to the Manchester Art Treasures Exhibition. The main discordant note was coverage of the Preston dispute of 1853–4, with an engraving of leaders addressing a meeting, accompanied by a hostile commentary.[6]

The more optimistic view drew on defensive justifications by leading employers and commissioners' and inspectors' reports (with their distinctions between responsible and irresponsible employers). The much-cited books of Andrew Ure, Edward Baines and William Cooke Taylor were key sources for this view.[7] These texts share a polemical commitment to entrepreneurial liberalism, but vary in their style, address and ability to encompass the nuances of their subject-matter. Ure's approach is that of a scientific taxonomy, with grandiloquent claims for the authority of natural philosophy in support of what is in many respects a technicist utopia. Ure begins from an overview of 'the general principles of manufacture', including the famous definition of a factory as 'the combined operation of many classes of work-people . . . tending with assiduous skill a system of productive machines continuously impelled by a central power'.[8] This is followed by Book II, on 'the scientific economy of the factory system', including analyses of the composition of textile fibres and chapters dedicated to the specific processes and machines appropriate for each branch of textiles. Finally, the 'moral economy' of the system is addressed in Book III, taking up contentious issues of living standards, health and morals.

Baines adopts a historical approach, including early evidence of cotton manufacture, its development in Asia and spread to Europe (chapters 1–6). His central chapters deal historically with the main mechanical inventions, then with recent commercial statistics of the cotton trade (chapters 7–15). The two concluding chapters deal, like Ure, with current controversies about factory reform and free trade.

Both books are extensively illustrated, in contrasting styles (I shall refer simply to 'Ure' or 'Baines', though the illustrations were of course commissioned from artists and engravers). Ure includes a frontispiece view of a new factory (Orrell, Stockport), and factory interiors of mule spinning and power-loom weaving (a large foldaway drawing, often reproduced in a cropped form, which makes the factory floor look

---

[6] *Illustrated London News*, 25 Oct. 1851, 2 Oct. 1852, 1 Oct., 12 Nov. 1853, 12 Sept. 1857.
[7] E. Baines, jnr., *History of the Cotton Manufacture in Great Britain* (1835); W. Cooke Taylor, *Notes of a Tour in the Manufacturing Districts of Lancashire* (2nd edn, 1842); A. Ure, *The Philosophy of Manufactures* (1835).
[8] Ure, *Philosophy*, p. 13.

proportionately more spacious).[9] There are also numerous technical diagrams, perspective drawings of machines and microscope enlargements of fibres. Baines, the successful journalist, offers the reader a rather more varied and pleasing visual range, including portraits of Arkwright (frontispiece), Peel and Crompton, Crompton's old house at Hall-in-the-Wood, carding, spinning, weaving and calico-printing scenes, two views of factory buildings, one of the Manchester Exchange, diagrams and drawings of machines and one of enlarged fibres. Smaller decorative woodcuts inset on the printed page (one of the new techniques of the period) show archaeological evidence of early cotton production, Indian hand-workers and cotton plants; the effect is to associate an aestheticised nature with the archaeological past and the colonial present, open to appropriation by a progressive modern industrial Britain.[10]

Both sets of illustrations have been selectively and widely reproduced, the factory scenes being the key points of this interest. These show interesting contrasts. Ure favoured an austere, angular, utilitarian style, while Baines' engravings have echoes of pastoral and genre painting, with softer, flowing lines. The mule-spinning scene in Baines was in fact specifically criticised by Ure for its romanticism and technical impossibility, which 'shows how incompetent a general artist is to delineate a system of machinery'.[11] Similarly, the views of factory buildings in Baines have stronger touches of the sublime and the picturesque, framed by rivers or canals. Finally, we should note the presence in Ure of authority figures (managers, proprietors, gentlemanly visitors to the works: Ure himself?) with diligent operatives in the background. The work-groups in Baines are ostensibly on their own, with a gender hierarchy established by mixed spinning and weaving groups focused on the male figures, balanced by an all-female card-room and all-male artisanal calico printers.

Another key text, Cooke Taylor's Tour, is not illustrated, but written in a strongly visual language.[12] Published in the depths of recession as covert propaganda for the Anti-Corn Law League, this emphasises the suffering, but also the stoic endurance and moral potentialities, of the operatives, viewed as victims of protectionism. The tropes of topographic writing are used to present Lancashire as a varied county, with connections to an older past, rather than simply a scene of industrial degradation

[9] Ibid., facing ch. 1, and p. 308; and cf. *Penny Magazine*, June 1843, supp. , p. 241; the classic, but now oddly neglected, study of this whole topic is F. Klingender, *Art and the Industrial Revolution* (revised edn, London, 1968); see also C. Arscott and G. Pollock with J. Wolff, 'The partial view: the visual representation of the early nineteenth-century industrial city', in Wolff and Seed (eds.), *The Culture of Capital*.

[10] Baines, *Cotton*, see listing of illustrations on contents pages.

[11] Ure, *Philosophy*, pp. 309–10 footnote.

[12] Arscott *et al.*, 'The partial view', pp. 214–15.

and conflict. The destitution of the handloom weavers is foregrounded, and associated with urban problems. The factory under favourable conditions and enlightened management is the site of potential improvement, apparent outside the towns where 'the influence of factories could be seen undisturbed'. Like numerous other commentators, Cooke Taylor describes the Ashworth mills at Turton, near Bolton, Ashton of Hyde and other exemplars of this bucolic industrial ideal. The account of Turton introduces the anecdote, much repeated in subsequent *reportage*, of how Ashworth's fruit was left undisturbed by hungry operatives in the 1842 strikes.[13]

Journalistic treatments of the manufacturing districts recycle much of this material, with a characteristic shift between particular workplaces, the essential characteristics of the 'factory system' and the industrial town or district. Manchester attracted particular attention (with for example more entries in *Poole's Index to Periodical Literature* than any other provincial English city). Manchester often stood for the whole cotton region, or even for modern industrialism. The city therefore remains, despite necessary revisions and qualifications, 'the symbol of a new age'.[14] What exactly that symbolism conveyed is more ambiguous. Attention shifted from industrial work to features of urban life: the unknowable social mix of the streets, the dangers and excitements of consumption and commercialised popular culture, shops everywhere 'streaming with light'.

Here almost every want that man feels can be satisfied . . . The factory, now so quiet, has given the people good wages . . . You see the husband and wife, both of them very young and neither looking very healthy, engaged in making purchases. The husband carries a baby, carefully wrapped and sound asleep, while the wife has a basket and the key of the house-door.[15]

This urban spectacle affords excitement and human interest; even the faults of the operatives (early marriage) are rendered comprehensible. It is the cessation of work that defines this urban space, when 'a population of not much under 100,000 is immediately released from a whole week's labour . . . The steam-engine is then a mere heap of cast-iron'; the workers regain their individuality on release from work, 'thousands of busy workers have each gone to satisfy his or her individual wants'.[16]

---

[13] Cooke Taylor, *Tour*, pp. 19, 23–4; cf., e.g., Ginswick (ed.), *Labour and the Poor*, vol. I, p. 36.

[14] *Poole's Index to Periodical Literature* (1891), vols. I, II, entries for Manchester, cf. Birmingham, Liverpool, etc.; A. Briggs, *Victorian Cities* (London, 1963).

[15] 'Saturday evening in Manchester', *Chambers Jour.*, new ser. no. 324, 16 March 1850, pp. 164–7; cf. local poets' treatments of similar themes in Maidment (ed.), *Poorhouse Fugitives*, pp. 152–4, 160.   [16] *Chambers Jour.*, 16 March 1850, pp. 164–5.

Work itself remains enigmatic, more difficult to describe in the language of popular journalism. The moment of transition, on entering or leaving the mill, is one of the stereotypes of social *reportage*. The observer at the factory gates, peering at the operatives and attempting to draw conclusions about their health and morals, is a familiar theme. For example, Turner Thackrah, a Leeds physician and one of the medical supporters of the ten-hours bill, gave extended treatment to factory work in the second edition of his well-known treatise on the *Effects of Trades*. He seems to have derived his information on cotton from a brief trans-pennine excursion. 'I stood in Oxford-row, Manchester, and observed the streams of operatives as they left the mills, at 12 o'clock.' There follows a description of 'almost universally ill-looking, small, sickly and ill-clad' children, men 'almost as pallid and thin'; the women looked better, 'but I saw no fresh or fine-looking individuals among them'.[17] Nearly two decades later, Angus Reach, reporting on conditions in Manchester for the *Morning Chronicle*, again stationed himself outside a mill off Oxford Road; his conclusions are fairly qualified, but the general tone is optimistic. 'They talk and laugh cheerily together . . . parties are formed round the peripatetic establishments of hot coffee and cocoa venders.'[18]

Visits inside the workplace – generally, the large, modern mill under 'enlightened' management – likewise followed a standard pattern, with a shift in focus from the workers to the machines and the progression of cotton 'from the pod to the piece'.[19] These descriptions became repetitive, as is perhaps signalled in the whimsically apologetic tone of *Chambers' Journal*: 'Behold us, then, note-book in hand, and with every faculty on the alert, set down in the steaming, smoking, buzzing town of Stockport.' The account of the technical processes was often perfunctory, playing up the wonders of the self-acting mule: 'and all this, thanks to the extraordinary skill of Mr Roberts of Manchester, without human intervention, excepting where here and there a little boy is seen crawling under them sweeping up the dust, or a girl is attending to a broken thread'.[20] This kind of industrial sight-seeing seems to have become something of a fashion, for concerned philanthropists, journalists or any tourist with appropriately respectable credentials; the keeping of visitors' books at

[17] C. Turner Thackrah, *The Effects of the Principal Arts, Trades and Professions . . . on Health and Longevity* (2nd edn, 1832; reprint, Edinburgh, 1957), p. 146.
[18] Ginswick (ed.), *Labour and the Poor*, p. 14.
[19] *Chambers Jour.*, new ser. no. 258, 9 Dec. 1848, pp. 372–6.
[20] Ibid.

mills, like that inaugurated for Prince Albert's visit to Barrow Bridge, is one index of this attention.[21]

A characteristic positioning of the observer–author–reader outside the factory gate, or passing through to view the technical marvels inside, constructed the factory as a bounded space. Industrialism itself is located in the geographic space of the 'factory districts'. In the words of the accompanying text to John Tallis' decorative map of Manchester (c. 1857): 'The extensive circumjacent tract as seen from the nearest range of hills looks not a little charming, but does so, not from its proper character of a landscape but from its profusion of groves, villas, mansions, factories and towns, with Manchester in the centre, and Stockport, Ashton, Oldham, Bolton, Bury and Middleton in the distances.'[22] Similarly, for the *Penny Magazine*, Lancashire could be regarded 'as one huge town, almost as one huge factory', defined by the 'connecting link between Manchester as a centre, and Bolton, Bury, Rochdale . . . &c. as branches'.[23] The Manchester Exchange was 'the very heart of the whole system', and so this centre turns out to be in commerce and exchange, as much as in industrial production. The language is that of Ure's construct of the factory as an integrated system moved by a central power, which is sometimes the steam-engine, sometimes the guiding intelligence of commerce and finance. The specialised cotton towns (increasingly, as most commentators noted, the sites of concentrated industrial growth) are made peripheral to the 'system'. Specific features of these towns are noted – Bolton as a former merchanting centre now devoted to manufacture, Oldham as a place whose eccentricities have not yet 'rubbed off' (the women wore head-scarves instead of bonnets, both sexes wore wooden clogs). Moving to the actual production process, the article notes the 'varieties' of cotton manufacture, but then sets this qualification aside; 'the interior arrangements of any one large factory' can provide 'something like a judgement of them all'. The factory chosen is, once again, Ure's state-of-the-art example, Orrell's of Stockport.[24] If the cotton

---

[21] Dean Mills, Visitors Book, in Haggas Bryan Coll., Bolton Archives, ZHB/1/12; *Illustrated London News*, 25 Oct. 1851; and see also, e.g., F. Engels, *The Condition of the Working Class in England*, ed. W.O. Henderson and W.H. Chaloner (Oxford, 1958), pp. 210–11; J. Uglow, *Elizabeth Gaskell* (paperback edn, London, 1994), pp. 555–6; and varied fictional treatments in B. Disraeli, *Coningsby* (Penguin edn, Harmondsworth, 1983), Book IV, chs. 1–3; G. Jewsbury, *Marian Withers*, 3 vols. (1851), vol. II, pp. 33–57; F. Trollope, *The Life and Adventures of Michael Armstrong the Factory Boy* (1840; reprint, Cass, London, 1968), pp. 236–8.

[22] A. Boynton-Williams (ed.), *Town and City Maps of the British Isles, 1800–1855* (London, 1992), p. 112; the hill mentioned may well be an imaginary viewpoint, and Manchester is not in fact at the 'centre' of the cotton towns, but towards the south-western edge.

[23] *Penny Magazine*, June 1843, supp. , pp. 241–3.   [24] Ibid.

region could be viewed metaphorically as 'one huge factory', then the interior arrangements of this actual factory would display the essential features of the system.

If this scheme is abstracted from the 'varieties' of the cotton industry, its application to the complexities of the West Riding posed further difficulties. Following its 'day in a cotton factory' with a 'day in a Leeds woollen factory', the *Penny Magazine* began from the historical peculiarities of the industry, describing domestic manufacture and the company mill as stages. However 'the factory *system* of cloth manufacturing' was analogous to that in cotton, 'being the growth of steam-power, mechanical invention and accumulated capital'; Benjamin Gott's famous Leeds mill was taken as an exemplar. The article then returns to the complexities of the industry, noting that Armley, another of Gott's mills, serviced domestic clothiers. It concludes with a description of the cloth-hall.[25] As for worsted, 'our present visit will partake somewhat of a rambling character', since 'we have found it desirable to extend our observations beyond the walls of one factory, and to glance round the circumstances and arrangements which give to an entire district the character of one great workshop'. This is followed by topographical descriptions of Bradford, a town lit up with 'that curious species of illumination resulting from the countless windows of large factories', and the industrial mix of Halifax and Calderdale (a staple of industrial topographies since Defoe). Finally, there are descriptions of handcombing and of Akroyd's mills at Halifax.[26]

The meanings of labour

The factory as workplace, set apart from its surroundings yet dependent on them, is the defining feature of the industrial topographies considered above. In this literature, the experience of industrial work itself remains enigmatic, the focus shifts from people to machinery, workplace to consumption and domestic life. This displaced and marginalised more radical narratives of work under the factory system.

More critical accounts might make ironic use of some of the tropes of topographical description. As George Crabtree wrote, he had set out 'not like ... Dr Syntax in search of the Picturesque', but to investigate the evils of the factory system; the picturesque landscapes of Calderdale, reminiscent of 'Alpine scenery', served as dramatic contrast to the hidden oppressions of overworking mills, whose presence is disclosed with gothic effects: 'But on a sudden, as though by magic, a Factory burst in our

[25] Ibid., 25 Nov. 1843, supp. , pp. 458–64.
[26] Ibid., 27 Jan. 1844, supp. , pp. 33–9.

view.'[27] In the *Memoir of Robert Blincoe* (1828, written by John Brown, a Bolton journalist, from Blincoe's testimony of his experiences as a factory apprentice, *c.* 1799–1813), Blincoe's arrival at a new and worse mill is symbolised in its remote and bleak location: 'The savage features of the adjacent scenery impressed a general gloom upon the convoy.'[28] The topography here is that of a *gulag*. In narratives like Blincoe's, or those of some of Sadler's working-class witnesses, the truth of the system is inscribed in the worker's body, emaciated by under-nourishment, weakened by prolonged labour and disease, tormented and deformed. In the iconography of radical caricature, such images belonged with those of military flogging, poor law bastilles, the new police and prisons.[29] The title-page of John Doherty's edition (1832) of the *Memoir* has a woodcut of its subject, shown in silhouette with crooked legs (plate 1).

Such narratives represented the factory, or its most oppressive instances, as the site of physical and moral degeneration and death. This view persisted, for example in the articles of Peter McDouall and some Chartist verse. McDouall adapts the image of the observer at the factory gate, injecting a note of gothic terror: 'The boy hesitates to enter, the little girl pauses before she enters the fatal workshop, and nature pulls violently to prevent them . . . but the bell has rung.'[30] The ostensible focus is on children, or sometimes on adult women, as victims, with working-class men allied to true philanthropists as their rescuers from unnatural bondage. There is also, perhaps increasingly, a language of struggle and bargaining over working practices and the control of machines, and the ten-hours campaign positioned adult men on this terrain. James Leach's much-quoted pamphlet, *Stubborn Facts from the Factories* (1844) emphasised the speed-up associated with new machinery. Assertions by short-time propagandists about distances walked by piecers during a working day were the main attempt to address this in public debate; at one lobby of Westminster the short-time delegates played spinners and piecers with Palmerston's dining-room chairs, in an attempt to explain the nature of the labour process.[31] The preoccupation with spinning and piecing, made to stand for all juvenile labour, or even for factory labour as such, is worth

[27] G. Crabtree, *A Brief Description of a Tour through Calder Dale, being a Letter to Richard Oastler* (1833), pp. 3, 17.
[28] J. Brown, *A Memoir of Robert Blincoe* (1832 edn; reprint, Caliban, Firle, Sussex, 1977), p. 45.
[29] A selection of such images is reproduced in Fox, *Graphic Journalism*, appendix.
[30] *McDouall's Journal* (1841), p. 77.
[31] J. Fielden, *The Curse of the Factory System* (1836); Grant, *The Ten Hours Bill*, pp. 56–7; R.H. Greg, *The Factory Question* (1837), pp. 72–3; Hodder, *Seventh Earl of Shaftesbury*, vol. II, pp. 18–20; [Leach], *Stubborn Facts*; *Report of the Central Committee of the Association of Millowners and Manufacturers, 1844* (1845), pp. 5–9; millowners' returns to questionnaires, Ashworth Papers, Lancs. RO, box marked 'Factory Act Returns'.

comment; young workers were as likely to be engaged in preparatory processes (and, in card-rooms, probably ran greater risks of permanent damage to health), while many piecers were in fact teenagers or young adult men. The blandly apologetic notion that simple machine-watching involved little physical effort and was therefore not exhausting was more or less discredited. But issues of the intensity of work were not pursued, perhaps in part because of the very insistence that it was the hours of work that needed to be reformed.

There was also a shift in the social imagery of industrial work. Journalistic accounts of the factory system depicted workers outside work, and machines in the workplace, effortlessly tended. At the same time, labour, and the position and aspirations of the 'working man' were becoming pervasive concerns, with the Chartist challenge, the 'condition of England' question and the gospel of work. Here work was represented as the attribute of adult men, the political protagonists of Chartism. The most characteristic images are of outdoor work or skilled artisans (navvies, building workers like those constructing the Crystal Palace, blacksmiths at the forge).[32] The worker himself is often portrayed as a vigorous and industrious free labourer, living by his honest toil. Such imagery conveyed a greater confidence about industrial society, as well as continuing tensions and anxieties. The focus on outdoor and artisanal labour perhaps appealed to more intuitively accessible forms of work, compared to the mysteries of piecing and the self-acting mule. Heavy engineering, with its skill-intensive techniques and promethean drama of the forge, superseded Andrew Ure's cotton mills as the leading edge of industrial progress.[33] Social anxieties shifted from the manufacturing districts to London, or to great cities generally, the sites of small-scale consumer goods production and casualised labour markets; the needlewoman was the most characteristic figure in images of degraded and dangerous work.[34]

Greater confidence and pride in industrial work were articulated in the rich regional cultures of the industrial north, notably in the dialect

[32] See Klingender, *Art and the Industrial Revolution*, chs. 7, 8 and plates 107–12.
[33] On engineering workers see esp. K. McClelland, 'Time to work, time to live: some aspects of work and the re-formation of class in Britain, 1850–1880', in Joyce (ed.), *Historical Meanings of Work*.
[34] S. Alexander, 'Women's work in nineteenth-century London', in J. Mitchell and A. Oakley (eds.), *The Rights and Wrongs of Women* (Harmondsworth, 1976); G. Stedman Jones, *Outcast London: A Study in the Relationship between Classes in Victorian Society* (Oxford, 1971); J. Treuherz *et al.*, *Hard Times: Social Realism in Victorian Art* (London and Manchester, 1987); for the growth of comparable anxieties in Manchester, A.J. Kidd, 'Outcast Manchester', in A.J. Kidd and K.W. Roberts (eds.), *City, Class and Culture: Studies of Cultural Production and Social Policy in Victorian Manchester* (Manchester, 1985).

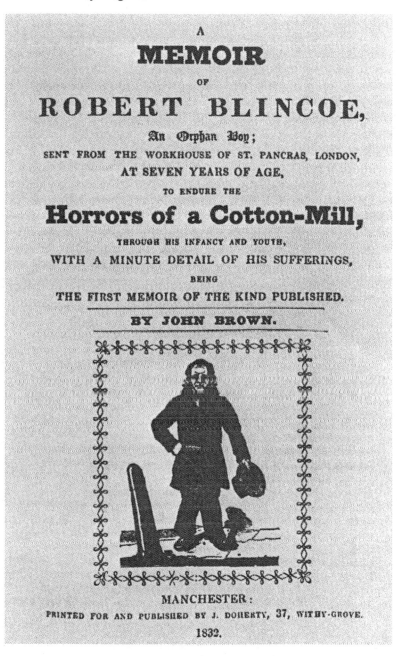

A

MEMOIR

OF

ROBERT BLINCOE,

An Orphan Boy;

SENT FROM THE WORKHOUSE OF ST. PANCRAS, LONDON,

AT SEVEN YEARS OF AGE,

TO ENDURE THE

Horrors of a Cotton-Mill,

THROUGH HIS INFANCY AND YOUTH,

WITH A MINUTE DETAIL OF HIS SUFFERINGS,

BEING

THE FIRST MEMOIR OF THE KIND PUBLISHED.

BY JOHN BROWN.

MANCHESTER:

PRINTED FOR AND PUBLISHED BY J. DOHERTY, 37, WITHY-GROVE.

1832.

Plate 1 Robert Blincoe, a survivor of child labour

writing that flourished (in print) from about 1840.[35] Ten-hours propaganda itself placed increasing emphasis on the superior strength, skill and
moral discipline of freeborn Englishmen – or 'Anglo-Saxons' – as the key
to industrial productivity and competitiveness.[36] The dialect tradition
may be read as a literature of adaptation and consolation, or, more positively, a celebration of the capacity to create meaning and derive pleasure
out of unpromising conditions. As Brian Maidment has pointed out,
dialect verse was not on the whole used as a vehicle for the more uni-
versalistic aspirations of radicalism and Chartism; nor could it be, given
the requirements of a nation-wide medium of political mobilisation.[37]

Dialect writing could however convey a more muted social indignation,
and a sceptical utopian sense of justice and common humanity. Life is
seen as harsh and unjust, but endurable with stoic courage and self-discipline. For example in Samuel Laycock's 'cotton panic' poems, the difficulties of weaving Surat cotton (used as a substitute for supplies
interrupted by the American war) are rendered slightly comical, part of
life's ups and downs:

> Every toime I go in wi' mi cuts to owd Joe,
> He gies me a cursin', an 'bates me an' o;
> Aw've a warp i' one loom wi' booath selvedges
> marr'd
> An' th' other's as bad for he's dress'd it to hard

In so far as anyone is to blame, it is 'yon Yankees'. In a later poem, the
return of operatives dispersed by the tramp in search of work is presented
as the resumption of the due course of things:

> Th' long chimnies are smokin' as hard as they con,
> An' th' machinery's wurlin' areawnd;
> Owd shopmates 'at havn't bin seen for some years
> Are o gettin' back to th' owd greawnd.

Factory work is hard, but not utterly intolerable, a matter of wry complaint rather than of cosmic struggle for survival.[38]

Didactic fictions, melodrama and the 'industrial novel'

Life in industrial towns enjoyed brief literary prominence, in the 'industrial' or 'social' novel of the 1840s and 1850s. As W. R. Greg noted, the

[35] Joyce, *Visions of the People*; Maidment (ed.), *Poorhouse Fugitives*.
[36] See, e.g., *Men of Newton and Hyde* (June 1853), *To the Operatives of Stalybridge* (July 1853), broadsides in Cassidy Coll., Tameside Archives; and see below, ch. 7.
[37] Maidment (ed.), *Poorhouse Fugitives*.
[38] Samuel Laycock, *Warblin's fro' an Owd Songster* (1893), pp. 51–2, 127.

discussion of 'employers and employed' had some impact on literary tastes; 'tales of rough passion or of tender sentiment' had given place to 'a new class of novels, of which "Mary Barton" and "Oliver Twist" are the type', characterised by 'an earnest spirit of universal social sympathy'.[39] It is of course debatable how far *Mary Barton* did constitute the type for a literary school (and it is scarcely deficient in 'passion', 'sentiment' or a lively narrative) but it was certainly read in a particular frame and, as Greg's comment indicates, the category was one produced by critics at the time. For subsequent generations of readers, too, the early Victorian novel has come to stand as the literary expression – or even the original inspiration – of an awakened social conscience.

The factory question was one topic of concern, and several works in the social fiction canon are set in the textile districts, notably Gaskell's two 'Manchester' novels (1848, 1855), Disraeli's *Sybil* (1845), Dickens' *Hard Times* (1854) and Charlotte Brontë's *Shirley* (1849; subsequent references to 'Brontë' are to Charlotte). As this list will indicate, the texts differed in attitude, intention and style; Brontë's *Shirley* is often seen as fitting the mould awkwardly, but so, in fact, do all these novels. The problems of industrialism provided a literary *topos*, often functioning as a complex metaphor for other concerns, rather than any unified genre. Fictional writing in this period explored a range of social issues and debates, which, perhaps by virtue of the imagery of 'industrial revolution', came to be loosely associated with industrialism and the factory. *Hard Times* and Gaskell's two 'Manchester' novels were perhaps the strongest influences in fixing these associations. The events of 1853–4 in Preston provided material for both writers, and occasioned a rather anxious negotiation around Dickens' editorial power in publishing both *North and South* and *Hard Times* in monthly parts.[40] For Dickens, the factory and the industrial town ('Coketown') stand as symbols of uniformity and human alienation. Gaskell, a more informed observer of industrial life, places more emphasis on difference and variety. I shall focus on fictional treatments produced from locations in the industrial north itself, including notably Gaskell and Brontë. This is placed in the context of earlier industrial fictions, of a more overtly partisan character, including Frances Trollope's *Michael Armstrong* and responses to it.

This is not therefore a comprehensive treatment of the industrial novel, or of its more general cultural context. The moment of the industrial novel was a brief period in the mid-1840s to early-1850s. During that moment, concerns with industrialism and class relations – perhaps

[39] W.R. Greg, 'The relation between employers and employed', in *Essays*, vol. II, pp. 256–7.
[40] G. Carnall, 'Dickens, Mrs. Gaskell and the Preston strike', *Victorian Studies* 8 (1964); Uglow, *Gaskell*, ch. 17.

reinforced by the Chartist crisis of 1848 – condensed a range of other tensions and issues. This was inherently unstable, and the concerns were again dispersed into sensationalism in one direction, or the novel of provincial life in another. The theme of industrialism was itself selectively treated, as it was in the corresponding documentary texts. Whereas the factory stood as an organising metaphor for social problems, active working-class dissidence was more often associated with male artisans (who were in any case more numerous than male factory workers). Even in novels directly depicting factory towns, artisans, needlewomen and domestic servants (and in *Hard Times* circus people) seem more acceptable characters than factory operatives.

These texts were however read in relation to a particular field of debate, affected by controversies surrounding the depiction of social realities. The construction of a literary canon of 'industrial' novels claimed to define a more 'mature' literary tradition, emerging from a prehistory of heavy didacticism and popular melodrama: 'social fiction, primarily used for advancing theses, became social literature'.[41] Quite apart from ideological intentions, the market for popular fiction, especially in periodical formats, also helped sustain features of didacticism and melodrama. The status of the novel itself – and of the middle-class women so strongly represented among its exponents, both the canonised and the now obscure – was shifting, within evolving hierarchies of the printed word.

Catherine Gallagher has drawn attention to some of the antecedents of industrial fiction, in the apprentice tale (the triumph of a courageous and resourceful young male hero over difficulty and hostile machinations, often to marry the master's daughter) and magazine stories about seamstresses (rescued from the greed and lechery of their exploiters, or expiring in a catastrophic *denouement*, in either case often through recognition of long-lost kinship with a true gentleman).[42] Like the language of factory agitation, such narratives are constructed in terms of gender difference, with men as active protagonists and women as objects of benevolent intervention. Workers' testimonies, such as that of Blincoe or some of Sadler's witnesses, might also be constructed in these terms.

Frances Trollope's *Adventures of Michael Armstrong* (serial publication 1839; book 1840) draws on these traditions. Trollope, the daughter of a Hampshire vicar and semi-estranged wife of an unsuccessful barrister and failed gentleman farmer (also the mother of a very famous novelist) began a successful literary career in middle age, with an account of travels in the United States (*Domestic Manners of the Americans*, 1832) followed by several novels and other travel books. Her sympathies appear to have

---

[41] Kestner, *Protest and Reform*, p. 18.   [42] Gallagher, *Industrial Reformation*, ch. 6.

been romantic Tory, but with a transgressive libertarian aspect and some hints of earlier radical leanings. A successful writer in market terms, she was regarded as outspoken and rather coarse, 'the sarcastic Mrs Trollope'. *Michael Armstrong* was undertaken at the suggestion of Lord Ashley, or at any rate with his endorsement, and researched in a brief trip to the industrial north, where Trollope met John Doherty, parson Bull and others.[43]

Trollope's descriptions of child labour are strongly influenced by Robert Blincoe, and therefore open to attack as referring to abuses long since removed. More recent critics have also noted the 'overdrawn characters' and 'patently absurd' plot.[44] Whatever their literary shortcomings, these features were integral to the book's impact, and probably to its popularity with 'Chartist' readers, at which Trollope expressed somewhat disingenuous surprise and alarm. The episodic plot relates to monthly publication, and to a readership that might read parts in isolation; this possibility would be reinforced by the illustrations that accompanied each part (further discussed later). The very absurdity of the plot may be a conscious device. The suffering inflicted on poor children is linked to caricature of the employer (Sir Matthew Dowling) and his associates – other employers, villainous managers and overlookers, mercenary and compromised professional men, society drones. The rather thickly laid on satire on *nouveau riche* pretension and arrogance echoes Trollope's portrayal of the Americans (and not least of the attitudes of slaveowners). The ludicrous plot points up the moral chaos consequent on irresponsible wealth and power. Michael is removed from his poor but loving home, to be made a symbol of benevolence in public, but abused in private, at the big house. This is to reward his good conduct in rescuing one of Sir Matthew's lady friends from a stubborn cow on the path. Michael is torn between the material improvement held out to him (especially the food sent to his ailing family) and the isolation and abuse he suffers in the Dowling household. His failure to express appropriate gratitude culminates at a ludicrous piece of amateur theatricals in celebration of Dowling's benevolence (see plate 2); he is punished by deportation to a particularly nasty mill (modelled on Blincoe's account of Litton in Derbyshire).

[43] W.H. Chaloner, 'Mrs Trollope and the early factory system', *Victorian Studies*, 4, no. 2 (1960); F.E. Trollope, *Frances Trollope: Her Life and Literary Work from George III to Victoria*, 2 vols. (1895), esp. vol. II, p. 178; see also the early chapters of V. Glendinning, *Trollope* (London, 1992). Further references to 'Trollope' are to Frances unless otherwise indicated.
[44] Kestner, *Protest and Reform*, p. 55; I. Kovacevic, *Fact into Fiction: English Literature and the Industrial Scene, 1750–1850* (Leicester and Belgrade, 1975), p. 100.

This is conveyed in some quite effective (albeit 'coarse') comic writing. The lampoon exposes the cruelty of a capricious and self-regarding pseudo-philanthropy – and, by implication, questions the claims made on behalf of the 'humane' employer. The satire is laced with sexual innuendo, hinting at the millowner's designs on servants, factory women and society ladies. When Michael in his smart clothes (cast-offs from his patron's family) revisits the mill, Dowling and the odious Dr Crockley try to recruit him to a kind of child pornography: '"Take scavenger, No. 3, there, round the neck; now – now – now, as she lies sprawling, and let us see you give her a hearty kiss".' And it is Dowling's flirtation with Lady Clarissa (rescued by Michael in the cow incident) that precipitates the whole action of the plot. Trollope makes play with the metaphor of steam-power and machinery to suggest Lady Dowling's suspicion of her husband; their marriage is 'a beautiful alternation of power, which the measured movement of the engine in their factories, first sending up one side, and then the other, might, perhaps, have suggested'.[45]

Michael's confinement in the isolated Deep Valley Mill, the attempt to find and rescue him by the genuinely benevolent Mary Brotherton, and his escape and subsequent adventures involve a series of journeys and episodic encounters. These enable Trollope and her illustrators to display 'evils' of the factory system: the dragging of children to work through the snow, as narrated to Mary by the clergyman Mr Bell (Bull); the fraudulent and oppressive nature of the Sunday School kept by 'a serious gentleman as owns a factory'; mad Sally, encountered on the moors, driven crazy by the trauma of incarceration after a childhood escape attempt.[46] The story of Sally merits further comment. A girl had been subjected to confinement under terrifying circumstances at the Gregs' Styal mill, quite recently when Trollope wrote; Doherty took an interest in the case, and may have told Trollope about it. As Joseph Kestner points out, apprenticeship and pauper migration were by no means dead issues in the 1830s.[47] Trollope, on the other hand, locates Sally's traumatisation in the fairly distant past (fifty years ago), perhaps to disguise the provenance of the story (if this was the Styal incident), perhaps also to create a picture of timeless oppression and suffering.

The first six parts of the novel were denounced at length in the *Athenaeum*. The review (possibly by Cooke Taylor, a regular *Athenaeum* contributor) follows the familiar lines of liberal defences of the factory system, framing its commentary on the text with more general comments about misrepresentation, aristocratic and popular prejudices and pro-

---

[45] Trollope, *Michael Armstrong*, pp. 719, 81, 103.   [46] Ibid., chs. 19, 22, 24.
[47] Kestner, *Protest and Reform*, pp. 52–5; and see above, ch. 4 n 106.

Plate 2 Amateur theatricals at 'Dowling Lodge' (Trollope, *Michael Armstrong*)

gressive improvement of the manufacturing population. On more strictly
literary grounds, the novel is condemned as melodrama, like the 'worst
comedies of the quondam German–English school'.[48] A subsequent
review of the book version, together with another of Trollope's novels,
accused her of 'double-dyed vulgarity', 'coarseness' and an obsession
with 'incurably underbred' wealthy characters, engaging in intrigues with
servants and other improprieties.[49]

Trollope provoked a counter-fiction, *Mary Ashley*, by Frederic
Montagu, a barrister (he also wrote a travelogue, *Gleanings in Craven*,
dedicated to the Duke of Devonshire as benevolent landowner, which
includes a fairly standard optimistic account of a mill, at Skipton).[50] *Mary
Ashley* adopts some of the same conventions of didactic fiction as
Trollope, but reverses the signs; the benevolence of a millowner rescues
Mary from inner-city poverty to work, under her father's eye, in the
factory. Like Trollope, Montagu includes a visit to the spinning-room,
but as the happy ending to the story rather than its unhappy beginning.
On entering the spinning-room, the benevolent lady visitor 'was much
pleased . . . to hear the sweet voice of a young girl singing the last verse of a
psalm'. The spinning-room is described as all-female at that moment (the
spinner, Mary's father, being, rather improbably, out of the room); while
the mill manager is a gentle and tender man, with 'dark and intelligent
eyes and a remarkable softness in his speech'.[51] Montagu imagines a
feminised and moralised workplace.

The engravings issued monthly with the parts of *Michael Armstrong*
(and undoubtedly widening its appeal) gave particular outrage to the
Athenaeum reviewer. Most of the illustrations were by Auguste Hervieu, a
French artist who accompanied the Trollopes on their travels, and was
associated with their literary projects, others were by the book illustrators
Thomas Onwhyn and Henry Buss, contemporaries and competitors of
Hablôt Browne ('Phiz').[52] The monthly illustrated format suggested
work aimed at a wide market, 'scattering firebrands among the people'
and inflaming the 'heated imaginations of our great manufacturing
towns, figuring as they do in every bookseller's window'.[53] As Celina Fox
has shown, conventions of appropriate visual representation, particularly
when addressing a 'popular' audience, were a matter of some cultural

[48] *Athenaeum*, no. 615, 10 Aug. 1839, pp. 587–90.
[49] Ibid., no. 649, 4 April 1840, pp. 274–5; see also 'Popular literature of the day', *British and Foreign Quarterly Review* 10 (1840), pp. 223–46.
[50] F. Montagu, *Mary Ashley, the Factory Girl, or Facts upon the Factory* (1839); idem, *Gleanings in Craven* (1838).   [51] Montagu, *Mary Ashley*, pp. 99, 103.
[52] Harvey, *Victorian Novelists*, pp. 16–17, 112.
[53] *Athenaeum*, no. 615, 10 Aug. 1839, pp. 588, 590.

confusion and anxiety in this period.[54] Trollope's daughter-in-law, writing a memoir in the 1890s, found it necessary to explain : 'These drawings furnish in some degree a scale whereby to measure the improvement of public taste and knowledge during the last half century'. Hervieu is, however, credited with 'humorous appreciation' and a 'quick eye for the grotesque and ridiculous'.[55]

As with the text of Trollope's novel, it is this eye for the grotesque that provoked outrage. These images challenged the utilitarian rationality or pastoral blandness of 'useful knowledge' and the more respectable illustrated magazines. Thus the well-known scene in the spinning-room (plate 3a) draws the machines in a crude and perfunctory fashion, a deliberately clumsy parody of the more standard engraving from which it is undoubtedly copied. The focus is on the figures, who have turned away from their work to witness the affecting scene of Michael greeting his brother. It is an emotive scene of moral order (the renewal of family ties) but industrial chaos. Trollope's illustrations show a range of settings in addition to the factory – wealthy and poor homes, figures in landscapes, inns, the apprentice house, a Sunday School – following a cycle, as does the plot, which begins and ends in Dowling Lodge. Scenes depicting the factory system generally have the mill looming somewhere in the background. In contrast with more conventional industrial scenes, some of the pictures show groups of mixed class and gender composition, without signalling the usual hierarchy of importance. The illustration of the factory interior scene from Montagu's counter-propaganda (copied this time from Baines' mule-spinning view) is, by implausible contrivance, an all-female group, focusing on the benevolent lady visitors (plate 3b).

Of the issues raised by Trollope, that of the cultural and moral formation of the employer class was the most consistent theme in subsequent industrial fiction. Elizabeth Stone's *William Langshawe the Cotton Lord* (1842) may be partly a response to Trollope. A Manchester writer, and daughter and sister of journalists and writers, Stone is concerned to portray Manchester and the cotton region as culturally diverse and evolving. Lengthy digressions, including documentary material and footnotes to establish the veracity of statements, vignettes of Manchester life and direct addresses to the 'gentle reader' as to its fitness as a topic for literary treatment, attempt to stake out this ground. A number of set-piece occasions (the races, a musical soirée, the Collegiate Church) display features of Manchester life, seen as a cultural centre for the cotton region. In the account of the races these features are established by their inactivity in

---

[54] Fox, *Graphic Journalism*.   [55] Trollope, *Frances Trollope*, vol. II, pp. 185–6

"*Love conquered Fear.*"

Plate 3 The factory as fiction
(a) Melodramatic confrontation (F. Trollope, *Michael Armstrong*)

Mary Ashley, at Work in the Middleton Mills.

Plate 3 (*cont.*)
(b) Benign hierarchy (Montagu, *Mary Ashley*)

race week; the Exchange is deserted, the Library is closed, 'the tall chimneys send forth no smoke'.[56]

Langshawe and his neighbours and associates are country spinners, marked by plain manners and occasional vulgarities, but redeemed by their practical energy and lack of affectation (one of Stone's asides is a commentary on the impractical and pretentious nature of current notions of lady-like education). Manufacturers like the Langshawes are shown as familiar with the homes of the poor, and endowed with a sense of charitable obligation; involvement in this is part of the practical activity commended for middle-class women, and Langshawe's daughter Edith is an example. She has often been round a cotton mill, and knows perfectly well where her family's wealth and comfort come from. Other millowners and their children are shown as less rough, and linked to a wider cultural network. Langshawe's business difficulties, attributed to a rash straying from the tried path of 'a safe trade and small profits' into 'speculation', are survived through fortitude and the restoration of northern simplicity in the reduced circumstances of a 'neat, small house'. This follows the dramatic cancellation of Edith's wedding to John Balshawe, the son of a neighbouring millowner, and known philanderer and seducer. Edith had only agreed to the projected marriage by force of economic circumstance, after protests that raise disturbing questions about the marriage–property nexus: 'I suppose he would make a bill of parcels of me, as he would of a bale of goods.'[57] This echoes attacks on the pauper migration schemes of the 1830s, a characteristic shifting of language between class and gender oppression. Balshawe's philandering provides the 'working-class' plot, concerning Nancy Halliwell, a mill-worker whom he seduces and alienates from her sweetheart, Jem Forshawe. Jem has always been 'weak-minded' and, in his embitterment, he declines from this to 'imbecility', drifts to Manchester, is sworn in to the union and murders a millowner's son. His happy end, in a somewhat perfunctory concluding chapter, is to be transferred to the incurable ward of the asylum.

The novel is a nuanced defence of the factory system and its employers, as the *Athenaeum* reviewer acknowledged. He nevertheless condemned its 'absurdly exaggerated ... picture ... a mere caricature'; the description of a cotton master doing business calculations during a church service is offensive, especially as it is 'intended to be the index to the character of a class', and does not provide a true picture of Manchester society. While the novel is 'not ... an attack on the Factory System, which, on the whole, it defends', the language of 'cottonocracy' and 'cotton lords' is derived from radical

[56] E. Stone, *William Langshawe the Cotton Lord*, 2 vols. (1842), vol. I, ch. 15, vol. II, chs. 9, 18.   [57] Ibid., vol. I, pp. 26–32, 62, 157–9, vol. II, pp. 68, 218.

critics.[58] A central symbol of the cottonocracy's preoccupation with accumulation at all costs is Edith's projected marriage, and the outspoken terms of her protest may be one source of the reviewer's offence. It should also be noted that the narrative itself links factory work with danger and destruction, perhaps partly as an effect of the conventions within which Stone was writing. As a factory worker Nancy is endangered by seduction, her rehabilitation occurs away from the factory, culminating in the prospect of marriage to a respectable shoemaker; Jem is dragged down into madness, terrorist conspiracy and homicide, albeit he was always feeble-minded. On the other hand, liminal figures outside the social relations of employment, including a Wordsworthian hermit and various rentier gentry characters, make benign interventions at crucial moments.

Some of these themes are reworked in the (deservedly) more familiar industrial novels of Gaskell and Brontë.[59] Indeed Gaskell for a 'time encouraged the rumour that Stone was the author of *Mary Barton* (the material does have obvious, though perhaps superficial, similarities).[60] Both Gaskell and Brontë attracted substantial metropolitan literary support. This is no doubt a reflection of their achievement as writers, but also perhaps of the opening of new spaces for an engagement with contemporary issues, and a wider settlement of opinion after the cultural confusions and partisan polemics of the 1830s and early 40s. The writing of 'acceptable' fictions set in the industrial north coincided with shifts in opinion, including the conversion of Macaulay and others to the ten-hours bill. *North and South* (1854–5) is the last published, least controversial and most explicitly 'contemporary' of the novels under discussion (*Mary Barton* is set in the recent past, images of the first Chartist crisis read in the context of the last one, and some other industrial novels have a wider gap). Industrial topics remained contentious, and *Mary Barton*, in particular, had a stormy reception. Its failure to make due obeisance to political economy, the difficulties faced by masters and their philanthropic contributions to continuing improvement were discussed at length in a famous review by W. R. Greg (himself, like Gaskell, a Manchester Unitarian).[61] Gaskell's local reception may also be to do with

---

[58] *Athenaeum*, no. 779, Oct. 1842, p. 846.

[59] C. Brontë, *Shirley* (1849; and Everyman edn, 1908, etc.); E. Gaskell, *Mary Barton* (1848; and Penguin edn, Harmondsworth, 1970); E. Gaskell, *North and South* (serial publn 1854–5, book 1855; and Penguin edn, Harmondsworth, 1970). In view of the ready availability of these works I have confined specific references to chapter numbers in brackets in text for direct quotations. On Gaskell and Brontë I am particularly indebted to Uglow, *Gaskell* and L. Gordon, *Charlotte Brontë: A Passionate Life* (Vintage paperback edn, London, 1995).   [60] Uglow, *Gaskell*, p. 215.

[61] W.R. Greg, 'Mary Barton', in *Essays*, vol. I; see also *British Quarterly Review* 9 (Feb. 1849), pp. 117–36; S. Dentith, 'Political economy, fiction and the language of practical ideology in nineteenth-century England', *Social History* 8 (1983); Uglow, *Gaskell*, ch. 11.

allusions to sensitive matters (such as Carson's pursuit of the heroine, or the mill fire which was not unwelcome to the owners) with real counterparts that Manchester insiders must have recognised, or speculated about.

Brontë expressed anxiety, with reference to *Shirley*, that she would 'make even a more ridiculous mess of the matter than Mrs Trollope did'.[62] The debate about realism in *Shirley* centred not so much on the industrial theme (on which Brontë was indeed fairly circumspect, partly by her use of a less recent historical setting) but on the portrayal of curates and of Yorkshire character, even of men in general. *Shirley* can certainly be read as a fiction of patriarchal power and resistance, perhaps more directly so than Brontë's other novels. Both *Frasers* and the *Athenaeum* complained about the 'grotesque' representation of most of the male characters – Moore, the millowner being 'a hero cut out by a lady's scissors [rather] than one engraved by "her master's" etching-needle'.[63] The ironic allusion to the recent 'shower of curates' in the novel's opening lines may also relate the portrayal of this category to the present, and to possible reservations about the march of civilisation.

One device used to ward off attacks, and to establish the novels' authorial space, is the claim to describe experience and observation. This is a reiterated theme in Brontë's letters, and, in a different way, in Gaskell's work.[64] The preface to *Mary Barton* claimed ignorance of political economy, but knowledge of the condition of the poor; and Margaret Hale is given similar lines in *North and South*. Women's positioning as liminal observers of the world of business (well captured in the account of Margaret Hale listening to the Manchester men's table talk) provides a space for a somewhat disingenuous insightful naivety. Gaskell certainly knew at least enough about political economy and trade to realise she was treading on dangerous ground, where the ignorance expected of women might be the best defence.

This positioning is symbolised in the treatment of the workplace and the characters' relation to it. Margaret Hale politely declines the offer of a visit to Thornton's mill, and instead visits, on her own initiative, the homes of the poor (her surprise that this was not accepted practice, as it was in the 'south', is another example of empowering naivety, but also of Margaret's own learning – the Manchester working class are not deferentially available for visiting in the same way). *Shirley* had, interestingly in

[62] T.J. Wise and J.A. Symington (eds.), *The Brontës: Their Lives, Friendships and Correspondence*, 4 vols. (Oxford, 1932), vol. II, p. 184: hereafter cited as *The Brontës*.
[63] *Athenaeum*, no. 1149, 3 Nov. 1849, p. 1109; *Frasers Magazine* 40 (Dec. 1849), pp. 692–4; *The Brontës*, vol. II, pp. 83, 313, vol. III, p. 30.
[64] See *The Brontës*, letters cited in previous note.

this context, originally been entitled 'Hollows Mill'.[65] The mill and the counting-house are represented as separate, mysterious and possibly desirable places. Caroline Helstone kept solitary vigil over 'the cottage, the mill, the dewy garden-ground, the still, deep dam' watching for the light from Robert Moore's counting-house window; later the absence of the elder Yorkes at their counting-house facilitates her transgressive access to Moore's sick-room (chapters 11, 33). But the male bourgeois space of the workplace is shown as dependent on female capital; Shirley Keeldar owns the land on which the mill stands, and Margaret Hale rescues Thornton from business difficulties (she is also of course the bearer of the cultural capital which the Hales bring to Manchester).

The humanisation of employment relations and the appropriate response to class conflict are formulated in terms of these gender perspectives. Class conflict is part of the masculine world, with working-class resistance represented by male characters (John Barton, Nicholas Higgins in *North and South*, the Luddites); working-class women in Gaskell are seamstresses, servants, housewives – or, significantly, perishing victims of earlier mill employment, their health broken (Bessy Higgins). Even in the relatively 'optimistic' narrative of *North and South*, factory work for women is associated with disease and death (and Gaskell is accurate enough in locating this threat in Bessy's card-room employment).

The handling of class relations displays debates about mutual sympathy and appropriate models of 'paternalism' – the metonymic or metaphoric relations between family and society.[66] This is foreshadowed in the plea for sympathy and the death-bed conversions in *Mary Barton*, and treated at length in a series of dialogues in *North and South*. This is not simply a matter of the redemption of industrial society by a humanitarian gentry paternalism; the learning is mutual. As Thornton insists, 'because they labour ten hours a-day for us, I do not see that we have any right to impose leading-strings upon them . . . I imagine this is a stronger feeling in the North of England than in the South' (chapter 15). Brontë was similarly aware of debates on the duties of property; as well as Carlyle and Ruskin, she admired Sir Arthur Helps as 'a beautiful mind . . . a heart full of kindness and sympathy'.[67]

The ideal explored in *Shirley* seems to be a romantic conservatism, tempered by a kind of intuitive sympathy with revolt and the familiar appeal to northern directness and plain dealing. Brontë's confrontational language of power and resistance, which had shocked some readers of

[65] Ibid., vol. III, p. 12.   [66] Gallagher, *Industrial Reformation*.
[67] *The Brontës*, vol. II, p. 326, vol. III, p. 22.

Jane Eyre, has some affinities to the popular rhetoric of Oastler or the Chartists. Shirley's residence at Fieldhead is associated with an image of 'manorial hospitality', which she chivalrously wishes to extend to the Luddites wounded in the attack on the mill (chapters 20, 29). Shirley's role as a female landowner raises some of the transgressive possibilities of the gentry *topos*. As Sue Harper has noted, the theme of gentry self-confidence and assertiveness as protection for unconventional behaviour is of long duration in British culture, with a particular appeal to working-class audiences, and a privileged historical site in the Regency period.[68] In *Shirley*, the limits of this are exposed in the Luddite episode, when the heroine's desire to intervene in events is rebuffed. Like *North and South*, *Shirley* concludes with the economic rescue of the male protagonist, marriage and the prospect of pursuing an industrial idyll: 'the houseless, the starving, the unemployed shall come to Hollow's Mill . . . and Joe Scott shall give them work, and Louis Moore, Esq., shall let them a tenement, and Mrs Gill shall mete them a portion till the first pay-day' (chapter 37).

These texts therefore give fictional treatment to themes in circulation in the social debates of the 1840s, with a characteristic emphasis on the merging of interests and the extending cultural resources needed for social leadership. This is linked to the way that they establish their regional settings as imagined places, articulated in relation to other places and an imagined nation. Industrial fiction leads in to the 'novel of provincial life'.[69] The use of dialect speech and ballads is one mark of this, and of claims to a kind of authenticity (also present in, for example, Stone's *William Langshawe*). William Gaskell was involved in the study of dialect and the preservation of oral tradition in Lancashire; and Samuel Bamford was among the defenders of *Mary Barton*.[70] The industrial town and town/country distinctions also figure in this representation of identity. Like some contemporaneous journalism, Gaskell's fiction exposes the excitement and human vibrancy, as well as the terrors, of the industrial city. As Margaret Hale tells Nicholas Higgins when he is contemplating migrating south in despair: 'You would not bear the dullness of the life; you don't know what it is; it would eat you away like rust.' The oppressions of southern rural life are evoked in a language that suggests debates on agricultural gangs, and perhaps plantation slavery, 'the great solitude of steaming fields' (chapter 37). Margaret herself discovers that the south has something to learn from the north, and that there is no going back. The industrial town is represented as a potentially livable

[68] Harper, *Picturing the Past*, esp. ch. 9.
[69] W.A. Craik, *Elizabeth Gaskell and the English Provincial Novel* (London, 1975); R.P. Draper (ed.), *The Literature of Region and Nation* (London, 1989); J. Lucas, *The Literature of Change* (Brighton, 1977).   [70] Uglow, *Gaskell*, pp. 202, 218.

human community, and at any rate a necessary destiny for many of its inhabitants.

In Gaskell's imagined north, the town and the factory are closely associated. Brontë's north is one of more scattered rural industries, set in a sometimes remote and bleak countryside; hence the northern character is shaped by 'the contrast of rough nature with highly artificial cultivation which forms one of their main characteristics'.[71] The association of the north with wild countryside and strong character is a tradition that long predates industrialisation.[72] The town/country distinction within the industrial north is taken up in Gaskell's *Life of Charlotte Brontë* in the opening description of the terrain round Keighley and Haworth (an imagined journey by train from Leeds). This is presented as a society 'in process of transformation', observed from the standpoint of the more developed society of Lancashire: 'Even an inhabitant of the neighbouring county of Lancaster is struck by the peculiar force of character which the Yorkshiremen display.'[73] This sense of difference perhaps leads Gaskell to exaggerate the isolation and peculiarity of Haworth (and a half-century or more of deindustrialisation has further reworked the myth for modern tourists).

Northern characteristics are linked to a wider national identity, even claimed as its point of origin; Lancashire dialect was advocated as the language of Chaucer, Shakespeare and the English Bible, while Yorkshire people could claim a 'rough Norse ancestry', and a Cromwellian puritan tradition was an inheritance from a more recent high point in the national past.[74] These characteristics might be asserted, not just against an effete rentier south, but also against, for example, the Irish presence in the industrial north.

North and South seems particularly significant in fixing the cluster of meanings around the notion of an industrial and urban north. Gaskell (who had probably been reading Anthony Trollope) contrasted her Keighley to 'any stately, sleepy picturesque cathedral town in the south', and Trollope returned the compliment by defining his Barset through its difference from 'its manufacturing leviathan brethren of the north'.[75] But distinctions such as urban/rural, industrial/agrarian or north/south could have complex and shifting functions; Gaskell herself created a fairly 'sleepy' northern town in *Cranford* (though, as she certainly well knew,

---

[71] *The Brontës*, vol. III, p. 83; this is applied to the local flora in *Shirley* (ch. 21; see p. 409 in Everyman edn).   [72] *OED*, entries for 'north', 'north country', etc.
[73] E. Gaskell, *The Life of Charlotte Bronte* (1857; Penguin edn, Harmondsworth, 1975), pp. 53, 60.   [74] Ibid., p. 61; Uglow, *Gaskell*, p. 202.
[75] Gaskell, *Life of Brontë*, p. 53; A. Trollope, *Doctor Thorne* (1858; and Bell and Sons edn, London, 1928), p. 1.

this world was linked to that of the nearby cotton region). In *North and South* a rural, deferential but morally integrated 'south' is contrasted to the Hales' encounter with an urban–industrial 'north', the site of market relations, anomie and class conflict, but redeemed by its energy and moral virtues of directness, independence and mutual, if sometimes antagonistic, respect. The urban/rural difference is also represented within industrial society, connoting a bucolic retreat from the town (as in the opening chapter of *Mary Barton*), or wildness, lack of cultivation and consequently rough manners. The images of the 'country mill' in the documentary literature oscillate between these poles, the sites of an integrated working community insulated from the corruptions of town life, or of oppression and confinement in remote and hidden localities, exercised by uncultured and irresponsible owners and their agents.

Conclusion

Documentary journalism and industrial fiction combined the *frisson* of social danger and the excitements of social exploration with potentialities of reconciliation and improvement. Factory agitation identified the textile districts as one important reference-point for such concerns, and this coalesced in images of an industrial north. At the same time, however, these images connoted other issues, such as social relations, sexual politics and proper modes of behaviour within the propertied classes themselves. The workplace became an important symbolic site, but one that remained enigmatic in most of this literature.

This and the preceding chapters have identified some of the ways in which the social relations and problems of factory labour might be represented. This began from an account of the early ten-hours movement, its 'popular' and 'patrician' elements and the shifting constructions of class and gender within its rhetoric. This led on to a discussion of the interventions of state officials and professional groups, and their influence in redefining the nature of factory reform. The previous chapter looked at the perspectives of employers, their activity in seeking to reshape agendas, and some of the tensions and dilemmas of inhabiting liberal entrepreneurial culture. Finally, this chapter has explored some of the ways in which this registered and circulated among reading publics.

Two connecting threads have emerged. One is the contesting and shifting of the terms of debate. Ways of talking about the factory, as a site of danger or of potential improvement, were partly what was at issue during this period. The slow and difficult progress of the ten-hours campaign was associated with a move to a more optimistic and harmonious vision of industrial society. Secondly, I have emphasised the variety of languages in

play in this contentious renegotiation. The discursive claims and boundary disputes of these languages – notably between the idealised marketplace of political economy, and principles of moral regulation and
hierarchy, often embodied in familistic metaphors – contributed to the
unsettled and explosive social debates of the second quarter of the
century.

Arguably, the late 1840s and 1850s saw a diminution of some of these
tensions; the authority of a modified political economy, within its defined
sphere, was less contested, though by no means without problems and
contradictions.[76] This was in part a renegotiated and moralised political
economy, whose market assumed certain forms of regulative intervention. In the second part of this book I propose to examine the implementation of that framework in more detail.

[76] See McClelland, 'Time to work' on this wider acceptance of political economy.

Part 2

Factory regulation, *c.* 1840–1860

6   Enforcement, resistance and compliance

The debates of the second quarter of the nineteenth century established the 'factory question' as part of an agenda for managing the consequences of economic and social change – whether that change was seen unambiguously as 'improvement' in the interests of all concerned, or as a cataclysm which could not be reversed, and to which society must therefore adapt. In this broader context, a viable form of factory regulation could eventually be negotiated and set in place. The *de facto* settlement of the 'factory question' formed one of a series of political and social settlements hammered out in the later 1840s and early 50s. The image of a uniform working day regulated by the clock and the factory bell, a more efficient and productive factory population improved in health and morals, and the role in this of employers and the state were incorporated in a vision of industrial progress.

Much of this was, however, constructed in retrospect, and assimilated by a concerned opinion at some distance from the industrial north. Recent studies have laid more emphasis on the uneven and contested nature of any 'mid-Victorian consensus', and the limited practical purchase of rhetorics of social conciliation.[1] It will be argued here that, although there was a discernible lessening of social tensions, divergent perspectives persisted. The implementation of factory legislation remained highly contentious, marked by an uneven and spasmodic transition from employer resistance to 'negotiated compliance', and by popular agitation which likewise challenged the terms of reference of state officials.[2]

As has already been argued, employer attitudes were rarely monolithic, but rather based on varying readings of the legitimate interests and rights of industrial capital and the dictates of competitive pressures. While certain prominent manufacturers, grouped around the Manchester

---

[1] Dutton and King, 'The limits of paternalism'; Kirk, *Growth of Reformism*; Saville, *1848*.
[2] See Carson, 'Conventionalization of early factory crime', and 'Institutionalisation of ambiguity'; Field, 'Without the law?'.

Statistical Society, were influential in the making of the 1833 Act and the approach adopted by the factory inspectors, the terms of that Act nevertheless remained contentious, especially given the context of continuing popular agitation. These articulate spokesmen for the manufacturing interest generally balanced off a recognition of some necessary role for state regulation – often seen as properly directed at other, less enlightened manufacturers – against anxieties about the timing of measures, market conditions, and the 'thin end of the wedge' threatening to open the way for further, less acceptable measures. It is now necessary to look in more detail at the process of regulation, and to place the views expressed in public debate in the context of employers' pragmatic responses.

This is approached, first, by investigating the geographical distribution of prosecutions and other manifestations of conflict over factory regulation. I analyse this at an aggregate level, in relation to industrial structure and technology. Some of the unexplained variation will suggest the importance of other factors, notably localised patterns of response to uncertain market conditions, problems of labour recruitment and specific accumulation strategies for dealing with these. Economic analysis will necessarily take on a cultural dimension. I explore this through more focused local comparisons, linking prosecutions in selected localities to a range of background information about the individuals concerned and their industrial and community contexts. I shall argue that this provides a fuller picture of patterns of response to factory regulation. It is also only at the local level that the relevance of popular pressure, and its impact both on employers and on the official state, becomes properly visible.

The incidence of prosecution

Contemporary comment, and much subsequent historiography, has attempted to associate systematic infringement of factory legislation with particular categories of employer. These are often represented as technically backward, obsolescent, essentially 'marginal' producers – smaller as against larger firms, water- as against steam-powered, 'rural' as against urban locations.[3] The fixing of this association was, as we have seen, part of the original debate, and it has been echoed in subsequent analyses. In the more recent historiography, however, the implied link between bad conditions and more marginal, smaller scale production is often incidental to arguments whose main focus lies elsewhere. There has been little direct study of reported factory act infringements and their social, eco-

---

[3] For example, Foster, *Class Struggle*, p. 181; Henriques, *Before the Welfare State*, p. 85; Marvel, 'Factory regulation'.

nomic and cultural correlates. The major exception is Marvel's econometric study of the incidence of prosecution.[4] The work of Carson, Bartrip, Peacock and Field has also initiated lively debate about socio-legal dimensions of the enforcement process, but their focus has been on judicial and bureaucratic decision-making rather than on specific industrial or community contexts.[5]

Marvel has demonstrated a correlation between the incidence of prosecutions and the proportion of water-power in a parish.[6] However the analysis is confined to the first year or so of enforcement activity (1834–6), and there are grounds for expecting any such association to be particularly pronounced at that period; moreover, as Marvel himself notes, there are some qualifications to be made, for example the relationship is far stronger in cotton than in other sectors of textiles.[7]

Another approach to the problem, also employed by Marvel among others, is to note the undoubted links between the thinking behind the Act of 1833 and views expressed by owners of large, technically advanced mills.[8] The existence of such links is well documented, and has indeed been one theme of the first part of this study; but, as is also argued there, the relationship between shared ideologies of economic progress and improved health and morals at a general level, and the framing and implementing of specific regulations is by no means straightforward, and allows ample scope for more immediate conflicts of perceived interest. As Howe has noted, the congruence of broad perspectives did not necessarily go along with easy acceptance of legislation in practice, particularly in the tense climate of the 1830s and 40s, with an embattled 'entrepreneurial class, facing, it believed, the hostility of aristocratic government and the working classes'.[9] There are, then, political and cultural dimensions underlying much employer resistance, which are not readily captured in econometric studies.

Table 6.1 calculates a measure of the relative incidence of cases (rates per 100 operatives) based on Dr Peacock's useful breakdown of numbers

---

[4] Marvel, 'Factory regulation'.
[5] Carson, 'Conventionalization of early factory crime', and 'Institutionalisation of ambiguity'; A.E. Peacock, 'The successful prosecution of the Factory Acts, 1833–55', *Economic History Review* 37 (1984); P. Bartrip, 'Success or failure? the prosecution of the early Factory Acts', *Economic History Review* 38 (1985); and reply by Peacock, ibid.; Field, 'Without the law?'.   [6] Marvel, 'Factory regulation'.
[7] Ibid., p. 398.
[8] Ibid., pp. 385–93; and cf. W.G. Carson, 'Symbolic and instrumental dimensions of early factory legislation', in R. Hood (ed.), *Crime, Criminology and Public Policy* (London, 1974), p. 135; J.Foster, 'The making of the first six factory acts', paper summarised in *Soc. for Study of Labour History Bull.* no. 18 (spring 1969), p. 5.
[9] Howe, *Cotton Masters*, p. 182.

Table 6.1 *Factory Act prosecutions, 1834–55, by parishes*

	No. of cases	Cases per 100 operatives		1838 returns Water: % of total h.p.	Children: % of total employed
Horner's district					
Saddleworth	97	2.8	C	21	6
			W	72	12
Rochdale	229	2.1	C	9	10
			W	39	19
Whalley	202	1.8	C	25	4
			W	48	17
Oldham	218	1.4	C	0	6
Ashton	132	1.1	C	8	3
Bury	146	1.0	C	26	6
Bolton	96	1.0	C	21	5
Blackburn	79	0.8	C	7	8
Preston	42	0.6	C	0	5
Manchester (includes Salford)	175	0.5	C	0	3
Saunders' district					
Dewsbury	108	7.1	W	13	22
Huddersfield	155	4.5	W	25	6
Wakefield	37	3.1	W	4	11
Bradford	297	2.5	Wo	5	15
Bingley	37	2.1	Wo	35	17
Halifax	220	1.7	C	37	8
			W	44	13
			Wo	18	24
Leeds	230	1.3	W	5	8
Almondbury	45	1.1	W	48	10
Keighley	24	1.0	Wo	51	13

Note: C: cotton, W: wool, Wo: worsted; where only one sector is indicated, this was the staple of the locality.

Source: A.E. Peacock, 'The justices of the peace and the prosecution of the factory acts, 1833–1855', DPhil, University of York,1982, table 8; Return of Mills and Factories, 1838, PP 1839 (41) XLII.

of cases brought by parishes; this is tabulated alongside figures for the proportion of water-power and the proportion of children employed (the calculations have unfortunately to be based on the factory returns for 1838, the last to be broken down further than by counties).[10] In Lancashire there does appear to be a continued higher level of prosecutions in parishes with more water mills (Saddleworth, though not in Lancashire, fell within Horner's inspection district and certainly fits the pattern). It is also, however, striking that Oldham and Ashton have higher prosecution rates, but far less water-power than Bolton and Bury. Horner himself regarded Oldham (a steam-powered parish) as the most 'barbarous' and intractable part of his district, together with Rochdale (where there was a higher proportion of water-power); and, like other commentators, he noted the turbulence, sectarian division and inadequate educational provision round Ashton and Stalybridge.[11]

In the West Riding, there is more water-power employed, but, as Marvel himself notes, a less clear-cut association between water-power and prosecution rates.[12] Indeed, Keighley and Almondbury, two parishes with high levels of water-power, in worsted and wool respectively, have the lowest prosecution-rates. Relationships between water-power and the employment of children appear to be similarly variable.

It is apparent that technology has some bearing on the incidence of prosecution. But it has to be considered in relation to market pressures and the varied trajectories of specific localities. The notion of an expanding, and unregulated, industrial 'frontier' may be more helpful than simple dichotomies based on technology and power-source. The whole area around Ashton, Stalybridge, Oldham and Saddleworth may fit this model, as does Whalley parish (including the rapidly mechanising weaving district round Accrington and Burnley). These areas to some extent fit the picture of the country spinner or manufacturer and the small, marginal firm. Ashton and Stalybridge, on the other hand, were dominated by the rapid growth of big, often combined spinning–weaving, enterprises, established by a particularly aggressive group of liberal entrepreneurs. In the uncertain market conditions of the 1830s and 40s

---

[10] The rate of prosecutions per 100 operatives seemed the best measure; rates per employer and per 100 'protected' operatives were also calculated, but made little difference to the rank order of parishes. Some of the places listed by Peacock have been combined to correspond to the administrative parishes used in the factory returns, no doubt some inaccuracies have crept in; it should be noted that some parishes (e.g. Halifax) covered an extensive rural hinterland, while others were more compact. The two inspectors' districts are treated separately to control for variations in enforcement policy.

[11] Lyell (ed.), *Horner*, vol. II, p. 14 (Horner's letter to his wife, 18 June 1841); Reports of Factory Inspectors: Horner, Oct. 1842 (on education in Ashton and Stalybridge).

[12] Marvel, 'Factory regulation'. pp. 388–90, 401–2.

such firms could be caught in the downswing over-exposed to investments in buildings and machinery. They may also have faced particular
managerial problems of adjustments to product mix and bottlenecks in
work-flow, which made them anxious to retain flexibility over hours and
other working practices (this may have been one factor in last-ditch
opposition to the ten-hour day, discussed in the following chapter).

Finally, it should be noted that the numerical incidence of prosecution
is not necessarily the best guide to the degree of conflict and public controversy. Such conflicts were particularly acute in the Ashton and
Stalybridge area, whose actual prosecution rate is only marginally above
that of some less troubled towns. Prosecutions reflect those cases that
came to court, and failures to prosecute could themselves fuel conflict.
The meanings of such episodes have to be related to their local contexts.

Resistance could be part of a political process, of pressure and bargaining over the *terms* of legislation, rather than either blanket resistance to all
legislation, or simple failure to comply with the law. The question considered in the remainder of this chapter therefore is not so much whether
employers resisted, as *how* and *why* that resistance varied locally in its
forms and intensity. The preponderance of one pattern over others in
employer attitudes seems to be subject to local variations, and has to be
analysed through local case-studies.

The pattern of prosecutions: local case-studies

Local configurations of response to factory regulation may appear more
clearly in a comparative analysis of prosecution returns, taking the localities, rather than industry- or sector-level variables of plant size and technology, as the focus of attention. A major concern here is to place the
involvement of particular employers in the context of available information about those individuals; this may serve to complement and qualify
the findings of larger-scale statistical correlations, with their danger of the
'ecological fallacy'. The interest is in identifying differences in local patterns of prosecution and other forms of conflict, as much as in the overall
incidence of that conflict. It will be argued that this more focused
comparative approach shows that factory act proceedings involved a
cross-section of employers in the locality, including leading firms. In so
far as there is a bias, it is a political one, to Liberal employers. This in turn
may be associated with newer capital and a fiercely competitive outlook.
Finally, it will be suggested that, for some of these employers, resistance
to regulation has to be seen as a political strategy. Conversely, the pressure
of popular campaigns also formed part of the bargaining over the implementation of legislation.

These conclusions are based on an analysis of all cases brought in selected localities for the period 1838–51; this period is taken because it covers the terms of office of Horner and Saunders in Lancashire and the West Riding respectively, and this administrative settlement allows us to hold constant enforcement style relating to turnover of personnel (though there was some turnover, especially in Horner's district, of superintendents, the inspectors' local-based deputies, whose personal approach to their duties must have had some bearing on the pattern of activity).[13] These years also of course comprise a period of marked social tension in all these towns, in which contentions over hours and other working practices played some part.

The localities are operationally defined in terms of parishes (with the exception of Stalybridge, which fell into two counties and three parishes, but for factory act purposes was under Horner's jurisdiction with Lancashire, as was the adjacent rural area of Saddleworth; Todmorden also bestraddled county boundaries, but was in Saunders' district along with the extensive rural part of Halifax parish). There is undoubtedly some inaccuracy and inconsistency in the figures, partly because information about locality was not always systematically presented in the published returns. My use of this material is based on counts of *cases*, that is proceedings against a specific defendant on a specific occasion, regardless of the number of separate *charges* brought in the proceedings; where cases were brought against the same defendant on several occasions each such occasion is counted as a separate case (such repeated prosecutions are in fact a point of particular interest in the following discussion).[14]

Table 6.2 presents figures for the numbers of cases, and figure 1 shows their distribution across categories of defendant. This indicates local variations in the proportion of cases brought against employers, as against parents, operatives, teachers or others who might be held liable under the law. This aspect of enforcement was one of the grievances expressed by

[13] See Peacock, 'Justices of the peace'; Thomas, *Early Factory Legislation*, for the administrative and judicial history of factory inspection. The following analysis is based on the annual returns of prosecutions, printed with various other Home Office statistics and latterly appended to inspectors' reports, and information in the inspectors' half-yearly reports; for full citations of these sources see table 6.2 and bibliography. Background information about the employers concerned was obtained from local directories, the local press, poll-books, etc. (often aided by the excellent indexing in local reference libraries) and from key secondary works including: Howe, *Cotton Masters*; Joyce, *Work, Society and Politics*; Kirk, *Growth of Reformism*; Koditschek, *Class Formation*; Reynolds, *The Great Paternalist*. Subsequent statements not otherwise referenced are based on employer profiles derived from these sources.

[14] Separate cases are defined as those brought with at least a one-month interval; in practice cases clustered around particular dates following inspectors' visits, etc., and there is little difficulty distinguishing separate cases against the same defendant from proceedings forming part of a single sequence.

Table 6.2 *Factory act prosecutions, 1838–1851, selected localities*

	Total cases	Factory act case firms[a]
Ashton, Stalybridge	35	30
Blackburn	52	40
Bolton	51	36
Oldham	115	98
Saddleworth	44	40
Bradford	157	108
Halifax, Calderdale	105	84
Huddersfield	41	34

Note: [a]Cases against employers, or against operatives, etc., with employer identified.
Sources: Prosecution Returns, PP 1839 XLII, 1840 XXXVIII, 1841 XVIII, 1842 XXXII, 1843 XLII, 1844 XXXIX, 1845 XXXVII, 1846 XXXIV, 1847 XLVI, 1847–8 XXVI, 1849 XXII, 1850 XXIII, pt ii, 1851 XXIII, 1852 XXI. See also nn. 13, 14.

the short-time movement, and it is questionable whether successful prosecutions in this category can be taken as an index of the efficacy of enforcement.[15] The highest proportions of cases against 'others' (operatives, parents, etc.) are at Bolton, Blackburn and Bradford, all towns with relatively high levels of expressed employer support for factory legislation.[16] The superintendent at Bradford was Robert Baker, the Leeds surgeon, and his preoccupations with education and moral reform may have affected the pattern of enforcement there. It is also worth noting that in the West Riding parishes non-employer defendants were more likely to be described as parents or other relatives, rather than as operatives in charge of the child concerned (they may of course have been both in some cases); the pattern of child employment in dispersed factory sites, combined with artisanal and out-work employment of adult men, may have given factory regulation a stronger community rather than workplace focus in this area.

The 'other, employer identified' category is of particular interest. These are cases against operatives, parents and others where the work-

---

[15] Both Peacock, 'Successful prosecution', and Bartrip, 'Success or failure?', make this assumption; for workers' grievances regarding this, Select Committee, 1840, Sixth Report, q. 8480 (J. Lawton).   [16] See above, ch. 4, table 4.1.

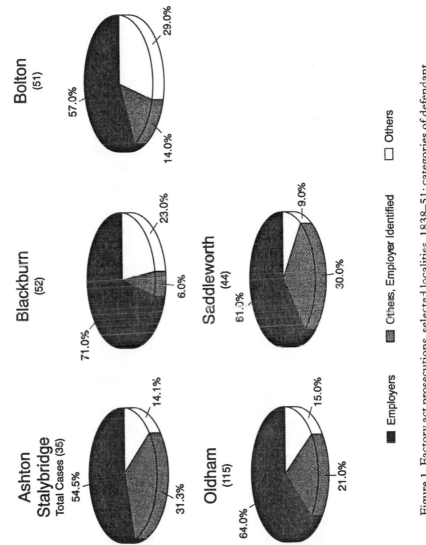

Figure 1 Factory act prosecutions, selected localities, 1838–51: categories of defendant

Ashton
Stalybridge
Total Cases (35)
54.5%
31.3%
14.1%

Blackburn
(52)
71.0%
6.0%
23.0%

Bolton
(51)
57.0%
14.0%
29.0%

Oldham
(115)
64.0%
21.0%
15.0%

Saddleworth
(44)
61.0%
30.0%
9.0%

■ Employers   ▨ Others, Employer Identified   □ Others

place is identified in the prosecution return (for example the name of the defendant, qualified as 'operative spinner at . . .'); sometimes this is found in cases where adjourned proceedings against a master are resumed against the employee. While the mention of the workplace in this way is probably not consistent (as may be apparent in its absence in the returns for Bradford), it may nevertheless be of some significance that the highest proportions of such cases are at Ashton–Stalybridge, Oldham and Saddleworth, areas of intense conflict over factory regulation. There is some evidence, discussed later in this chapter, that cases of this type formed part of concerted employer campaigns to deflect legislation.

The yearly movement in numbers of cases (figure 2) broadly follows that discovered by Peacock for the inspectors' districts concerned. This is probably conditioned partly by trade cycles, as the inspectors themselves suggested, with the sudden scramble for orders in the upswings of the mid-1840s and early 1850s encouraging longer working and neglect of age restrictions.[17] But these upswings coincided with battles to implement the 1844 and 1847 Acts, and it is hard to disentangle these factors. Administrative timetables (for example the inspectors' preoccupation with the parliamentary enquiry of 1840–1), the inspectors' itineraries and various other contingencies no doubt account for some of the variation between localities.

The factory acts were packages of regulations, and prosecution could relate to a range of possible infringements. Figure 3 shows the proportion of cases involving different categories of offence (one defendant could of course be charged with several offences). Offences have been roughly classified into those concerning the hours worked (the key issue so far as many short-time activists were concerned), including meal-breaks and statutory holidays, as well as exceeding the legal day or week; certification and other 'administrative' matters (age certificates, school attendance, registers and time-books, statutory notices of hours); and health and safety (whitewashing the mill from 1833, the safety clauses of the 1844 Act). The analysis is confined to charges against employers, since by definition certain types of possible infringements could be committed only by an employer. The classification is to some extent artificial. Regulations about certification and the keeping of the various registers and time-books were linked to the restriction on hours; and the drawing up of charge-sheets was partly a matter of court-room tactics.[18]

---

[17] Cf. Peacock, 'Justices of the peace', pp. 34–6; Reports of Factory Inspectors: Horner, Jan. 1843, June 1851.

[18] Select Committee 1840, q. 67–74 (Horner); Bartrip, 'Success or failure?', pp. 424–5.

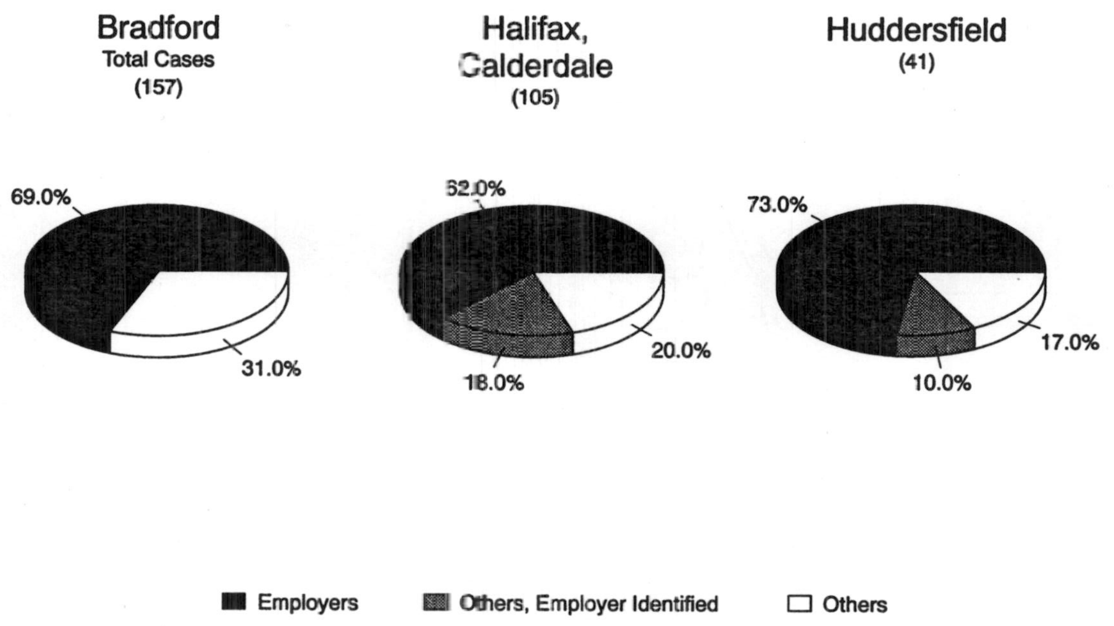

Bradford
Total Cases
(157)

69.0%

31.0%

**Halifax,
Calderdale**
(105)

52.0%

20.0%

18.0%

Huddersfield
(41)

73.0%

17.0%

10.0%

■ Employers   ▨ Others, Employer Identified   ☐ Others

Figure 1 (*cont.*)

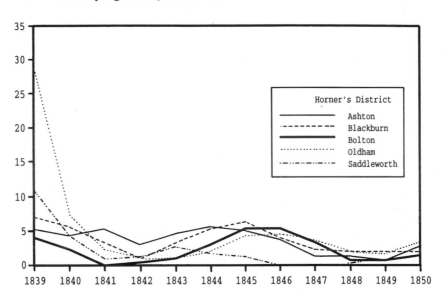

Figure 2 Numbers of prosecutions: three-year moving average

Employers believed to be infringing the major restrictions imposed by the acts might be most easily prosecuted for an administrative technicality – while others, like the Ashworths, might make non-compliance with such technicalities part of a symbolic contest over authority.[19] In other cases inspectors seem to have 'thrown the book' at recalcitrant employers.

The composition of charges suggests the greater prominence of the hours issue in Bolton and Blackburn, the two cotton towns with the highest levels of stated employer support for regulation (see table 4.1). Here, a conception of the standard working day may have informed enforcement policy. The greater salience of the hours question in cotton is borne out by a sectoral breakdown in the mixed industrial areas of Halifax and Saddleworth. In Halifax, hours charges figured in half the cases involving cotton firms (sixteen out of thirty-two), compared with eleven out of twenty-eight for worsted and three out of ten for wool; in Saddleworth, the figures are nine out of thirteen cotton firms, compared with four out of eleven wool. The fact that different inspectors were responsible for these two localities suggests that the pattern arose from industrial conditions, rather than the policies of individual inspectors. Informal pressure by groups of employers, as well as by workers, probably played some part; as Horner noted in evidence to the parliamentary enquiry of 1840–1, manufacturers' vigilance over their competitors' practices was a major source of information about overworking mills, especially those infringing the ban on night-work.[20] In such cases factory act enforcement may fit the model of the 'responsible' employer policing his rivals' working practices. But any employer consensus on these lines was insecure; even in towns where it was most developed, major employers (Ashworth in Bolton, Pilkington in Blackburn: see below, appendix to this chapter) might mount stubborn resistance across the board. And acceptance of a standard working day as an aspect of 'fair competition' did not preclude contention about the length of that day.

Hours figure less strongly in cases elsewhere in Horner's district, at Ashton and Stalybridge, Oldham and Saddleworth. In these areas of prolonged conflict over regulation there was a very high proportion of cases involving certification charges. The same applies to Huddersfield in the West Riding. Certification charges may therefore reflect situations where the inspectors' authority was less accepted. Some of the reasons for this

---

[19] Boyson, *Ashworth Cotton Enterprise*, ch. 9.
[20] Select Committee 1840, qq. 30–40 (Horner); a ban on night-work was the most widely supported measure in Lancashire employers' responses to the Factory Commission questionnaire.

Percentages

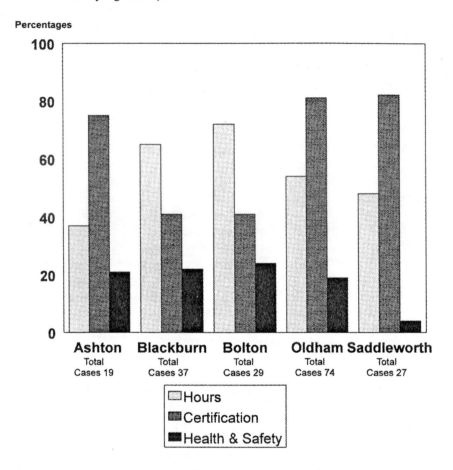

Figure 3 Prosecutions, 1838–51: charges laid against employers

resistance will become apparent from fuller profiles of the employers concerned, and of their local contexts.

Various, inevitably patchy, sources have been used to produce such profiles. For the purposes of this analysis cases in the 'others, employer identified' category have been combined with cases against employers, to constitute a data-set of 'factory act case firms' (total numbers as shown in table 6.2). Despite the patchiness of available information, comparisons of these firms with all firms in the locality are of some value. They enable us to assess the typicality of those involved in proceedings, and provide some test of assertions about the marginality of such firms.

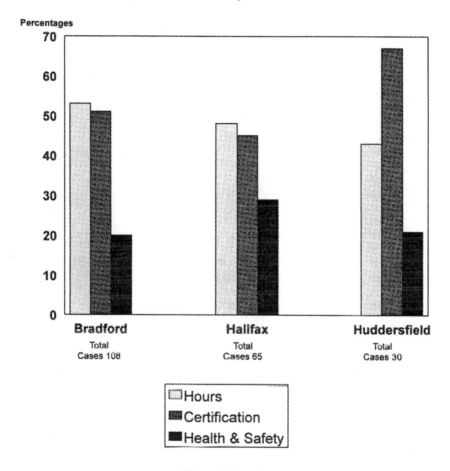

Figure 3 (*cont.*)

Except for a few stable and successful firms (which are however quite well represented among those involved in factory act cases), there is little comprehensive background information about the size, technology or market situation of individual firms. I have however used directory listings to compute survival rates as a general indication of the typicality of firms involved in prosecutions (table 6.3). There are inevitable difficulties and uncertainties in identifying firms, given the characteristic structure of shifting family partnerships. What is really of interest is the continuity of the firm's owners as members of a local employing class, and this cannot readily be captured by this method. It is in fact quite likely that the identification rules adopted underestimate survival rates both for factory act case firms and for all firms (though there is no

Table 6.3 *Survival rates of factory act case firms*

| | % surviving to 1865/6 | |
	Factory act case firms	All firms (average of 1838/1850 cohorts)
Ashton, Stalybridge	43	45
Blackburn	40	36
Bolton	42	38
Oldham	36	34
Saddleworth	50	24
Bradford	19	27
Halifax	39	35
Huddersfield	24	36

Source: see table 6.2. Firms in cases traced in local directories, precise dates of cohorts depended on available directories, figures for all firms based on main sector(s) of textiles in locality. See also n. 21.

reason to think that this creates a systematic bias such as to invalidate comparisons).[21]

The figures suggest that the profile of factory act case firms was broadly similar to that of all firms in the localities. The biggest divergences are in Bradford, Huddersfield and Saddleworth. In Bradford and Huddersfield it would appear that factory act case firms were somewhat less stable than the generality of firms listed. Many of the factory act case firms not surviving in these two localities were actually not traced in directories at all, even at the date of the offence.[22] These may well have been small concerns hiring room and power and working on a commission basis, or rural

---

[21] Cf. Davidoff and Hall, *Family Fortunes,* pt ii; major textile firms were beginning to retain the same business name over changes in personnel, but numerous concerns seem analogous to those more fluid forms described by Davidoff and Hall. Firms were treated as positively identified where either the surname and first name(s)/initial(s), or the surname and address (business, in some cases home) were the same; in partnerships, survival by these criteria of either partner counted. In some cases particular names were very common in the trade locally, possibly a reflection of a maze of interlocking family partnerships too dense to explore for the present limited purposes, and these firms had to be treated as unidentified.

[22] These are however identifiable as employers, either by the nature of the charges, or because the names are cited in such a way as to suggest a partnership.

Table 6.4 *Factory act case firms, Bradford*
worsted spinning

No. of frames	Factory act case firms		All firms	
	No.	%	No	%
Under 20	25	69	69	73
20–39	2	6	13	14
40–59	5	14	8	8
60 and over	4	11	5	5
Total	36	100	95	100
Not listed	72			

Source: MS list of firms (1839), Bradford Archives,
DB.17, case 24, no. 8.

manufacturers oriented to the Huddersfield or Bradford markets. Such
cases may fit the picture of the offending small employer, but they must
be set beside the involvement of leading local firms in all the towns
studied. Names familiar from recent studies of the industrial north can
frequently be encountered in the prosecution returns.[23] In Saddleworth,
an area with a relatively high frequency of prosecutions which appears to
fit the stereotype of the outlying region of overworking rural water mills
(cf. table 6.1), firms involved in cases seem to be more stable than all
firms in the locality. It was not a diminishing category of marginal producers that were the targets of enforcement activity, at any rate during the
period analysed.

Comparison with a number of other sources bears out the impression
that factory act cases involved a cross-section of local firms. The most
comprehensive industrial census identifying individual firms is for
Bradford in 1839 (table 6.4). This listing includes about a third of the
factory act case firms, whose size distribution is, if anything, biased to
the upper ranges. If those not listed are all assumed to be marginal small
producers it would modify this picture considerably, and some
allowance should certainly be made for a bias to the more substantial
enterprises; however those not traced also include firms not yet in existence in 1839, some outside Bradford, and several described as 'manufacturer', 'stuff finisher' or other headings, rather than as spinners. Ten

[23] For example employers mentioned in the works cited above, n 13; cf. below, ch. 6
appendix.

of the factory act case firms not included in the 1839 list in fact survived to 1866.

In the cotton towns, Horner's industrial census of 1841 indicates that combined spinning and weaving firms are, if anything, somewhat over-represented among factory act cases in Blackburn and the Ashton and Stalybridge area. In Oldham, on the other hand, it is the specialised spinning firms typical of the locality which are over-represented.[24] The combined firms generally comprised the largest units in the industry, and their rapid expansion was a feature of the 1830s and 40s in Blackburn and round Ashton and Stalybridge; the commitment of fixed capital under uncertain market conditions, and problems in managing large integrated units, may well have contributed to their involvement in factory act proceedings. Horner's figures are less helpful with regard to counts spun, (generally expressed as numbers for length of yarn per weight of raw material); Horner drew a single line between fine and coarse spinning at 60s, which effectively obscures the crucial expansion in the highly competitive medium counts. A very patchy survey of mule spinning by the masters' association includes too few firms to draw any strong conclusion, but it again suggests, on extremely small numbers, that factory act case firms conformed to the general profile of the locality.[25]

The profile of factory act case firms would therefore appear, on the limited evidence considered here, to be broadly similar to that of their peer group, so far as structural variables are concerned. It is also neces-

[24] Combined and specialised firms in factory act cases (distribution for all mills in brackets):

	Combined		Specialised	
Ashton, Stalybr.	13	(25)	17	(82)
Blackburn	18	(25)	22	(89)
Bolton	11	(18)	25	(43)
Oldham	16	(42)	82	(105)

Classification of factory act case firms as described in directories; figures for all mills from survey by Horner, Reports of Factory Inspectors, Dec. 1841; note that Horner's census was of *mills*, not firms.

[25] Counts spun by factory act case firms (distribution for all firms responding in brackets):

	Below 40		40–59		60–79		80 and over		Not listed
Ashton, Stalybr.	1	(3)	—	(4)	1	(6)	—	(1)	28
(Blackburn – no returns)									
Bolton	—	(4)	—	(1)	1	(1)	2	(6)	33
Oldham	3	(14)	—	(4)	3	(6)	—	(1)	92

From MS returns of survey of piecing, Ashworth Papers, Lancs. RO, Box marked 'Factory Act Returns'.

Table 6.5 *Voting behaviour of factory act case firms, Liberal support*

	Factory act case firms % Lib.	Total traced	All firms % Lib.	Total traced
Ashton 1841	73	15	51	45
Blackburn 1847	30	20	15	13[a]
Bolton 1841	67	12	60	83
Oldham 1847[b]	17	35	13	187
Bradford 1847	79	42	67	63
Halifax 1847[c]	0	14	5	19
Huddersfield 1837[d]	79	14	68	75

Notes: [a] More factory act case firms traced due to multiple prosecutions.
[b,c] Majority split votes (Fox-Duncuft Oldham, Wood/Edwards Halifax) account for low Liberal vote.
[d] Includes cases prior to 1838, in view of early date.
Source: firms traced in poll-books. In two-member seats voting for both Liberals, or plumping for either counted; in partnerships only one voter was counted (there were no cases of partners voting differently); in repeated prosecutions the same voter is counted again in respect of each separate case.

sary to consider political, religious and cultural divisions. Voting behaviour, as recorded in poll-books, gives some indication of these patterns (table 6.5). The figures suggest a Liberal bias among factory act case firms. These findings should be treated with caution, in view of the problems of record linkage, the small numbers traced and the complications of cross-party voting in some instances. But it is notable that the bias is in the same direction in all the towns, except Halifax. Here, there was a higher proportion of Radical/Chartist votes among factory act case firms. This may actually fit the pattern, paradoxically in view of the ten-hours commitment of the Chartist candidate, Ernest Jones; Jones ran in tandem with Edward Miall, the standard-bearer of militant Dissent, who appealed to the more radical sectors of a divided liberal bourgeoisie.[26]

The association between Liberal voting and involvement in factory act proceedings is particularly marked in Ashton, Bradford and Huddersfield, all straight Liberal/Conservative contests, with little cross-voting. In all three towns. political alignments can be placed in a wider local context,

[26] J.A. Jowitt, 'Parliamentary politics in Halifax, 1832–1847', *Northern History* 12 (1976); K. Tiller, 'Late Chartism: Halifax 1847–58', in J. Epstein and D. Thompson (eds.), *The Chartist Experience* (London, 1982).

linking entrepreneurial practices to political and religious differences, which together defined distinct sub-cultures within the local business community. In Ashton and Bradford, it is possible to identify emergent groups of Liberal Dissenting millowners, who were engaged in a scramble to accumulate and committed to investments in plant and machinery in unstable and fiercely competitive market conditions. Some of the anxieties that this generated, and the essential ambivalence of entrepreneurial Dissenting ideologies, have already been considered in chapter 4. But, whatever the dilemmas of accumulation, the state was not the favoured agency for resolving them. At times of economic pressure, room for manoeuvre was perceived to be severely constrained, and at all times these groups remained suspicious of a Tory Anglican aristocratic Establishment. The Liberal bias of factory act case firms may also be an effect of politically motivated targeting of major Liberal employers in these towns.

The Ashton Liberal community felt itself besieged by Chartism and operative short-time committees on one hand, and the populist Toryism of J. R. Stephens on the other. Here, the division appears to be between larger and smaller capital. Linking the turbulence of the area to the deficient state of education and divisions among the masters, Horner estimated that 27 Dissenters employed 14,400 while 36 Anglicans employed 6,575.[27] Paradoxically, the member for Ashton, Charles Hindley, was a parliamentary advocate of the ten-hours bill, but this does not seem to have affected the stubborn resistance to factory regulation maintained by some of his leading constituency supporters. In Bradford, this period saw the consolidation and expansion of a restructured worsted industry, with new generations of (often 'migrant') entrepreneurs challenging the quasi-monopoly position of established, more often Tory, manufacturers committed to earlier forms of gentlemanly capitalism.[28]

There is also evidence of divisions among Huddersfield merchants and manufacturers, which can be related to the complicated changes occurring in the local woollen industry. The 1837 Huddersfield election was a highly charged occasion, with Richard Oastler, as a Tory with some radical support, challenging the Ramsden Whig dominance of the borough. The factory issue seems to have had unusually close links to political divisions in Huddersfield; for example signatories of the 1832 petition against proposed legislation traced in the poll-book were all Liberal voters.[29] This can be related to deeper divisions in the Huddersfield manufacturing community over work and marketing practices and the proper balance of factory and domestic production. What was at issue was not simply a difference

[27] Reports of Factory Inspectors: Horner, Oct. 1842.
[28] See Koditschek, *Class Formation*, esp. pt ii.
[29] Names in Sykes, *History of Huddersfield*, pp. 321–3.

between large and small capital, but more subtle differences between the artisanal small master and the small capitalist manufacturer.[30] Whereas the domestic manufacturer 'brings his goods to Huddersfield market, and there sells them to the merchant in an unfinished state, and the merchant finishes them', the new-style manufacturer concentrated the various processes under his control, and by-passed the cloth-hall; he probably also functioned as a merchant vis-à-vis the domestic clothier, undermining 'the old John Bull system of trade'.[31] There is some evidence for links between 'old' or 'new' manufacturers and political attitudes; those 'merchants and manufacturers' voting Liberal in 1837 were more likely to have been founded in the preceding fifteen years (four out of thirty-nine listed 1822, compared with four out of twenty Oastler voters) but also more likely to survive twenty years later (twelve out of thirty-nine listed 1857, compared with four out of twenty).

In specific local instances there does appear to be some foundation for the stereotype of hard-faced opposition to factory legislation by newly wealthy Liberal Dissenting masters. However the converse of Tory identification with factory reform does not necessarily follow; it is more a retrospective stereotype based on the activities of highly idiosyncratic Tory populist figures like Oastler and Stephens than any consistent party alignment discernible at the time. As a Halifax 'Liberal elector' recalled, following Tory attempts to appropriate the cause of factory reform in 1877, Tory manufacturers had been among those lobbying and petitioning against Sadler.[32] And there are instances of prominent Tories (such as Bolling in Bolton or Hopwood in Blackburn) becoming involved in factory act proceedings.

The absence of consistent party alignments over the factory issue is apparent from hustings speeches in the towns studied. The factory question was generally raised by ten-hours supporters (often, presumably, non-electors), who sometimes had to 'remind' the candidate of his commitment to the issue, while opponents, whether Liberal or Tory, preferred a discreet silence.[33] Some of the ambivalence of would-be populist

---

[30] Cf. Behagg, *Politics and Production*; for Huddersfield in this period, W.B. Crumpp and G. Ghorbal, *History of the Huddersfield Woollen Industry* (Huddersfield, 1935), pp. 108–22; Marland, *Medicine and Society*, ch. 2.

[31] Select Committee on Manufactures, Commerce and Shipping, PP 1833 (690) VI, q. 1877 (J. Brooke, woollen manufacturer); Select Committee on Handloom Weavers' Petitions, PP 1834 (556) X, qq. 3788–90 (R. Oastler).

[32] *Halifax Weekly Courier*, letter from 'Liberal Elector', 3 March 1877.

[33] This generalisation is based on reports of election meetings in the local press, 1835–52; for electoral politics in textile towns see Howe, *Cotton Masters*, ch. 3; Jowitt, 'Parliamentary politics in Halifax'; D.G. Wright, 'A radical borough: parliamentary politics in Bradford, 1832–1841', *Northern History* 4 (1969). Factory reform was a cross-party issue at both parliamentary and constituency levels; cf. Lubenow, *Politics of Government Growth*, pp. 138–150.

politicians is reflected in the pages of Miall's *Nonconformist*. While welcoming factory agitation as 'accustoming the operatives to think for themselves . . . raising them to a position of self-reliance and respect, which feudalism will hereafter find it impossible to subvert', the paper nevertheless opposed the demand for a ten-hours bill as delusory, a stance maintained until November 1846, then not mentioned as an issue, despite predictable coverage of Miall's Halifax campaign.[34] Aggressive economic liberalism was never a particularly popular cry, except in the more benign guise of free trade, universal peace and prosperity in the days to come; and economic doctrine was itself being reworked in the 1840s to embrace both free trade and factory reform.

Opposition to legislation was more often expressed in petitions, lobbying, the suborning of official opinion and evasion and defiance at the local level. In this perspective, the views of a Liberal like Hindley in Ashton (or even of Fielden in Oldham) might appear not particularly 'dangerous' – or at any rate to be the price for sustaining other interests, such as political reform, education and religious issues. There is little evidence from poll-books of any swings in employer voting related to the presence of pro-ten-hours candidates. Fielden's defeat in 1847 may be a partial exception (as he himself alleged), but it can equally be seen as a manifestation of the fissiparous divisions in local radicalism, the emergence of a convincing 'Liberal' alternative in W. J. Fox (a pledged supporter of the Ten Hours Bill) and an instance of the cross-party voting apparent elsewhere in a realigning election.[35] While the factory issue no doubt played some part in electoral politics – and probably a larger one in the popular theatre of the non-electors at the hustings – other resources, ultimately the economic power of large employers, could be deployed in a struggle to turn around unacceptable legislation.

Factory act cases have to be seen as part of a political process of conflict and bargaining over the terms of legislation. The various factory acts arose from particular parliamentary circumstances, and comprised packages of measures, some of which could prove more operationally significant than others; rendering parts of the law 'unworkable', while awaiting a favourable political conjuncture to codify its modification, constituted a plausible strategy for anxious employers. The element of political calculation should not be exaggerated; the bulk of cases probably arose from the purely pragmatic adoption, under market pressures, of working practices deemed illegal, or from simple managerial inertia. But there is evidence

[34] *The Nonconformist*, 17 April 1844, p. 244; 18 Nov. 1846, p. 772; and 1844–7, *passim*.
[35] Weaver, *Fielden*, pp. 268–74; cf. R.A. Sykes, 'Some aspects of working-class consciousness in Oldham, 1832–1842', *Historical Journal* 23, 1 (1980); M. Winstanley, 'Oldham radicalism and the origins of popular Liberalism', *Historical Journal* 36 (1993).

that a significant minority of cases were linked to a fairly conscious strategy of resistance.

Cases dismissed, withdrawn or shifted on to operatives or others could form part of such a strategy. Such cases were more likely to involve firms surviving to 1865–6 in Ashton (55 per cent surviving, compared with 43 per cent for all factory act case firms) Blackburn (63 per cent compared with 40 per cent) and Saddleworth (64 per cent compared with 50 per cent). In these areas at least, the ability to deflect factory act proceedings seems to be associated with successful accumulation strategies. Elsewhere, although there is no overall pattern of this kind, it is certainly possible to adduce individual instances of leading employers having cases withdrawn or dismissed. Some instances are presented in the appendix to this chapter.[36] Employers involved in cases include several members of those manufacturing dynasties producing magistrates, mayors, parliamentary candidates and MPs. In the four Lancashire towns considered, eight out of twelve local manufacturers standing as parliamentary candidates (1837–52) were at some time involved in factory act cases.

Prominent employers were in some instances repeatedly involved in proceedings; the celebrated confrontation between Horner and the Ashworths was only the most dramatic and best-publicised example of a wider pattern (see appendix). Involvement of prominent employers went beyond a few gentlemanly test cases; it could reflect a consistent policy of testing the law to destruction, or where possible directing its force on to operatives or others.

Two further points may be noted about the firms considered in the appendix. First, they are mostly identified with the expanding medium-range sector of the cotton industry which was subject to the fiercest competitive pressures in this period. Although Ashworth is sometimes described as a 'fine spinner' his product, like that of Mason of Ashton, belongs to the medium-fine range, rather than to true fine spinning more often associated with Bolton. There is less direct evidence about the product range of the Blackburn firms, but Blackburn was particularly associated with the manufacture of coarse and medium fabrics for the growing Indian trade. Secondly, the political affiliations of these firms are of some interest. Like employer sympathy for factory regulation, this fairly determined employer resistance was evidently a cross-party phenomenon; but its most vociferous exponents are associated with Liberalism (as are their sympathisers on the bench, where Whig county justices, and the Manchester borough court were more inclined to convict

[36] Other cases include Wareing & Sons, May 1839, J. Cheetham & Co., June 1838 (Oldham); J. Lockwood, Nov. 1839, W. Learoyd, Sept. 1847 (Huddersfield); R. Crossley, June 1846, J. Holdsworth, Aug. 1846 (Halifax).

substitute offenders).[37] The inspectors even alleged that Pilkington's parliamentary motion for a return of mills was intended to divert them from enforcement duties.[38]

Cases of the kind under discussion often became local *causes célèbres*, exploited by political rivals of the employers concerned, but also attracting a class-based sense of popular outrage.[39] What has been referred to as the 'excitable rhetoric of Oastler' must be placed in this context.[40] Popular denunciations, however excitable, do seem to have had some bearing on the enforcement process. For example, several employers mentioned in George Crabtree's exposure of conditions in Calderdale were among the first cases brought in that area once the 1833 Act came into force.[41] And, as we have seen, there was some foundation for Oastler's identification of overworking employers on his home ground at Huddersfield with Liberal Dissent. Oastler's best-known polemic was his 'law or the needle' speech at Blackburn in September 1836, when he hinted at industrial sabotage as a possible response to employers' lawlessness. [42] The background to this is rather obscure; although the speech is often taken to refer to the dismissal of a case by the local bench, no case had been brought at Blackburn for some time prior to that date. Earlier cases had however included the dismissal of the second Hopwood case in December 1835 (see appendix). Oastler may have been responding to continuing popular resentment about this incident, or perhaps to refusal by the magistrates to hear a case (or, more likely, to intercede by drawing it to the attention of the inspector, who would have had to lay the information). This would bear out Bartrip's view that any assessment of enforcement must consider decisions to prosecute, not simply the outcomes of those complaints that reached the court room.[43] Different, customary understandings of the law, and anger at the authorities' refusal to act on them, may also be involved here. If the Blackburn short-time committee had indeed approached the local justices with their complaints, this may have reflected the earlier system of supposedly ineffectual factory act enforcement by common informer; workers' representatives continued to express the demand for a simple law (such as restriction on the mill-engine) that might be enforced in this way.[44]

---

[37] Peacock, 'Justices of the peace', p. 186, and 'Successful prosecution', p. 203.

[38] Minutes of Meetings of Factory Inspectors, 13 Feb. 1854, PRO, LAB 15.3.

[39] Dutton and King, 'The limits of paternalism'; Rose, Taylor and Winstanley, 'Economic origins of paternalism', pp. 94–5, for examples of polemics about employment practices; J.R. Stephens' *Ashton Chronicle* and various local radical papers gave extensive coverage to factory grievances.   [40] Peacock, 'Successful prosecution', p. 197.

[41] Employers mentioned in G. Crabtree, *A Brief Description of a Tour through Calder Dale, being a Letter to Richard Oastler* (1833), traced in prosecution returns.

[42] Driver, *Tory Radical*, pp. 326–30.   [43] Bartrip, 'Success or failure?'.

[44] Select Committee 1840, qq. 8311–13, 8381, 8384 (J. Lawton).

Popular demands for a law that would empower workers to enforce 'fair' employment as they understood it were at variance with the formalism of inspectors, magistrates and the Home Office. In the Ashton–Stalybridge area, the scene of longstanding contention over factory regulation, the inefficacy of inspection was related to a range of employment grievances, including arbitrary fines (used to fund a Sunday School), probationary periods on low pay, and obligatory renting of cottages: 'I and my mates, who often talk these things over, are at a loss to know where the inspector lives; what he reports when he comes round; and what the government really intend when they propose laws for the regulation of factories.'[45] The enforcement of factory regulation involved negotiated relationships to these popular understandings, as well as 'negotiated compliance' on the part of employers.[46] The introduction of a salaried inspectorate appears as an important landmark in Whiggish histories of 'social reform'; but at the time it was viewed with suspicion. As Foster has pointed out, the system of enforcement by common informer, however limited, could in some localities empower workers' representatives.[47] There was a continuing undercurrent of scepticism, with repeated emphasis on a simple law enforced by local initiative: 'the men, women and children of the Factories, together with their parents, were necessarily the most capable of exercising the guardianship and protection of the young hands. *Hear, hear.*'[48]

There was a tactical shift by the short-time movement to pressure for enforcement of the existing law, including the election of workers' delegates as unofficial inspectors and lobbying of the inspectors and Home Office.[49] This pressure, and the challenge of more radical customary conceptions of law and its enforcement helped push the inspectors to take a stronger line – and perhaps to broaden their scope beyond those undercutting 'country mills' to which their attention had been drawn by leading manufacturers. Horner was careful to maintain public distance from the popular movement, but there is evidence that it did contribute to prosecutions. Horner's rule of ignoring anonymous tip-offs was set aside in the case of Hopwood's weavers (the last of the cases at that firm in the

---

[45] *Ashton Chronicle*, 19 Aug. 1848.
[46] Carson, 'Conventionalization of factory crime'; Field, 'Without the law?'; and see Joyce, *Visions of the People*, chs. 4–6, for the relevance of popular notions of custom, law and morality.
[47] Foster, 'The first six factory acts'.
[48] Speech by John Fielden, in *Report of the Important Proceedings of a Public Meeting . . . held in Oldham, 11 Nov. 1836* (1836), p. 14; cf. speech by Oastler at Blackburn, reported (from *The Times*) in *The Nonconformist*, 24 April 1844, p. 265.
[49] Clegg to Fielden, 8 June 1836, Fielden Papers, John Rylands University Library, Manchester; Select Committee 1840, qq. 8471–4 (J. Lawton).

appendix), where he acted on a letter from 'a few sufferers': 'And now, Sir, we beg to state that the above is a correct statement of facts, the truth of which may be proved any day by your coming over . . . and taking them by surprise.'[50] Hopwood's long record of defiance of the factory acts, the substantial local employer opinion supporting regulation, and the battle over implementing the 1847 Act no doubt made Horner more receptive to this appeal. In another case about the same time, an anonymous letter led to the conviction of Messrs Bracewell of Barnoldswick, one of the major firms resisting the ten-hour day.[51] Certain elements of popular understandings of factory regulation do seem to have entered enforcement practice. Smoke coming from the chimney, or the mill lit up at night were *prima facie* signs calling for investigation, though it was then necessary to prove that restricted workers were present on the premises.[52] The gradual acceptance of state regulation arose from negotiated relationships with popular short-time movements, as well as with employers.

Customary understandings played an important part in the negotiated interpretation of law. Employers' notions of fair competition, as well as of their proprietary rights as providers of capital and employment, formed part of this network of customary assumptions. At the same time, workers saw factory regulation in terms of empowerment to enforce their conceptions of fair employment, beyond the formal requirements of statute. These customary understandings varied between industrial and community contexts, and were often challenged and disrupted by state intervention or innovating employers.

The idea of a normal working day, based on the permitted hours of restricted workers, was central to notions of fair competition and fair employment. It was informally incorporated into aspects of regulatory practice, though it was by no means stipulated by any clause of the relevant legislation. Employer consensus in this respect was fragile, and could not be made to hold without the external pressures of popular agitation and state mediation. These issues were to be focused in struggles over the interpretation of the 1847 Act, which form the theme of the next chapter.

[50] Reports of Factory Inspectors: Horner, Oct. 1850.
[51] Ibid.   [52] Select Committee 1840, q. 39 (Horner).

APPENDIX: PROMINENT EMPLOYERS IN FACTORY ACT CASES

Based on employer profiles, as for tables 6.2, 6.3, 6.5.

YP: young persons; C: children; W/D: withdrawn.

Thos. Mason, Ashton, spinners (medium-fine counts), Liberal, Dissenter, mayor

May 1837: working Good Friday (YP) – one of several cases in Ashton, W/D on test case; May 1845: case v Mason's book-keeper, registers not in order, fined £2, overlooker also charged, fined £2; Nov. 1846: school attendance, fined £2, overlooker also charged re registration, fined £2; Jan. 1849: hours (YP) – W/D on test case.

H. & E. Ashworth, nr Bolton, spinners/weavers (medium-fine counts), Liberal, Dissenter, JP, MP

June 1837: certification ('technical' offence), fined £3 – refused to pay, furniture seized, bought back at auction by loyal workpeople; May 1840: hours (C) – convicted, no penalty 'not wilful', parent fined £1 for benefiting from child's wages; April 1841: hours (C) – parent (beerseller) fined £1; Nov. 1841: hours (C) and false certificates – three spinners fined £3 each; Feb. 1849: hours (YP) – dismissed on test case.

E. & W. Bolling, Bolton, spinners, Tory, Anglican, MP

May 1840: false certificate – teacher sentenced to one month suspended; Oct. 1840: hours (YP), not keeping register – dismissed.

Robert Hopwood, Blackburn, spinner/weaver, Tory, Anglican, alderman

Nov. 1835: night-work (YP) – fined £5; Dec. 1835: hours (YP), false time-book – dismissed; Dec. 1845: safety (injury from machinery) – fined £10; Nov. 1846: registration offences – fined £2, C employed under age – dismissed, also case v operative, fined £1 10s; March 1850: hours (YP), fifty cases – fined £70.

Pilkington Bros., Blackburn, spinner/weaver, Liberal, Dissenter, MP

Aug. 1845: safety, child injured under mule –dismissed; June 1849: child under mule – fined £2.

7 The ten-hour day

By the mid-1840s, the principle of legislative regulation for textile factories had gained fairly wide acceptance among politicians, economic pundits and other opinion-formers. There was also a measure of acceptance by employers, with regard at least to some of the stipulations of the factory acts. However, the length of the working day for restricted categories (children, young persons, from 1844, adult women) remained a contentious issue, as did the extent of limitations on the hours of adult men, either as the necessary price of protecting the restricted workers, or as anyhow desirable in its own right. Workers' short-time campaigns centred on the demand for a ten-hours bill, and the conception of a standard working day fixed in relation to these hours.

The later 1840s are often considered to have witnessed a sea-change in attitudes to these popular demands, including the 'conversion' of political economists and some prominent Whig politicians, together with pressure from dissident Tories unhappy about Peelite accommodation of commercial and manufacturing interests.[1] In this context, John Fielden successfully introduced a new factory act (1847) which reduced the legal day for young persons and women, from twelve to ten hours. The political conjuncture of what Marx described as the 'epoch-making' years 1846–7, following the repeal of the corn laws, provided the immediate background to this, but it is possible to exaggerate the element of 'gentry revenge' in these events, just as it is possible to exaggerate the specifically Tory contribution to the whole process of factory reform.[2]

The present concern is less with these shifts in parliamentary politics – though they will be touched on again, in relation to the placing of 'industrial England' in redefinitions of the nation – than with the further evolution of the local and regional attitudes and responses explored in the preceding chapter. Whereas 1847 might appear in chronologies of central politics as a landmark in attitudes to the factory question, in certain

---

[1] For changes in economic opinion see Robson, *On Higher than Commercial Grounds*.
[2] Marx, *Capital vol. I*, p. 395; cf. Lubenow, *The Politics of Government Growth*, pp. 138–50; Mandler, *Aristocratic Government*; Weaver, *Fielden*.

textile-manufacturing localities it produced further conflicts over interpretation. The failure of the 1847 Act to deliver its promise of a standard
ten-hour day led to disturbances over working time, and ultimately to
tightened legislation (1850 and 1853). This chapter considers employers'
views about the Ten Hours Act as it came into force; subsequent patterns
of local conflict; and finally the relationship of these events to mid-nineteenth-century constructions of Britain as an 'industrial nation'.

Employer opinion and the Ten Hours Bill

There is some evidence of a softening of employer opposition to short-
time working, following the economic crisis and social unrest symbolised
in the Chartist strikes of 1842. This experience may have predisposed
some manufacturers to look more favourably on further regulation,
despite evident pressures for extended working in the scramble out of
recession.

One hostile manufacturer wrote to Chadwick (April 1844) explaining
growing support, or at least acceptance of the Ten Hours Bill. Exponents
of this trend included: 'Those who really think that the toil or confinement is too severe; and that unless something is done to shorten the hours
of labour it will be quite useless to attempt . . . to educate and civilize the
industrial classes.' Other categories included those unafraid, 'some of
them from thorough ignorance', of the threat of foreign competition; *pro-
vocateurs* hoping to engineer a crisis in which the working class would rally
to the Anti-Corn Law League; adherents of popular economic fallacies
that shorter hours would raise the price of goods and thereby revive trade;
and those whose calculations were based on political opportunism as
'representatives of popular constituencies'.[3] Less impressionistic evidence about the distribution of these or other attitudes among employers
is, as always, fragmentary and difficult to interpret. Attitudes might in any
case display an ambivalent pragmatism. Chadwick's correspondent
himself thought that 'we shall come eventually to shorter hours' but
expressed characteristic alarm about the 'recklessness' and 'ignorance' of
an over-impressionable legislature.[4]

The strongest declaration of employer support for ten hours was a West
Riding masters' petition (May 1842). This argued that, in addition to
improvement in health and morals, shorter hours would counter the tendency to over-production which had enabled 'persons, who are disposed to

[3] Letter to Chadwick (writer unidentified), quoted Robson, *On Higher than Commercial
Grounds*, p. 153: I have been unable to locate this letter in the Chadwick Papers, which
were uncatalogued at the time of use by Robson.
[4] Robson, *On Higher than Commercial Grounds*, p. 153.

take advantage of it, to glut the markets with goods the produce of excessively low wages'.[5] The petition claimed 294 signatories; names are unfortunately not appended, but that total would account for up to 30 per cent of woollen and worsted mills, or up to 28 per cent of all mills returned in the county in 1838.[6] Similar arguments for shorter hours were presented in official reports from Saunders, the inspector responsible for the West Riding.[7] There were a number of initiatives by West Riding employers to reduce hours on a voluntary basis, but to eleven hours rather than ten.[8] There was also strong opposition from some West Riding masters, notably at Huddersfield, where a meeting in April 1844 voted overwhelmingly against any reduction at all.[9] The 1842 ten-hours petition was produced in the depths of recession, and it is a matter of speculation how far its signatories maintained the same views in the upswing of the mid-1840s.

Among Lancashire cotton masters positive support for the ten-hours movement was certainly a minority trend. Its best-known advocates were John Fielden and the Blackburn Tory manufacturer, W.H. Hornby, and his managing partner, William Kenworthy. Across a political spectrum, from Fielden's radicalism to Hornby's Toryism, these manufacturers expounded a similar economic analysis.[10] The dictates of religion and morality, and the 'duty, imperatively incumbent upon every humane and philanthropic manufacturer' were linked to the need to stabilise markets and the potential advantages accruing to superior technology and an industrious and skilled labour-force. Fears of foreign competition were exaggerated; 'fluctuations caused by speculations' were a more serious threat to the nation's prosperity.[11] Both Fielden and Hornby and Kenworthy were relatively isolated within cotton employer circles; Hornby claimed that his stance had made him unpopular with his political friends (possibly a reference to Robert Hopwood, another Blackburn Tory, with a record of intransigent resistance to factory regulation).[12]

[5] Petition of Master Spinners and Manufacturers of the West Riding, PP 1843 LII.
[6] Jenkins, 'The validity of the factory returns', p. 41. As Jenkins points out, the returns were of mills, not firms; on the other hand, different partners in a firm may all have signed the petition separately, so estimates of levels of support must be at best approximate.
[7] Reports of Factory Inspectors: Saunders, June 1841, pp. 15–16; May 1847, pp. 47–8.
[8] W.G. Rimmer, Marshall's of Leeds, Flax-Spinners, 1788–1886 (Cambridge, 1960), p. 209; The Ten Hours Advocate, 26 Sept. 1846.
[9] Memorial from Huddersfield Manufacturers, in Home Office Papers, PRO, HO 45/5205.
[10] For Fielden, see Weaver, Fielden; for Hornby, Dutton and King, 'The limits of paternalism: the cotton tyrants of north Lancashire, 1836–54', pp. 70–1; Joyce, Work, Society and Politics, pp. 9–10, 149–50, 182–3, 189–91.
[11] W. Kenworthy, Inventions and Hours of Labour: A Letter to Master Cotton Spinners, Manufacturers, and Millowners in General (1842), pp. 13–4.
[12] Blackburn Standard, July 1852; for Hopwood, see above, ch. 6 and appendix; and on Blackburn politics, see Walsh, 'Working class political integration', esp. pp. 458–62.

There is nevertheless more to this stance than political idiosyncrasy or populism. Populist politics (whether of a radical or Tory cast) certainly had some relevance for both Fielden and Hornby, but their roles as owners of large cotton firms in the conditions of Blackburn and the Lancashire–Yorkshire border round Todmorden could also produce particular readings of the true interests of manufacturers and their workers. These were regions of handloom weaving, where competitive advantages accrued to large enterprises installing power-looms, while the traditions of the 'merchant-manufacturer' may also have influenced the accumulation strategies of major employers.[13] As political opponents in Fielden's Oldham constituency did not fail to point out, his advocacy of factory reform and fixing weavers' wages was combined with the rapid adoption of new machinery in his own factories.[14]

Arguments about efficiency and improved productivity provided another rationale for reducing hours. In retrospect this came to appear realistic and far-sighted; Marx was to theorise about the effect of state intervention in encouraging a shift to more 'intensive', rationalised methods of exploitation.[15] But, in the context of the 1840s, it cut against what employers, political economists and others believed to be the practical experience of industrial management. The mandatory extension of a few celebrated experiments seemed a risky course. The best-known such experiment was the reduction to eleven hours in 1844 by Gardner and Bazley at Preston. This fine-spinning and manufacturing concern seems to have pursued a strategy of finding niches in expanding and diversifying consumer markets; Bazley was a major figure in debates about industrial design and the importance of an educated work-force, linked to a vision of the elevation of taste and morals by the wider availability of a variety of quality textile products.[16] There were also initiatives to reduce hours by voluntary agreement in the West Riding, by Marshall's of Leeds, and the Halifax worsted masters. One of the latter group, Edward Akroyd, had argued on rather similar lines to Bazley about moral improvement through the cheapening of a wider range of goods, though in the rather different context of an embattled defence of free trade and machinery in the crisis month of August 1842.[17]

Initiatives to reduce hours may thus have arisen from 'optimistic'

[13] Cf. J.S. Lyons, 'The Lancashire cotton industry and the introduction of the power-loom, 1815–1850', PhD, University of California, Berkeley, 1977; Weaver, *Fielden*, esp. ch. 1.

[14] B. Grime, *Memory Sketches* (1887), pp. 51–2.

[15] Marx, *Capital vol. I*, p. 635.

[16] Dutton and King, 'The limits of paternalism', p. 62; Howe, *Cotton Masters*, pp. 186, 220–1, 226–7; Bazley, 'Cotton as an element of industry', and his *Lecture upon the Labour of Life* (1856).

[17] *Halifax Guardian*, 6, 13 Aug. 1842 (letters by E. Akroyd); and see also above, n. 8.

readings of the market, and the capacity of British manufacturing to maintain its position by orderly expansion of production. Commenting on the Gardner and Bazley experiment, Horner noted the importance of hand-labour in fine spinning, and doubted whether the productivity gains would be replicated in other, more typical sectors, where production was assumed to be governed by the speed of machinery.[18] It should also be noted that these experiments were on a voluntary basis, possibly intended to deflect legislative campaigns for the ten-hour day, while reinforcing images of the reciprocal interests of enlightened employers and rational and disciplined workers. Announcing the reduction to eleven hours, Marshall made the offer of a productivity bargain in fairly explicit terms:

And we trust that the voluntary reduction of the hours of labour on our part, will be met by a readiness on the part of our work-people to perform their share also, in a cheerful endeavour to make their labour more valuable to their employers, when their hours of work are shortened . . . This is the more necessary in a manu-factory such as ours, where the work is generally not paid by the piece, but by the day.[19]

There is little doubt that the prospect of a legal ten-hour day was viewed with alarm by most Lancashire cotton masters, and by many of their counterparts in the West Riding textile industries. Last-ditch peti-tions by Lancashire millowners (spring 1847) argued on well-worn grounds that the 'proposed interference' would deprive 'multitudes of men' of their livelihoods, threatening the future of 'British manufacturing industry'. Some of the language here echoes that of Kenworthy, perhaps deliberately, while inverting his argument.[20] Signatories of these petitions seem to have comprised a cross-section, with relatively higher propor-tions in Manchester and the main towns, where employer opinion was no doubt more organised. Ashton and Stalybridge had a particularly high level of support (52 per cent of firms listed in the directory), followed by Oldham (39 per cent); the proportion is rather lower in Bolton and Blackburn (26 and 24 per cent respectively). This distribution is in line with longstanding local patterns of employer response (chapter 6, above). The leading Bolton fine spinners (as opposed to medium-fine spinners, like Ashworth) were not among the signatories.

More privately, opponents of the Bill may have been resigned to its success, at least in the short run. As Edmund Ashworth complained to

[18] Reports of Factory Inspectors: Horner, May 1845, pp. 19–22.
[19] 'Eleven Hours' Time: Notice to the Workpeople of Marshall & Co.' (*c.* 1846), Marshall Papers, Brotherton Library, University of Leeds, MS 200/ 15.33.
[20] Memorial . . . by Certain Millowners Against the Factories Bill, PP 1847 XLVI, pp. 108 (Feb. 1847), 348 (May 1847); Memorial of Master Manufacturers in the County of Lancaster, PP 1847 XXVI, pp. 628–9; cf. Kenworthy, *Inventions and Hours of Labour.*

Chadwick, 'facts and arguments have seemed to avail nothing . . . the question has now obtained too firm a hold on the public mind to be staved off'.[21] Conversely, the tone of ten-hours propaganda at this period was one of reasoned optimism, claiming to be the bearer of the consensus of all people of goodwill.[22] The motives of employer opposition were probably mixed, ranging from a pragmatic negotiating stance of resistance to ten hours, to deep-seated fears about the future. As Marx argued, resistance was made more difficult by the deepening recession of 1847–8, and many of those resigned to the success of the Bill may have looked to reverse it in more favourable circumstances. Engels, writing in 1850 from Manchester rather than in retrospect in the British Museum, anticipated the nullification of the 1847 Act, and consequent awakening of working-class consciousness.[23]

Conflicts over working hours, 1848–53

The phasing in of the 1847 Act was followed by a series of legal test-cases and other factory act proceedings, but also by continuing industrial guerrilla warfare over work-schedules, which contributed to a general atmosphere of social unrest.

Horner noted with some puzzlement that the pressure to work longer was most intense in the Ashton–Stalybridge and Oldham areas, despite the apparently identical industrial profile of other, less disturbed areas.[24] However the main numerical clustering of cases concerning hours was elsewhere, in Rochdale and the Burnley–Accrington–Colne weaving belt.[25] Most of these were not contested, and may thus be routine infringements, perhaps involving the stereotype of the 'small employer'; there was a relatively low level of signatories of the masters' petition from this area. In the areas of most intense contention over working hours and the principle of a standard day, there were fewer actual cases, but more public controversy and popular dissatisfaction with the failure of the law to enforce ten-hour working.

Defended cases, which were either dismissed or withdrawn, include

---

[21] E. Ashworth to E. Chadwick, 29 April 1847, Chadwick Papers, University College, London, no. 101.

[22] See, e.g., *The Ten Hours Advocate* (appeared 1846–7), *passim*.

[23] P. Phillips, *Marx and Engels on Law and Laws* (Oxford, 1980), pp. 86–109. The firm of Ermen and Engels signed the 1847 petition against the Ten Hours Bill, and indeed figured in a subsequent case about hours. As Phillips points out, there are interesting differences in emphasis between Marx and Engels.

[24] Reports of Factory Inspectors: Horner, April 1851, pp. 3–4.

[25] Prosecution returns, 1848–53, appended to Reports of Factory Inspectors. All subsequent information on specific cases not otherwise referenced is based on this source.

two each in Manchester, Ashton–Stalybridge and Heywood, a case involving Ashworth at Bolton, and one each in Oldham, Tyldesley, Saddleworth and Marsden. These test-cases, various administrative and legal manoeuvres, and attempts to close legislative loopholes occurred against a background of continuing localised conflicts, especially in the Ashton–Stalybridge and Oldham areas (extending to their rural hinterlands of Saddleworth and Glossop). These conflicts, including strikes, demonstrations, mass pickets and crowd actions, fit a geographical pattern already identified over the whole process of factory regulation from 1833. After 1847, this longstanding pattern became focused in contentions over work-scheduling practices. Split shifts of protected workers (so-called 'false relays') could be used to work longer, as could adult men without female or juvenile co-workers. Hugh Mason of Ashton became famous for his obdurate insistence on working twelve hours, showing, as he claimed, the feasibility of running for extra hours with adult men only: 'a fact to which . . . its due weight should be attached', as the *Morning Chronicle* correspondent noted.[26]

These practices were not suddenly invented to evade the Ten Hours Act. Images of a standard working day, regulated by the steam-engine and by the interdependence of different categories of worker, may be misleading. Such images squared the circle of regulating the hours of adult men, while not formally submitting their 'free labour' to legal restriction; they also reinforced visions of regular, disciplined and uniform factory labour, governed by the movements of Andrew Ure's 'automaton'.[27] In reality, variable work-scheduling did occur, reflecting the diversity of factory work-processes, imbalances in production-flows and the differentiation of the labour-force in terms of gender, age and socially constructed 'skills'. The imposition of uniformity was limited by worker resistance, often structured along gender lines, but also by the requirements of fluctuating markets and a variable product mix. Employers themselves undercut the image of mechanised regularity by their demands for rapid accumulation and flexible response to market conditions.[28] The introduction of a standard working day cannot therefore be seen as a technologically defined requirement of factory production.

[26] J. Ginswick (ed.), *Labour and the Poor in England and Wales: Letters from the Morning Chronicle* (London and Totowa, New Jersey, 1983), vol. I, p. 92.

[27] Ure, *Philosophy*, pp. 13–23, 330.

[28] For critiques of concepts of the rationalisation of work see, e.g., A. Cottereau, 'La gestion, entre utilarisme heureux et éthique malheureuse: l'exemple des entreprises industrielles au XIXè siècle, en France', paper for international conference 'Nouvelles tendances en gestion', Montreal, 1986 (I am indebted to the author for a copy of this paper); R. Whipp, '"A time to every purpose": an essay on time and work', in Joyce (ed.), *Historical Meanings of Work*.

There is evidence of varied working hours in some mills some time before the issue of split shifts arose in 1848. Operative witnesses from Stalybridge reported to the 1833 Factory Commission that card-rooms and weaving-sheds sometimes ran later than the spinners; while spinners themselves might be obliged to work longer without piecers.[29] In an account of his mill community at Bollington (1841), Samuel Greg, jnr, stated that different departments had different stopping-times, allegedly to mitigate the dangers of crowds of young people at the factory gates; in similar vein it was claimed that the split shifts adopted after 1847 kept young workers away from 'sweethearts and other temptations'.[30] Whatever the moral justifications offered, differing work-schedules were probably related to imbalances between processes and production bottle-necks, which may well have intensified with the restructuring and market fluctuations of the 1830s and 40s. The adoption of split shifts, extended working by adult men and other expedients seems to have been a response to market conditions and production difficulties, as well as a tactic to nullify the 1847 Act. After disputes over extended working in Cheetham's weaving-sheds (Stalybridge) there was agreement that adult male winders and weavers would work late alternately to clear a bottle-neck in the supply of warps.[31] Employer resistance to a standard day was related to the desire to retain this kind of flexibility.

The failure of the 1847 Act to deliver a standard ten-hour day led to rather confused battles, exposing ambiguities and divisions in the short-time movement itself, as well as in the outlook of officials and politicians. The issue of gender is at the centre of these confusions. Demands to regu-late the labour of 'dependent' categories could, as is often suggested, be deployed tactically to shorten the hours of adult men. This persistent theme in short-time agitation, together with quite explicit statements about the desirability of a common ten-hour day, certainly has to qualify any simple interpretation of legislation as aimed at the blanket exclusion of women from working in textile factories; such a strategy would indeed require that men worked longer in order to make themselves preferable as employees – the very matter that led to so much contention.[32] But if

---

[29] Factory Comm., Supp. Report, PP 1834 XX, D.2, pp. 74–6.
[30] [S. Greg], *Two Letters to Leonard Horner, Esq. on the Capabilities of the Factory System* (1841), p. 18; *Some Remarks on the Ten Hours Bill, by a Stalybridge Manufacturer* (1849), p. 3.
[31] *The Champion of What is True and Right*, vol. II (1850): issues of this journal are undated, but this incident must have followed the passing of the 1850 Act in August.
[32] See C.E. Morgan, 'Women, work and consciousness in the mid-nineteenth-century English cotton industry', *Social History* 17 (1992); Valverde, '"Giving the female a domestic turn"'; Walby, *Patriarchy at Work*, esp. pp. 100–34; for an expanded version of the present argument, Gray, 'Factory legislation'.

factory legislation was intended to introduce *de facto* the same hours for men, the form in which this was achieved still worked to construct gender difference. In a sense, the form of factory legislation enabled adult male workers to have their cake and eat it: to sustain a definition of themselves as the free agents postulated by political economy and evangelical religion alike, while yet enjoying the protection of a legal working day.

Shorter hours for men were often presented as the necessary consequence of shortening the legal day for restricted categories. This representation perhaps helped justify a legislative standard day in terms of economic orthodoxy, but it obscured a more complex situation. Trade custom, enforced if necessary by assertions of manly independence against 'unfair' employers, was to bring about the standardisation of hours. Men could see themselves as achieving the hours of protected workers, apparently by their own efforts, as well as seeing themselves as privileged agents in a struggle to provide protection for dependent categories. The effects of patriarchal interests on factory reform are both more complex and more pervasive than a simple model of exclusionary strategy would suggest.

The confused conflicts which followed the implementation of the 1847 Act to some extent disrupted, but never displaced, these masculine working-class identities. The spinners' short-time strategy had long assumed that trade custom, enforced by collective action in conjunction with 'fair' employers, would establish a uniform working day. At Bolton, a centre of spinners' organisation, this seems to have been achieved with relatively little conflict; all but two mills (including, predictably, Ashworth) had adopted the shortened hours by March 1849.[33] At Ashton and Stalybridge, the short-time committee, probably again based mainly on spinners' organisations, issued a series of placards, exhorting workers 'to take the peaceable and constitutional method of ceasing labour at Six o'Clock'. After enforcing short-time working in Ashton, 'they carried the moral warfare to Stalybridge, then to Mossley, then to Hyde, and then to the beautiful, but slave-driven valley of Glossop . . . a display of moral courage unequalled in the struggles of a people'.[34] The address of these broadsides is to 'free men' claiming 'liberty . . . to cease labour at an hour recognised by nearly every other trade in the empire'. There is a corresponding appeal to employers 'to meet our wishes on the question of factory labour' in free and fair negotiation between equals; a 'uniform system of working' was required to establish 'the harmony of fair trading'. Every reasonable employer should agree to this proposition, both because

[33] *Bolton Chronicle*, 31 March 1849; for the development of spinners' organisations, see Fowler and Wyke (eds.), *Barefoot Aristocrats*, chs. 1–3.
[34] *Fellow Workmen* (June 1853), broadsheet in Cassidy Coll., Tameside Archives, MS DD.13; see also Joyce, *Visions of the People*, pp. 102–8, 362–5.

it would enable the industry 'to go into the markets of the world and compete with all comers', and because 'surely, gentlemen, we live for some higher object than the mere acquisition of money'. [35]

The specific occupational reference in these appeals is mainly to spinners and piecers (including, presumably, young adult senior piecers). But there is also a more diffuse appeal to 'the people':

Then, Piecer Boys of Glossop, up with your souls and down with your jackets at Six O'clock, and the will of a united people, taking that which Parliament has been unable to give, will settle the Ten Hours Question, make factory life endurable, and place the Operatives on the same footing as their brethren of other trades throughout this empire.[36]

This address both invokes the wider popular political nation of 'this empire', which had willed the Ten Hours Act, and embraces a wider range of factory workers than the 'piecer boys'. This may register ambiguities in the position of the spinners, and the involvement of other groups, such as power-loom weavers, including women. As Horner noted, the greatest agitation for a ten-hours bill had been in Ashton, Stalybridge and Oldham: 'the chief agitators were unquestionably adult males … [yet] there is no difficulty in these places to get adult males to work the longer time'.[37] The effectiveness of the spinners' campaigns to enforce ten-hour working may thus have been undermined by the availability of spinners and older piecers prepared to work longer. Exhorting the Oldham spinners to follow the piecers' example and take action, the Ashton short-time committee played on masculine pride: 'Are the laws of nature to be reversed – boys to display the heart of lions, and their fathers those of hens?'[38]

Weavers seem to have been as important as spinners in workplace conflicts over hours. Women weavers actively resisted split shifts from the outset.[39] Yet the language of manly independence was often made to stand for the struggles of an extensively feminised work-force, in which women were at least as militant as men. A letter in the *Ashton Chronicle* complained that men at Leech's, Stalybridge, were transferred to another weaving-shed, where the engine 'runs that [extra] time for men – Englishmen, independent labourers, free agents as we are called'.[40] At

[35] *To the Manufacturers of Ashton and Neighbourhood* (April 1853); circular to employers, *The Late Factory Bill* (n.d.); *To the Manufacturers of Great Britain and Ireland* (July 1853): Cassidy Coll.
[36] *The Queen, her People and the Ten Hours Bill* (May 1853): Cassidy Coll.
[37] Reports of Factory Inspectors: Horner, April 1851.
[38] *The Factory Operatives of Oldham* (July 1853): Cassidy Coll. It may be doubted whether many Oldham spinners were literally the fathers of these particular piecers; the 'boys' were most likely young adults.
[39] Morgan, 'Women, work and consciousness', pp. 37–8.
[40] *Ashton Chronicle*, 13 Jan. 1849.

Cheetham's, after the banning of split shifts by the 1850 Act, the adult male weavers refused to work longer: 'The men actually stopped their looms and turned out and spoke out like men, and said they would not do it.' The day before this incident weavers at Cheetham's, probably mainly women, celebrated the prohibition of split shifts with a mock funeral: 'orange wine, raspberry wine, porter, biscuits, pork-pies, brandy-snaps, acid drops, &c., &c., were served . . . Many of the weavers did little work today. The manager of the weavers caught them in the midst of the frolic, but went his way laughing and did not interfere.'[41]

This report provides a rare glimpse of the informal cultural politics of struggles over time. The workplace celebration was itself a reappropriation of time and space, suggestive of popular notions of licensed excess and the 'good time'.[42] It forms an interesting contrast with the Bolton operatives' 'Exhibition and Bazaar', likewise a celebration of the achievement of shorter hours. This was an altogether grander, but not necessarily more enjoyable event, held at the Temperance Hall and firmly inscribed in the institutional space of 'rational recreation'. The occasion rated a characteristically bland engraving in the *Illustrated London News*, as part of the more acceptable face of industrial society.[43] It is tempting, but possibly misleading, to reduce such contrasts to occupational or ideological difference; they are as much to do with differences between the languages of formal, institutional life and less self-consciously elevated and edifying modes of expression. As Joyce has persuasively argued, the 'respectable' public culture of mid-Victorian liberalism did not simply displace customary forms; both could be faces of the same working-class culture.[44] This is of some relevance to the varied meanings of work-time and its regulation, which will be further discussed below (chapter 8).

It is, however, likely that differing local and occupational experiences had some bearing on divisions emerging in the short-time movement itself. Some sections of the movement, apparently centred on Oldham, called for legal restriction on the moving-power (i.e. stopping the mill-engine by law after ten hours); while others, as we have seen, looked to voluntary agreement and trade practice to align men's hours with a standard day. Ashley's proposed parliamentary compromise of a ten-and-a-half-hour day, together with removal of some of the legal anomalies, was a further bone of contention. The 1850 Act instituted a ten-and-a-half-hour day, which was eventually to form part of a relatively firm compromise settlement, but was subject to considerable criticism as a dilution of

---

[41] *The Champion*, vol. II (1850), pp. 287–8.
[42] Cf. Joyce, *Visions of the People*, esp. pp. 308–11, 340.
[43] *Illustrated London News*, 2 Oct. 1852; see also *Bolton Chronicle*, 25 Sept. 1852.
[44] Joyce, *Visions of the People*, esp. pt iii; cf. Eley, 'Edward Thompson, social history and political culture'; Moore, 'Women, industrialisation and protest', pp. 133–6, 176–80.

the ten-hours position. This division may reflect a difference between the
better organised and pragmatically inclined spinners and such groups as
weavers, card-room hands and possibly senior piecers blocked by a shortage of places for spinners.[45] But it may also be that the spinners' organisation was itself fragile, and that the 'realism' of parliamentary lobbyists
among the leaders was not so convincing to the rank-and-file. The changing situation could change attitudes, with slow progress (and some evidence of bad faith) in the legislature, and continued employer resistance
at local level. While advocates of restricting the moving-power, such as
Oastler, Stephens and local Chartist leaders, no doubt also had a personal
influence on their audiences. The ten-hours issue figured in the 1852
election, especially at Oldham, in the form of debates about restricting
the moving-power, rather than the principle of the ten-hour day.[46]

Stopping the mill-engine may, as Valverde has suggested, constitute a
more radical position, which could 'unite the working-class rather than
divide it along age and gender lines';[47] it would also have been a more
substantial breach in the principles of *laissez-faire*. But both restriction of
the engine, and the alternative strategy of regulating men's hours by trade
custom and collective bargaining, could be justified in terms of shared
notions of (adult male) labour as property and the rights of freeborn
Englishmen. It was argued that adult men needed regulated hours in
order to conserve their property in their own persons and labour; and this
claim of labour to the same protection as other forms of property was,
after all, a staple of radical argument.[48] At an Oldham election meeting,
'the man in the gallery wanted to know if life and health were not of more
value than protection to the present law of the country which enabled
working men to break down their constitutions?'.[49] Legislative intervention was needed, not to put men in the position of protected dependants,
but 'to do that for them which they cannot do for themselves', to
empower men to achieve what they all desired but none could achieve
individually; longer hours were imposed 'against the will and in spite of
the entreaties of the employed'.[50] Arguments for radical state interven-

[45] Driver, *Tory Radical*, chs. 37, 38; Foster, *Class Struggle*, p. 233; Fowler and Wyke (eds.), *Barefoot Aristocrats*, pp. 45–6.
[46] Grime, *Memory Sketches*, pp. 108–9, 134–8.
[47] Valverde, '"Giving the female a domestic turn"', pp. 626–7.
[48] See, e.g., Hall, *White, Male and Middle Class*, esp. pp. 137–41.
[49] *The Address of W.J. Fox, Esq. MP, and Proceedings of the Public Meeting ... 25 April 1852*, in 'Election Scraps, Oldham 1852', Oldham Reference Library.
[50] *The Ten Hours Bill: The Factory Operative's Guide and Labourer's Advocate*, June 1853, copy in PRO, HO 45/5128; *Report of the Speeches Delivered at a Great Ten Hours Meeting ... Over Darwen, 18 March 1853* (1853), p. 6, in J.M. Cobbett Coll., Goldsmiths' Library, University of London; cf. J.S. Mill, *Principles of Political Economy* (Penguin edn, Harmondsworth, 1985), pp. 329–30.

tion to enforce a standard working day regardless of sex or age still incorporated gender difference. Such measures were represented as enabling adult men to preserve their inalienable property in person and labour; women were to enjoy the benefits of protection, preserve feminine moral virtue and become better wives and mothers.

The establishment of a standard day by trade custom and voluntary agreement seems to have commanded broader support, and the eventual legislative settlement of the question after 1853 was based on this approach, with further tightening of clauses concerning protected workers (children on this occasion). But the threat of growing support for restrictions on the moving-power, with the problems this would have posed for economic orthodoxy, had some bearing on this outcome. There was also continuing social disturbance in some places in the factory districts, related to contentions over working hours. This context, as relayed especially by Leonard Horner in his written reports and probably also through informal lobbying, must have entered into the calculations of politicians, key officials and opinion-formers. It may also have impressed on hitherto reluctant employers the advantages of a standard working day as the price of relative industrial peace.

Social disturbance and managerial authority

The battles over implementing the Ten Hours Act should therefore be placed in the context of wider social tensions in the cotton districts, including the Chartist crisis of 1848 and its aftermath, and the wage-disputes of 1853–4. These generalised tensions may also be linked to specific problems of management and industrial authority in large textile concerns.

The period of intense conflict over working hours, centred in Ashton–Stalybridge, Oldham and adjacent areas, was framed by the Chartist disturbances of 1848, affecting various places throughout the Lancashire and West Riding textile districts, and the wage-disputes of 1853–4, culminating in a prolonged and bitter lock-out in Preston.[51] Connections between these disturbances and the ten-hours question have been obscured, partly by the insistence of working-class short-time leaders (as well as sympathisers like Ashley) on keeping the hours question distinct and adopting a language of reasoned moderation and social harmony. This may be compounded by a 'compartmentalist' approach

---

[51] For Chartism in 1848, see Saville, *1848*; Tiller, 'Late Chartism: Halifax, 1847–58', pp. 312–44. For industrial conflicts, Dutton and King, 'The limits of paternalism', and their book, *Ten Per Cent and No Surrender: The Preston Strike, 1853–4* (Cambridge, 1981); Kirk, *Growth of Reformism*, pp. 247–53.

to popular activity, encouraging face-value readings of such protesta-tions.[52]

The phasing in of the Ten Hours Act coincided with the Chartist crisis of 1848, whose substantial dimensions in the industrial north have been emphasised by Saville.[53] The atmosphere in Ashton and Stalybridge was evidently highly charged. Liberal millowners in this area had long been assailed by populist polemics, and this tradition persisted in the events of 1847 and after. Standing at Huddersfield in 1847 on a platform of mili-tant Dissent, James Cheetham was the subject of unspecified allegations, apparently about his activities as an employer and magistrate at Stalybridge: 'his opponents were not satisfied with sending spies into his neighbourhood to pick up all that private malice could pervert or a lying tongue invent'.[54] Although press reports of this exchange are rather enig-matic, the recent passing of the Ten Hours Act must have been part of the context. As tension rose in the spring of 1848, Hugh Mason, the Ashton spinner and leading Liberal, wrote to the Home Office in somewhat hysterical tones, enclosing a copy of the *Ashton Chronicle*, and complain-ing of Stephens' 'vile abuse of Whigs and millowners', all the more alarm-ing since his 'talents are of a very high order'; Stephens was blamed for inciting the operatives in their 'fiendish joy' at recent mill fires.[55] This hints at a theme of mill arson more explicitly stated in July, at Bolton, where the mayor warned of rumoured plans by the Irish 'confederates' to fire mills, and urged employers 'to use all the influence in your power with your hands in dissuading them from joining any assemblies in the streets'.[56] At Oldham in May, crowds stopped mills, pulling plugs and breaking some windows, following meetings to protest at the sentencing of James Mitchell, the Irish leader.[57]

It was claimed that such actions were the work of 'strangers', rather than of regularly employed factory workers, who might indeed be recruited in defence of their workplaces.[58] Mason's letter, on the other

---

[52] Cf. F.K. Donnelly, 'Ideology and early English working-class history: E.P. Thompson and his critics', *Social History* 1 (1976).
[53] Saville, *1848*; the law came fully into force in July 1848.
[54] *Halifax Guardian*, 31 July 1847; *Leeds Mercury*, same date has a somewhat more circum-spect report.   [55] Letter from H. Mason, 6 March 1848, in PRO, HO 45/2410B.
[56] Confidential circular from mayor of Bolton, 28 July 1848, in PRO, HO 45/2410B. Industrial arson may merit fuller study; such fears were doubtless encouraged by public-ity surrounding rick-burning: see D. Jones, *Crime, Protest, Community and Police in Nineteenth-Century Britain* (London, 1982), ch. 2.
[57] Oldham magistrates, 31 May 1848, PRO, HO 45/2410B.
[58] Oldham magistrates, 2 June 1848, PRO, HO 45/2410B; the mayor of Bolton urged employers to point out 'the injury done to the interest of the working classes' by the alleged activities of the Irish clubs; on working-class 'volunteering' in 1848, see Saville, *1848*, pp. 114–17.

hand, suggests the mobilisation of factory operatives' antagonism to employers, at any rate in the Ashton and Stalybridge area, and there is evidence that crowd pressure was directed at 'unfair' employers, especially in the struggle to spread ten-hour working to the hinterlands of Saddleworth. Fears remained, as Chartism was repressed, trade revived and the battle over the working day began in earnest.

Reporting the absence of 'political excitement' in March 1850, the military commander nevertheless noted 'discontent . . . manifested by many of the operatives in the Manufacturing Towns' over the recent Exchequer Court judgment legalising split shifts.[59] The Saddleworth magistrates reported in some alarm in September the 'feeling in Oldham and its neighbourhood amongst the Factory Work people to compel the Masters to cease working their mills with adult hands at six o'clock'. In Oldham itself, this had led to 'one or two large assemblages about the mills at the time of stoppage', but little serious incident; but now that mills had to light up they could become 'a mark for the mob', especially in relatively isolated locations round Saddleworth. One such 'mob', consisting of 500 to 600 young men who 'appeared to be big piecers', marched to Lees and Hey, then to various mills in Saddleworth, forcing them to stop. The men employed there wanted to work the extra hours, and the masters 'will work if they can be protected', but felt intimidated: 'during the darkness of winter evenings outrages assassination or incendiarism may be committed with impunity'. As the magistrates pointed out, 'the movement may be general', since its object 'is one of a general nature'.[60]

The exact extent of any such 'movement' and its relationship to organised short-time committees must remain obscure. The main stress of ten-hours propaganda was on 'the peaceable and constitutional method', but the actual enforcement of standard hours rested on collective action, ranging from the gentlemanly negotiation of the Bolton spinners to more turbulent forms. Echoes of Luddism and 1842 seem to have been present in the minds of alarmed magistrates and employers, and probably also of operatives. And, through a long tradition of popular protest, appeals to constitutional rights could legitimise mass defiance of magistrates, employers or other representatives of authority and property. A placard against the magistrates' ban on a short-time demonstration at Glossop, headed 'VR' and 'given at our Court of Constitutional Law and Common Sense', alluded to the events of 1688 and various legal authorities on the

---

[59] Earl of Cathcart to Home Office, 4 March 1850, PRO, HO 45/3131.
[60] Letter from Saddleworth magistrates and attached deposition, 28 Sept. 1850, PRO, HO 45/3139. The number of piecers mentioned must have been recruited from several mills, or perhaps also unemployed workers.

right of popular assembly.[61] In the event the rally passed off peacefully, attended by about 3,000 from Manchester, Ashton and Stalybridge, and seems to have discouraged further overworking in Glossop.[62] While formally constituted short-time committees, and especially many of the spinners' leaders, probably did want to distance themselves from the more turbulent forms of action, this must be understood in a broader context. Constitutional formal organisation and crowd violence were merely the extreme points on a continuum of popular action. It may also be the case that formal organisations had only limited influence over local actions (or, for that matter, over those adult male spinners whose willingness to work extra hours was partly at issue). Crowds of big piecers assembling outside mills as night fell, or women weavers resisting split shifts, step forward from a background of workplace and community solidarity which has left only limited institutional and documentary traces.

Shaftesbury's remark, from a safer mid-Victorian retrospect, that the ten-hours movement was conducted 'without violence, without menace, without strikes' thus needs considerable qualification.[63] Apart from industrial conflicts and crowd actions ostensibly directed at the enforcement of standard hours, the whole context of social disturbance in the factory districts can rarely have been far from the considerations of politicians and officials. The atmosphere remained highly charged for some time after the supposed decline of Chartism, as fears of incendiarism and outrage testify. Trade unions and wage-disputes, culminating in the events at Preston in 1853–4, focused employers' concerns, leading to a wave of pamphleteering. These pamphlets generally emphasised the laws of the marketplace, the autonomous authority of employers and their proper relation to the employed; some of the more 'hard-line' contributions emanated, predictably, from Stalybridge.[64] Although most of this literature ostensibly focuses on wages and combinations, it also alludes, in more or less explicit terms, to the short-time movement. The fallacy that artificial scarcity of labour 'by combination and unions, and the working

[61] Broadsheet headed *VR* (June 1853), Cassidy Coll.
[62] *Ten Hours Bill*, June 1853, copy in HO 45/5128.
[63] Shaftesbury, speech in Manchester, 1866, quoted in Robson, *On Higher than Commercial Grounds*, p. 262; see also his speech at inauguration of Oastler memorial, Bradford, *Bradford Observer*, 17 May 1869.
[64] See, e.g., W.R. Greg, 'The relation between employers and employed', reprinted in his *Essays*; 'A Lancashire Man' [J.A. Nicholls], *The Strike: A Letter to the Working Classes on their Present Position and Movement* (1853); *Some Remarks on the Ten Hours Bill, by a Stalybridge Manufacturer* (1849); S. Robinson, *To the Persons Working in the Dukinfield Old Mill* (1854); [H. Johnson, jnr], *Free Trade and Free Labour* (1854); cf. Howe, *Cotton Masters*, pp. 166–8 and bibliography. Manchester Central Library has extensive holdings in this literature.

fewer hours to the day' could permanently raise wages was one aspect of the 'strong prejudice against Political Economy' unfortunately lodged in the operatives' minds.[65]

The confused and localised battles over hours were perhaps overshadowed in contemporary opinion, and in subsequent historiography, by the set-piece industrial drama of the Preston strike and lock-out. Like the local short-time struggles, these wage movements involved a broad improvised organisation of weavers, card-room workers and others, convened through mass meetings around the slogan of 'ten per cent and no surrender' – an echo of 'ten hours and no surrender', or even 'the Charter and no surrender'.[66] Short-time committees often attempted to keep the hours issue distinct from wage or other demands, but the potential links were apparent. Many of the leaders in the 'ten per cent' struggle emerged from Chartist and short-time activity; one such figure, the Royton Chartist, J.B. Horsfall, argued in his journal *The Ten Hours Bill* that employers should not be allowed to take 'revenge' for the Ten Hours Act in the form of wage-cuts.[67] These links were never fully made, and it is arguable that one outcome of the conflicts of this period was a tendency to greater institutional separation of wage-bargaining, factory regulation and popular politics, establishing the framework for more manageable class relations. But, for beleaguered employers, strikes, state regulation, short-time agitation and populist local 'demagogues' were all forms of 'interference' with their authority, freedom of action and competitive viability. Orderly, institutional negotiation through the state or collective bargaining may then have appeared the least of several evils.

Confrontations over hours or wages can be seen as dramatic manifestations of underlying problems of managerial authority and industrial organisation affecting the large combined textile firm. The battle over hours began with the adoption of split shifts and other expedients in Ashton and Stalybridge, where such firms had rapidly expanded since the 1830s.[68] In general, hours played a more prominent part in conflicts over factory regulation in the cotton districts than in the West Riding. Cases about registration, certification and health and safety, extending over the period after the 1847 Act, and again affecting large combined enterprises, were more important in the woollen and worsted districts. Major worsted firms, including Crossley and Holdsworth (Halifax), Illingworth, Rand, Wade

---

[65] [Johnson], *Free Trade and Free Labour*, pp. iii, 5.
[66] Dutton and King, *Ten Per Cent*. Cf. Driver, *Tory Radical*, pp. 483, 487; F. Peel, *The Risings of the Luddites, Plugdrawers and Chartists* (3rd edn, 1895), p. 346, for other instances of the 'no surrender' slogan.
[67] *Ten Hours Bill*, June 1853, in HO 45/5128. Cf. Dutton and King, *Ten Per Cent*, ch. 3; Kirk, *Growth of Reformism*, pp. 247–53, for the nature of strike organisation and leadership.
[68] Kirk, *Growth of Reformism*, pp. 50–1.

, and Waud (Bradford), were involved.[69] Rand, a leading public advocate of factory reform, was convicted of a variety of offences relating to register-keeping, whitewashing the mill and meal-breaks; his partner or manager undertook to 'place the mill under proper management'.[70] There were also safety cases in Lancashire cotton firms; in Blackburn (like Bradford a town with a relatively high level of declared employer support for factory regulation), the prohibition of cleaning under self-acting mules while in motion gave rise to several cases. Safety regulations often provoked more unified employer opposition than other aspects of factory legislation, and, as the battle over hours died down in Lancashire, attention shifted to the 'fencing controversy' of the mid-1850s.[71] Safety regulations might raise sensitive issues of managerial practice. There were also wage-disputes and other difficulties, particularly affecting the weaving departments of large firms, in both cotton and worsted; these included several firms involved in factory act cases or other conflicts over regulation.[72]

A range of comment on the ambivalent and sensitive position of overlookers (semi-supervisory workers, often adult men in charge of women or juvenile production workers) provides one indication of underlying managerial problems. Both J. R. Stephens, in his detailed hostile commentaries on factory abuses, and W.R. Greg, in a moralised liberal defence of the rights of employers, emphasised the importance of the moral formation of overlookers.[73] As Stephens argued, in a characteristically flamboyant polemic:

bad masters have about them a number of cringing sycophants, lying lickspittles, and of your own class; but your worst foes . . . [W]e no more look for tenderness and sympathy toward the weak and the sickly under his power, than we should from the evil one himself . . . Who can hear of the virtuous daughters of honest and industrious people being, on every trifling ground or without any occasion for it, called every name that was ever applied to the most abandoned of their sex?[74]

The reported participation of overlookers in the short-time movement, on the other hand, was welcomed as a sign of their possible redemption.[75] At a Manchester meeting a resolution was adopted, citing the overlookers' responsibility 'for all matters and things in cotton mills' as justifica-

[69] See above, n. 25.   [70] *Bradford Observer*, 12 Feb. 1846.
[71] P.W.J. Bartrip and S.B. Burman, *The Wounded Soldiers of Industry: Industrial Compensation Policy, 1833–1897* (Oxford, 1985); Howe, *Cotton Masters*, pp. 188–9.
[72] Boyson, *Ashworth Cotton Enterprise*, p. 149; Dutton and King, 'The limits of paternalism', pp. 69–70 (Hopwood, Blackburn); Moore, 'Women, industrialisation and protest', pp. 173–4 (Waud, Bradford); and disputes over work-schedules at Stalybridge mentioned above, nn. 31, 39–41.
[73] *Ashton Chronicle*, e.g., 7 Oct. 1848; Greg, 'Employers and employed', pp. 298–9. Cf. Joyce, *Work, Society and Politics*, pp. 100–3, 338–9; Reynolds, *The Great Paternalist*, p. 289.
[74] *Ashton Chronicle*, 7 Oct. 1848.   [75] Ibid., 7 April 1849.

tion for their activity as 'loyal subjects' to uphold law.[76] In addition to suffering some of the economic insecurities of all factory labour,[77] overlookers must have borne the brunt of organising complicated and unpopular shift systems, with the added burden of liability for breaches of a law whose interpretation was in dispute. The loyalty of overlookers thus became a sensitive issue. A pamphleteering 'Stalybridge manufacturer' took particular exception to the calling of a short-time meeting for overlookers and managers in the town.[78]

There may therefore be grounds for seeing the short-time issue as one dimension of a wider crisis of employers' authority, to which the pamphlet literature by cotton masters (discussed above) was a defensive response. Trade unions, factory legislation or demagogic criticism of internal working arrangements constituted 'interferences' in the free and equal contract of employer and employed; there are frequent shifts in the language, from 'masters and men' to 'employers and employed' or 'labour and capital', a characteristic move in liberal arguments, with the implication of legal and moral equality. [79] Conversely, from rather different premises, critics like J.R. Stephens looked to the restoration of 'straitforward (*sic*), upright, manly dealing'.[80] This criticism is presented in a series of fictional dialogues, in which the master is brought to see the justice of his men's complaints: 'You must look into things more yourself, master, and not leave so much and entrust so much to these lickspittles and go-betweens'; truck and other grievances are the master's responsibility, not his overlooker's (a point of some relevance to the shifting of blame in factory act cases). Ill-judged and over-ambitious diversification, for which workers must carry the costs, is another significant item in the litany of complaints presented in this dialogue.[81]

Fictionalised dialogues of this kind construct a utopia of moral equality, mutual respect and fair dealing. Patrick Joyce has traced the embedding of such notions in the popular culture of the industrial north.[82] While the ostensible tone is often one of nostalgia, a reference back to the time when 'we all lived very homely', and the master in infancy was nursed by a worker's wife, this imaginary world signified active claims to fair treatment.[83] Both the aggressive economic liberalism of some

---

[76] *Manchester Guardian*, 21 March 1849; see also *Bolton Chronicle*, 21 April 1849.

[77] Johnstone, 'The standard of living of worsted workers', pp. 120–1, 143, 266, makes this point with reference to worsted overlookers; cotton overlookers require comparable attention.   [78] *Remarks on the Ten Hours Bill*, p. 1.

[79] See sources cited above, n. 64.   [80] *Ashton Chronicle*, 9 Dec. 1848.

[81] Ibid., 14 Oct. 1848.   [82] Joyce, *Visions of the People*.

[83] *Ashton Chronicle*, 14 Oct. 1848; my analysis here is indebted to Sonenscher's reading of the figure of the 'bon sans-culotte' in French artisanal culture: Sonenscher, 'The *sans-culottes* of the Year II'.

employers and the responses of Chartists or populist traditionalists took up the ground of manly independence and free and open dialogue and bargaining between 'masters' and 'men'. Liberal employers generally saw factory regulation, trade unions and other 'interference' as impeding this dialogue, while their opponents asserted the need for regulative frameworks to create the conditions for fair bargaining.

The factory question and the 'industrial nation'

Struggles over the standard working day constituted a platform for debates about employment relations in mechanised industry. Apart from any specific resolution of these issues, the process of debate itself marked an important moment. The industrial north came to be seen as a distinct regional social space, a *habitus* where employers and workers might co-exist, quarrel and cooperate at different times. Appeals to free and fair competition, manufacturing superiority based on technical progress and an industrious people, and a national interest in industrial prosperity were appropriated to different viewpoints. An emerging sense of industrial relations as a game that had to be played, with worthy and honourable opponents, formed part of this shared *habitus*. As in any such cultural construct, some definitions were privileged over others. It was the 'respectable dissent' of male trade unionists and potential citizens that was taken as the authorised representation of working-class interests.[84]

There were wider resonances, outside the industrial north, contributing to redefinitions of national identity. The struggle over the ten-hour day was one of a series of events, which realigned political and cultural attitudes in the later 1840s and early 1850s. A regulated factory system formed part of the image of orderly progress, counterposed to the cycles of revolution and reaction, and underlying social stagnation held to characterise 'other countries'.[85] For much contemporary opinion and subsequent historiography the 1847 Act symbolised a politics of social conciliation, complementing the repeal of the corn laws. As Robson has shown, the 1840s saw the gradual evolution of a modified liberal economic doctrine, combining corn law repeal with factory reform.[86] From metropolitan political perspectives, continuing disturbance in the factory districts and subsequent legislative responses were minor footnotes. Supporters of the ten-hours cause might themselves downplay this con-

---

[84] Rose, 'Respectable men'; for the notion of a *habitus* see P. Bourdieu, *The Field of Cultural Production* (London, 1993); Harper, *Picturing the Past*, p. 4.

[85] The phrase 'other countries' is from Dickens' *Our Mutual Friend*, as memorably adopted in E.P. Thompson, 'The Peculiarities of the English', in *The Poverty of Theory and Other Essays* (London, 1978), pp. 36–7.   [86] Robson, *On Higher than Commercial Grounds*.

tinuing battle, partly no doubt because of its divisive impact on the short-time movement. The well-known near-contemporary account of 'Alfred' (Samuel Kydd) ends on a celebratory note at 1847, enumerating the contributions of 'much of the energetic and philanthropic mind of the country', united across religious and party lines.[87] Factory legislation, like the anti-slavery movement at its peak, could symbolise the philanthropic enlightenment of a Christian nation.

Regulation of the factory work of protected categories was one touchstone of the 'paternal and providing state'.[88] Over-emphasis on 'Tory paternalism', counterposed to *laissez-faire* liberalism and Whig indolence and ineptitude, can be misleading. Factory reform, like other social issues, often cut across party lines. The 'conversion' of Whig politicians was part of the background to Fielden's parliamentary success in 1847. And it was Palmerston's firmness at the Home Office that put through the last strengthening measure in 1853.[89] Patrician disdain for manufacturers' lobbies may have played some part in this, as did links between Whig politicians and particular networks associated with social and moral reform; Palmerston had family links to Ashley, and shared Leonard Horner's Edinburgh University background.[90] Popular pressure, and continuing unrest in the factory districts – on which Horner was an assiduous commentator – inflected a spectrum of less immediately engaged opinion towards the *de facto* imposition of a standard working day.

This apparent settlement of the factory question had some relevance to articulations of national identity around the middle of the century. A number of factors made for a sharpening sense of national and ethnic difference during the 1840s.[91] The significance of anti-slavery for debates about industrial labour has been widely discussed, and I have touched on this issue in earlier chapters. Debates about post-Emancipation Caribbean society, the increasing prominence of India as a field for moral improvement and commercial expansion (not least for the cotton industry) and Irish 'problems' (both in Ireland and the perceived Irish presence in British towns and cities) all functioned as imaginary others for a white protestant British consciousness. The immunity of the balanced constitution, fortified by judicious doses of Whig reform, to the revolutionary fevers of 1848 gave rise to a rhetoric of national difference. This was linked to the theme of moral improvement, an industrious and thrifty

[87] 'Alfred', *Factory Movement*, 2 vols. (1857), vol. II, p. 289.
[88] Cf. Oakley, 'Utilitarian, paternalistic or both?'.
[89] D. Roberts, 'Lord Palmerston at the Home Office', *The Historian* 21 (1958–9).
[90] S. Collini, D. Winch and J. Burrow, *That Noble Science of Politics* (Cambridge, 1983), ch. 1.   [91] See Hall, *White, Male and Middle Class*, pt iii.

people and manufacturing superiority. The moral and physical qualities of the people were the key to a dynamic and expanding society, for example in Farre's commentary of the 1851 census occupation tables, with its mixture of functional social hierarchy (class I headed up by HM the Queen), political economy ('productive labour') and fantasised racial history (Vikings in boats, Anglo-Saxons on farms, Celts in the hills).[92]

The protracted debates about factory labour, and their symbolic settlement in the legislation of 1847–53, established an imagined industrial north as part of this expanding productive nation. These conceptions were then echoed in debates about factory regulation, at both parliamentary and local levels. As Macaulay argued, in his famous 'conversion' speech:

Never will I believe that what makes a population stronger, and healthier, and wiser, and better, can ultimately make it poorer ... If ever we are forced to yield the foremost place among commercial nations, we shall yield it, not to a race of degenerate dwarfs, but to some people preeminently vigorous in body and in mind.[93]

This keynote speech appropriated and transformed longstanding elements of short-time rhetoric. There are thus echoes of Cobbett's mockery of the idea that British supremacy might depend on '300,000 little girls in Lancashire' working long hours; as well as the Evangelical theme that what is morally wrong cannot be be truly advantageous.[94] Similar arguments are encountered in the appeals of local short-time committees, with a particular emphasis on 'the people' as 'the real movers of every thing that creates wealth, and maintains England in its proud pre-eminence amongst the nations of the earth', and an address to the 'spirit of SELF RELIANCE' which has underpinned the achievements of 'the Anglo-Saxon race'.[95]

Industrial dynamism was thus linked to the character of the English as a free people. This address was shared by employers and workers, and across a political spectrum defined by different varieties of protestant constitutionalism. It both unified and divided its implied publics. It formulated contentious demands on the part of those working-class men claiming a place in the popular political nation. If gendered and racial constructions of the freeborn Englishman provided ground for cross-class negotiation concerning factory regulation, and employment rela-

[92] Census of England and Wales, 1851, Report: Occupations of the People, PP 1852-3 LXXXVIII, pt i, pp. lxix–c.   [93] Quoted in Nardinelli, *Child Labor*, p. 23.
[94] Cobbett, quoted Nardinelli, *Child Labor*, p. 19; and see also, e.g., 'Alfred', *Factory Movement*, vol. I, pp. 272–4, for an example of Evangelical language.
[95] *To the Operatives of Stalybridge* (July 1853), *Men of Hyde and Newton* (June 1853): Cassidy Coll.

tions generally, this also provided a frame of reference for continuing conflict and debate. Divergent meanings could be attributed to the mutuality of interests within a properly regulated factory system, which figured so prominently in the rhetoric of 'mid-Victorian' social harmony. The nature of that harmony and the impact of factory regulation in the apparently more settled years after 1853 now require more detailed consideration.

8   A reformed factory system?

The apparent resolution of the factory question was often represented as part of a 'mid-Victorian' social settlement, also comprising free trade, Gladstonian finance and the wider acceptability of a reworked political economy.[1] A number of factors made for relative industrial stability, after the rapid expansion, violent fluctuation and stormy popular protest of the second quarter of the nineteenth century. As is often the case with such processes of social settlement (Keynesian policy and the 'welfare state' after 1945 is a more recent example) it is difficult to disentangle the effects of specific policies and institutions from the economic conditions with which they come to be symbolically linked. What is beyond doubt is that, in the general context of trends in the 1850s, the dying down of controversy over working hours helped implant the factory acts as symbols of better times.

This chapter examines constructions of stability and consensus in factory communities, and the contributions of state reform and employer initiatives. First, I consider some of the effects of legislation within the workplace. That legislation had important symbolic functions, standing for the mutual interests of enlightened government, responsible employers and the respectable working class. The second part of the chapter focuses on this imagery and its enactment on public ceremonial occasions in factory towns. Finally, I comment briefly on the extension of regulation to other sectors of industry and the projection of the textile factory as a model of the well-ordered and rational workplace.

The experience of work

During the third quarter of the nineteenth century textiles retained their significance as a major industrial sector, especially in the export economy, but were joined in this by engineering and the capital goods sector. There

---

[1] See esp. E.F. Biagini, *Liberty, Retrenchment and Reform: Popular Liberalism in the Age of Gladstone, 1860–1880* (Cambridge, 1992), chs. 2, 3; Joyce, *Work, Society and Politics*; Kirk, *Growth of Reformism*; Robson, *On Higher than Commercial Grounds*.

was continued and intensified mechanisation, but in the context of a more measured and less volatile secular growth. In cotton, output and employment continued to grow in the three decades after 1850 (interrupted by the serious setback of the 'cotton famine' of the 1860s), but the rate of expansion levelled off as compared to earlier decades; and this levelling off was more pronounced for output than for numbers employed.[2] The self-acting mule and the power-loom were applied to a widening range of yarns and fabrics. According to von Tunzelmann, this became viable, not just because of refinements to the machines concerned, but because more efficient steam-engines made it economical to run faster, and the rise in output offset the increased labour costs of repairing breakages to finer grades of work (for example piecing costs on the self-acting mule). Increased volume sustained profits in the face of lower margins of value added – a new way to pursue the old adage of 'a safe trade and small profits'.[3] Mechanisation and the factory system were consolidated in wool and worsted, particularly the latter. The worsted sector provided some of the leading examples of the large, integrated firm and high-profile employer 'paternalism', facilitated by the exploitation of leads in new technology and market niches in new fabrics. The more 'typical' firm in worsted, like its cotton counterpart, was a smaller unit competing to supply a range of standard products.[4]

One aspect of this greater stability was a restabilisation of gender divisions and of family forms adapted to waged work in factory industry. In part, this simply reflected a diminution of the extreme pressures on working-class family incomes in crisis years. However the celebrated rise in living standards was less marked than bland accounts of 'mid-Victorian prosperity' imply; initially, it probably owed more to greater regularity of employment than to improvements in earnings.[5] There was certainly no rapid shift to the male breadwinner as sole wage-earner, but it became easier to see him as the *principal* earner. Cotton mule spinning had been consolidated as a male occupation, with elements of skill and quasi-apprenticeship; this control was maintained, and possibly in some respects reinforced, on the growing numbers of self-acting machines.[6] In worsted, the decline of hand-labour in combing and weaving had passed its crisis, and the continued need for hand-workers in some grades of work or to supply sudden increases in demand made for a less cata-

[2] Calculated from figures in Kirk, *Growth of Reformism*, p. 89.
[3] Von Tunzelmann, *Steam-Power*; Stone, *Langshawe*, vol II, p. 6.
[4] J. Hodgson, *Textile Manufacture and Other Industries in Keighley* (1879); James, *History of the Worsted Manufacture*; Reynolds, *The Great Paternalist*.
[5] See Kirk, *Growth of Reformism*, ch. 3.
[6] Fowler and Wyke (eds.), *Barefoot Aristocrats*, pp. 52–3; Freifeld, 'Technological change'; Lazonick, 'Industrial relations'.

strophic process of transition than had been witnessed in the 1830s and 40s. Employment of diminished numbers of hand-workers, provision of allotments and in one case of pensions ensured the ancillary supply of labour, while projecting an image of employer benevolence.[7] At the same time, the incorporation of processes into the mill and the general expansion of the industry provided male skilled and supervisory jobs, within a heavily feminised work-force.[8]

In weaving, the transition to the factory had shifted the gender balance (though there had been women engaged in handloom weaving, and not necessarily just in conjunction with the rest of the household). Men employed in power-loom weaving tended to monopolise better paid kinds of work, and had access to a career ladder leading to various more specialised and supervisory jobs.[9]

Finally, it should be noted that the diversification associated with railways, engineering and the capital goods sector generally created male jobs at many places throughout the textile region, as did the process of urban development. Boys who left the mill in their teens might enter these sectors.[10] Patriarchal fears of the family turned upside down, which had been so important both to popular agitation and humanitarian concern, became less acute.

Factory legislation reinforced and consolidated these trends, though it certainly did not cause them. In the first place, it may have been a stimulus to further mechanisation; von Tunzelmann notes that investment in high pressure steam-engines coincided with the statutory shortening of hours after 1847 (though his analysis does ignore the protracted resistance to that shortening). As Marx argued, machinery was adopted to intensify labour and produce more in a shorter time: 'This occurs in two ways: the speed of the machines is increased, and the same worker receives a greater quantity of machinery to supervise or operate.'[11] Both these things can be seen happening from the late 1840s, with improved engines, higher running speeds and more looms or spindles per operative. This was largely a matter of the piecemeal adoption and fine-tuning of basic innovations made in the preceding decades (often through modifications to existing machinery *in situ*). '[W]hen the labour force benefited from a shorter working day (in 1847), it did so through even greater "intensification"'.[12]

[7] *The Fosters of Queensbury* (1884), pp. 17–18; *History of the Firm of James Akroyd & Son Ltd.* (1874), pp. 13–14; Hodgson, *Textile Manufacture*, p. 42.
[8] Reynolds, *The Great Paternalist*, pp. 289–95.   [9] Rose, *Limited Livelihoods*, ch. 7.
[10] See, e.g., *Autobiography of Thomas Wood, 1822–1880* (privately printed, 1956; copy in Keighley Reference Library).
[11] Von Tunzelmann, *Steam-Power*, pp. 216–25; Marx, *Capital vol. I*, ch. 15, 3 (c), p. 536 (quoted by von Tunzelmann from a different edition).   [12] Ibid., p. 225.

The burdens and rewards of that intensification were, as usual, unevenly distributed. As 'a factory woman' from Chorley wrote to the *Working Man's Friend*: 'Thank God for the Ten Hours Bill for such a woman as I!' Lack of time and energy and low pay nevertheless precluded the domestic ideal advocated by the magazine's columnist 'Lydia':

> [We] are not able to sit and work together, like Lydia and her husband. Indeed, as to sitting, there is but little of that in a factory, I can assure you; it is oftener *running*, for the machinery is so rapid in its motion that it turns out as much work now in the ten hours as it used to do in the twelve.[13]

The shorter hours were associated with tighter discipline and the driving of workers, often of women production workers by male overseers. Abram commented on the roughness of supervision and driving in the weaving-sheds, part of the price weavers paid for their high joint family earnings in good times.[14] There are similar comments on driving at mills in Royton, a former 'jacobin village' near Oldham; here, the hands had lost their 'outs', 'when the males can ramble in the fields, view the beauties of nature, and recruit their exhausted strength; and the females can walk home to superintend the preparation of the forthcoming meal'.[15] Employers insisted on their money's worth from a shorter working day.

The process of implementing regulation helped define and consolidate employers' authority, often with some ambivalence and reluctance to accept the responsibilities involved. The keeping of registers and time-books – part of the 'regulatory burden' of which employers incessantly complained – systematised managerial practices. The juridical definition of a 'factory' (a matter which had led to quibbles in some cases) constituted the workplace as a bounded space. 'If the building stands separately, and the only entrance door opens into a road or street, then the building itself is considered the Factory: but if it stands in a yard . . . then all the premises within the gates are parts of the Factory'; an employed person was one doing 'any kind of work whatsoever within the entrance walls of any factory, whether for or without wages'.[16] Time, as well as

---

[13] *The Working Man's Friend and Family Instructor*, 13 April 1850, pp. 53–4.
[14] W.A. Abram, 'Social condition and political prospects of the Lancashire workmen', *Fortnightly Review* new ser. 4 (1868), pp. 431–2.
[15] J.B. Horsfall, *Royton: Its Associations for Mental Improvement, its Self-educated Men &c.* (1854), pp. 4–5: copy in Oldham Reference Library; and see earlier comments on the persistence of 'outs', J. Broadbent, Waterhead Mill, J. Potter, Werneth, in survey of piecers' distances (1844), Ashworth Papers, Lancs. RO, box labelled 'Factory Act Returns'.
[16] R. Baker, *The Factory Acts Made Easy* (1851), pp. 34, 36. Cf. H. Lefebvre, *The Production of Space*, trans. D. Nicholson-Smith (Oxford and Cambridge, Mass., 1991)

space, was legally defined; mills in a locality had to take their time from a single designated public clock (often the railway clock).[17]

If employers were subjected to certain restrictions by legislative requirements, they also found managerial authority thrust upon them. John Brigg and Co. (Keighley) asked the inspector to endorse their management appointments, with a declaration to be signed by the appointees accepting responsibility for compliance with the factory acts in their departments; the inspector refused to involve himself, as 'we have no authority to confirm or disallow any arrangements you may make with your own men'. Other items in the same collection include a mill time-book for the late 1830s and early 1840s, which gives a rare glimpse of the routine practice of factory regulation. It shows holidays for 'old Christmas' (the 6th of January), local fairs, and three days' closure during the strikes of August 1842, duly recorded as a holiday given because of 'rioting'.[18] There are also used and marked copies of the acts themselves and of Robert Baker's widely circulated guides to them. The pressure to regularise management and work-practices provided a framework for the elaboration of a practical culture of work, attuned to the ways of mill life, symbolised above all in the divisions of the normal working day. The acculturation of both managers (who might also be owners, or members of the owner's family) and workers was a precondition for such developments as the 'Oldham Limiteds', but also for the proliferation of the average, competitive small to medium-sized mill.[19]

Finally, it is important to note the impact of regulation and more formal management structures on gender and age divisions. Age restrictions and the associated educational requirements implied a particular model of the life-cycle, and of regularised transitions from schooling to waged work. Periodic waves of concern and public debate also encouraged more systematic job segregation within the workplace. Discussions of labour requirements and the supposed aptitudes of particular categories of worker must have reacted back on employers' own perceptions of the optimal work-force.[20] Quite apart from legislative requirements, the terms of debate empowered adult men in the renegotiation of the division of labour. That debate both foregrounded women workers as an object of moral concern, and rendered them all but invisible in the resulting legislation. Restrictions were extended to adult women by the 1844

[17] Brigg & Co., correspondence with factory inspector, May 1859, box labelled 'Factory Act', Keighley Reference Library: I am much indebted to Mr I. Dewhirst for showing me this. [18] 'Factory Act', Keighley Library.
[19] Farnie, *Cotton Industry*, pt iii; and see H. Catling, *The Self-Acting Mule* (Newton Abbot, 1970), pp. 149–78, for a graphic account of working practices.
[20] See, e.g., employer questionnaires, Factory Comm., Supp, Report, pt ii.

Act, following an orchestrated campaign in line with parallel developments at that time (including the Children's Employment Commission
and the Mines Act). However reference to women is confined to a perfunctory stipulation that they were henceforth 'to be employed as young
persons'; other clauses of the Act, and subsequent acts (including the Ten
Hours Act of 1847) refer simply to 'young persons', now deemed to
include women.[21] In Baker's handbook on the acts there is a characteristic slippage, between the universal male juridical person ('he') and
female names in the examples given of the various certificates and registers. Protected workers connote femininity.[22]

The effect was not of course to exclude women or girls from factory
employment, but to regulate their participation and probably to reinforce
preexisting patterns of job segregation and exclusions from specific processes. The interpretation placed on accident clauses helped consolidate
male control of machine maintenance and thus of some of the best-paid
and most secure jobs in the mill hierarchy.[23] While the general emphasis
on moral control and segregation encouraged 'responsible' employers in
this direction – though not to the extent of putting women in charge of
female work-areas. Denunciations of the evils of married women's work
led to bans in some mills, often those owned by high-profile 'industrial
paternalists'.[24]

Gendered concerns with moral control extended from the workplace to
the community and constructions of a reformed working-class family.
Ten-hours propaganda itself placed increasing emphasis on the respectable and rational use of the time gained – rational recreation and self-
improvement for men, domestic duties for women.[25] Addressing a
celebration of the successful Ten Hours Bill, Ashley drew attention to the
'use which might be made of this leisure for the moral improvement of the
factory people, and especially the female workers'.[26] The Bolton Factory
Workers' Bazaar, again a celebration of the shorter day, displayed 'evidence of nimble fingers, clear heads, or persevering minds'.[27]

The effects of factory legislation are to be found in this symbolic realm,
as well as in the impact of specific legal requirements. This public symbolism associated the factory acts with improvement, class conciliation and
the moralisation of employment relations. There is some evidence that
this in practice meant tighter time-keeping and intensified effort, as well

[21] 7 & 8 Vict., c.14; cf. Robson, *On Higher than Commercial Grounds*, pp. 173–5.
[22] Baker, *Factory Acts*, e.g. pp. 8, 85–6, 116.
[23] Gray, 'Factory legislation', pp. 70–2.   [24] Rose, *Limited Livelihoods*, pp. 45–7.
[25] See, e.g., *The Ten Hours Advocate* (1846–7), *passim*; Ginswick (ed.), *Labour and the Poor*,
     vol. I, pp. 117–9.   [26] Quoted in Grant, *Factory Legislation*, p. 137.
[27] *Bolton Factory Workers Exhibition and Bazaar* (1852), p. 4.

as greater stability of employment and halting and uneven increases in earnings. The meaning of short time shifted from the radical political economy of self-regulation endorsed by law. Instead there was a bureaucratic model of enforcement, though necessarily a negotiated one in practice, and a strengthening of the responsibility and authority of employers. Annual outings (sometimes days off with pay) replaced the 'outs' which had interrupted a longer working day. The widespread communal celebration of reciprocal good feeling symbolised in the factory acts may well have silenced those who bore more of the costs and shared fewer of the rewards of producing more in a shorter time. Many women were excluded in this way, and Sonya Rose has drawn attention to their rebelliousness as a source of potential disruption of the mid-Victorian settlement. As she points out, the language of institutionalised negotiation established industrial relations as a masculine domain, even when those supposedly represented were women.[28] Like wage-bargaining, factory reform was inscribed in this public sphere.

Rituals of reconciliation

Acceptance of factory legislation figured in the rhetoric of progress and improvement, celebrated in the civic public spaces of the Victorian industrial town.[29] This was initially a rather nervous shifting, from the register of ongoing polemic to that of mutual congratulation. For short-time activists, celebration of the gains made was also a matter of vigilance in their defence. Philip Grant described the Ten Hours Act as a 'charter of liberties'.[30] As has been emphasised in the previous chapter, the hours question remained unsettled into the 1850s, with complicated tactical divisions in the short-time movement itself, as well as employer resistance and political manoeuvring. Speaking at the Bolton Bazaar, canon Slade (a close ally of the Tory Bollings, who had long resisted factory regulation) was careful to place the event in a context of uncontroversial improvement and philanthropy. 'I consider that we are assembled for the purpose of profiting as much as may be from that [ten-hours] measure. Whether I approved of it or not, I should deem it my bounden duty to do my utmost to carry it out in the most advantageous and efficient manner.'[31]

From the 1860s, the factory agitation could be evoked in the framework of a blander, consensual public rhetoric, whose volume mounted with the extension of the franchise to many working-class men. The

[28] Rose, 'Respectable men'.
[29] For the construction of civic space see esp. Vernon, *Politics and the People*; Pearson, 'Knowing one's place'.   [30] Grant, *Factory Legislation*, p. 5.
[31] J.A. Atkinson, *A Memoir of the Rev. Canon Slade* (1892), pp. 146–7.

popular, but still rather controversial, figure of Richard Oastler was incorporated. In a compilation of 1868 in aid of the new Leeds Infirmary Oastler is remembered among the *Eminent Men of Leeds*; the very next entry is devoted to Sir George Goodman, first mayor under the reformed municipality in the 1830s, and the target at that time of one of Oastler's inimitable polemics.[32] Both presumably qualified as local worthies, striving to do good according to their lights. This assimilation of Oastler to a civic pantheon culminated in his memorial at Bradford, the town where 'he donned his armour, and . . . went forth on his crusade'. The commissioning of the statue and other arrangements were superintended by a committee of Oastler's old associates (notably Matthew Balme, the Bradford Sunday school teacher and ten-hours activist), together with colonel (of Volunteers) Edward Akroyd, a more recent convert to the cause.[33]

The statue shows Oastler with two factory children, 'the boy in corduroys and smock, the girl in striped dress with pinafore in front, and both wear Yorkshire clogs'. The boy was looking down 'in modest attitude' (or, according to the *Illustrated London News*, 'rather shamefaced and modest attitude'), while the girl 'looks up to him who is their protector and advocate'.[34] W. E. Forster visited the sculptor's studio and wrote to Balme:

If I could find any fault it was with the children that they were too healthy looking – rather like what Oastler & his fellow-workers have made Bradford mill-children than what they were when he struggled for them – but it is too much to expect of a sculptor that he would not make his figures as good looking as in him lies.[35]

The unveiling attracted a large crowd, with a procession headed by 'factory children, young persons and general operatives', followed by workers from various mills, others grouped by occupation or trade (some probably trade unions), friendly societies and contingents from other places (including one from Keighley carrying a 'relic of the old fight', in the shape of the remains of a banner carried at the York county meeting of 1832).[36] Speakers at the ceremony and a subsequent dinner included Shaftesbury and inspector Baker. The latter alluded to 'the merry faces, the well-dressed lasses, and the appearance of comfort', which he attributed to the success of factory legislation. The commemoration was however framed by references to the 'excessive vehemence' of Oastler's

---

[32] *Memoirs of Eminent Men of Leeds* (1868), pp. 54–61; cf. R. Oastler, *The Unjust Judge* (1836).   [33] *Bradford Observer*, 15 May 1869.
[34] Ibid., 17 May 1869; *Illustrated London News*, 15 May 1869.
[35] Forster to Balme, 7 Dec. 1867, Balme Coll., Bradford Archives.
[36] *Bradford Observer*, 15, 17 May 1869.

language; sending apologies for absence, Akroyd noted his own opposition at the time to the ten-hours movement, and Oastler's latter-day
regret for 'expressions of personal hostility towards his opponents'. Now,
however, these differences had been set aside and 'throughout the whole
of the factory districts there is one universal feeling of respect and gratitude to the memory of a great and good man'. A more overt note of controversy was introduced by an apparently abrasive speech by Edward
Miall (now radical MP for the town) and comments in response by
Shaftesbury, questioning Miall's sincerity, while praising that of his less
radical partner as MP for Bradford, W. E. Forster. After some cheering
and heckling Shaftesbury 'abandoned this line of remark'.[37]

Both the language of mutual self-congratulation and the occasional
notes of controversy recur in the civic and work-related ceremonies that
defined the position of the employer as social leader. In Bradford, the
practice of works outings seems to have become established in the context
of shorter hours and the worsted boom which accompanied their introduction.[38] More stable industrial conditions gave increased scope for
such gestures and also employer support for schools, churches and other
community facilities. Periodic and eventually routine displays of collective gratitude could be readily interpreted in a reassuring framework of
paternalism and deference. Where employer initiatives were linked to
housing provision (as at Akroyd's Halifax mill communities, Mason's
Oxford Mills in Ashton, Saltaire, the major Blackburn employers and
several others) it could produce the image of 'a community to themselves
... under the eye of the employer'.[39] This image, reassuring as it may have
been, does not encapsulate the complexity of employment and community.

Employers' social and cultural leadership was constructed across a
number of spheres, which might fit awkwardly together. It was fundamentally conditioned by economic calculation, as commentators like W.
R. Greg had insisted in the controversies of the 1840s.[40] Referring to the
splendid new Sunday School at Ashton (to which he had been a prominent contributor), Hugh Mason computed the risk he ran by keeping his
mills open during the cotton famine at 'two or three schools such as
ours'.[41]

Housing development on pieces of land not required for industrial
plant was a widespread form of investment, by small as well as big
employers. This came to be more strongly projected in terms of enlight-

---

[37] Ibid.   [38] Koditschek, *Class Formation*, pp. 424–5.
[39] [D. Power], *On the Responsibilities of Employers* (1849), p. 53.
[40] See above, chapter 4.   [41] Rogers, *Autobiography*, p. 116.

ened management by certain high-profile 'paternalists'.[42] Given this economic framework, employers varied in the attention paid to building
standards and the management of housing; this did make some difference
at the margins, and marginal improvements in conditions could be very
important to working-class people. (There might also be more or less
coherent attempts to give the development a recognisable architectural
identity, as in Akroyd's leaning to gothic.) In the best-known cases the
houses seem to have been of somewhat better standard at higher rents
than comparable housing otherwise available to workers; they were occupied by a core labour-force of skilled and supervisory workers and the
regularly employed.[43] A number of factors must qualify the image of the
cohesive factory village 'under the eye of the employer'. Dealings with
working-class tenants required sensitive management; any hint of truck,
tied cottages or overt dictation of religious or political behaviour could
undermine the reputation of the fair employer. Moreover the fit between
available housing and the labour requirements of the mill was rarely
precise; while demographic turnover meant that the working population
was, by definition, a shifting one.

Similar considerations affected employer activities in the religious and
educational fields. Here again, the relevant community of support might
overlap, but not coincide with the work-force. In the Dissenting tradition
in particular, the emphasis on conscience, inner conviction and voluntary
assent were in some tension with any employer-led conformism, however
much adherence may in practice have been a matter of family background, peer-group pressure and worldly convenience. Large employers
often provided facilities for persuasions they did not share, or even provided the chapel premises but left the choice of denomination to the
workers. W. A. Abram (admittedly a Liberal source) alleged that religious
and political discrimination (among varieties of protestantism: catholics
were another matter) was a characteristic of Anglican more than
Nonconformist masters.[44] Recognition of the contributions of leading
employers might come from their co-religionists, rather than their
workers as such. In Abram's Blackburn, the opening of the Park Place
Schools by Pilkington, a leading Congregationalist employer, was marked

[42] The following comments are based on S.M. Gaskell, 'Housing estate development,
1840–1918, with particular reference to the Pennine towns', PhD, University of
Sheffield, 1974; L.D.W. Smith, 'Textile factory settlements in the early industrial revolution', PhD, University of Aston, 1976.
[43] See O. Ashmore and T. Bolton, 'Hugh Mason and the Oxford mills and community',
Transactions of the Lancashire and Cheshire Antiquarian Society 78 (1975); Reynolds, *The
Great Paternalist*, ch. 6.
[44] Abram, 'Social condition of the Lancashire workmen', p. 438; cf. Reynolds, *The Great
Paternalist*, pp. 306–7; Rose, *The Gregs*, pp. 26–7.

by the presentation of an inscribed silver trowel from the teachers, 'as a token of respect for the kindness of himself and brothers in erecting that splendid building'; some years later Mrs Pilkington was presented with yet another trowel, by the Reverend Fraser, 'as the representative of the congregation assembling in Chapel-street Chapel, and more especially . . . the teachers and scholars'.[45] The foundation of Congregational churches at Ryecroft, Ashton (serving Mason's Oxford Mills colony) and Stalybridge reflected initiatives within the parent congregation at Ashton (Sunday School teachers being a key group of activists); the big millowners who underwrote the finances, appearing as trustees rather than deacons, retained their membership in the central Albion Chapel.[46]

The penumbra of activities that surrounded Nonconformist congregations, especially their schools, established themselves as popular institutions, symbols of collective self-help as well as employer philanthropy or 'social control'. Marking the Jubilee celebrations of Stalybridge Sunday School, as well as of the monarch, Samuel Laycock connected the school with the progress of the town ('our Stalybridge friends are not lagging behind') and reminded the young of the struggles of the past:

> Have you thought of these hardships, denials, and strife
> Ye who think easy births the great objects of life?[47]

This may be Victorian occasional verse of a banal moralising kind (and by no means Laycock's best work), but it probably did speak to its public. Laying the foundation stone of Albion Sunday Schools (claimed to be the biggest, best and most modern in the country), Hugh Mason applauded the donations of 'all classes', from the scholar's pennies, to the '£5 of the self-actor minder', to the three-figure sums of his own class. '[W]e have subscribed voluntarily, freely, liberally . . . another triumph of the voluntary principle (cheers).' Mason was followed by Guinness Rogers, the minister, who linked the growth of religious independency to the progress of the town 'now peopled by tens of thousands of intelligent and industrious workers', thanks to 'the power of steam, that mighty agent in our modern civilisation'.[48]

Sunday School teaching was important in opening new roles and widened cultural possibilities for women of all classes (including employers' wives and daughters) and working-class men (like Samuel Laycock).

---

[45] *Blackburn Standard*, 8 Jan. 1851, 27 Aug. 1859.
[46] Material on Congregational churches in Tameside Local Studies Library, esp. : *Half a Century of Independency in Ashton-under-Lyne* (1867); D.S. Johns and A. McCulloch, *The Congregational Church, Stalybridge, 1831–1931* (1931); *Ryecroft Independent Chapel Manual* (1867).   [47] Laycock, *Warblins fro' an Owd Songster*, p. 335.
[48] *Ashton Reporter*, 30 March 1861.

Mason opened his speech by referring to the part played by his wife and advocating a more public profile for such women – especially since titled ladies appeared in public to launch warships with 'barbarous names'. This makes a neat counterpart to another speech by Mason at this time; opening the reading-rooms attached to the mills he emphasised that few of the households in his 'colony' had wives employed outside the home: 'the place of the mother was at home . . . (hear, hear)'.[49] Philanthropy was a proper sphere for women; waged work was not.

Anglican employers faced a different set of institutional mediations, with greater powers of patronage but the need to negotiate these through an ecclesiatical hierarchy. Edward Akroyd built a splendid gothic church overlooking one of his factories at Haley Hill, Halifax. 'In chosing this position, the founder sought to impress upon the workpeople in their daily avocations the aspect of a temple to the living God.'[50] Akroyd had sought permission for a family side-chapel, without the customary condition of continued residence in the parish; this was refused, on the grounds that 'at the present day this will not do'.[51] At Queensbury, previously a 'hotbed and stronghold of Chartism and Infidelity', a church had been built in 1845, with financial support from Foster, whose Black Dyke Mills dominated the village.[52] In 1857 the factory inspector (Redgrave) became involved in easing out the incumbent, who had apparently allowed the school to fall into neglect and misappropriated funds intended for books, a state of affairs, as Redgrave put it, 'hampering to yourself and others on the Bench who are anxious to help the Clergyman in doing good'. The matter was to drag on for about two years.[53]

There was thus no straightforward overlap between employers' economic power, influence over their workers and civic philanthropy, though a closer fit may have been attempted by Anglicans than their Nonconformist counterparts. There may however have been sufficient cohesion to sustain the desired image in relevant contexts. Employers' reputations for fairness and benevolence figured particularly in electoral politics, where they were however always open to polemical challenge.[54] Akroyd's reputation was assiduously mobilised when he stood at Huddersfield in 1857. Of his workers, 3,000 were said to have signed a loyal address, conveyed to Huddersfield by a deputation, enumerating the

---

[49] Ibid., 31 March 1861.   [50] *James Akroyd & Son Ltd.*, p. 35.
[51] Legal correspondence regarding church at Haley Hill, Leeds Archives RD/AF/2/3/14.
[52] *Memorial of Church of the Holy Trinity, Queensbury, 1845–1945* (1945), copy in Foster Papers, Brotherton Library, University of Leeds.
[53] Correspondence with factory inspector Redgrave, 3 Sept., 23 Dec. 1857, 23 July 1859, Foster Papers, box 111.107, 161, 445.
[54] See Joyce, *Work Society and Politics*; and cf. Vernon, *Politics and the People*, pp. 270–2.

Plate 4 Stalybridge Congregational Sunday School, c. 1862

benefits he had provided and expressing confidence that 'the zeal which you have always displayed in promoting our comfort and welfare, will be extended for the benefit and prosperity of the Nation at large'.[55] Challenged on his attitude to factory reform, Akroyd declared that he never worked after 6.00 p.m. and expressed support for legislation 'to protect the young and the women, those who were not able to protect themselves'; however 'the stalwart honest faces and bold manly figures before me' were able to protect themselves. Akroyd's questioner agreed that he had 'come forward like a gentleman . . . he has answered the questions manfully and is worthy of our respect. (Loud cheers)'.[56]

The ritual of loyal addresses, workers' support at the hustings and pulling the candidate's carriage home in triumph seems to fit a pattern of deferential 'factory politics'.[57] However this does not necessarily overlap the mill community; Akroyd stood at Huddersfield, not the already rather crowded political space of his own Halifax industrial base. Activities as a fair employer formed part of a reputation mobilised in electoral politics, rather than necessarily a direct basis of political power.

The language of deference and gratitude mobilised in politics replicates that of more routine occasions, more closely linked to the workplace and the immediate community: factory outings, the opening of community buildings, events in the employer's family. Expressing gratitude for a works outing (a new feature in 1849) workers at one Bradford firm hoped 'that their benevolent employers may be long spared to enjoy health, prosperity and wealth'.[58] Such addresses might be expensively written on vellum and accompanied by symbolic gifts, like the silver cup and salver presented by workers from Hopwood's Blackburn mills in acknowledgment of a works trip; these artifacts were 'much esteemed at the time, and . . . now most highly prized by the family'.[59]

Occasions like this provide important evidence in the continuing debate on 'paternalism'. What do they represent, how are they to be decoded? They were, first, episodes of ritual exchange. The workers' symbolic gift – which, given the cost of the artifacts presented, was also a real gift from their point of view – reaffirmed their independence. Like any gift, these presentations were also a claim on the recipient, just as the employer's benevolent conduct was a claim on workers' loyalty. The language of deference was a language of negotiation. Thanks for past benev-

[55] *Which of the Candidates is Most Worthy of the Support of Working Men?* (21 March 1857), election broadside, Kirklees Archives.
[56] *Huddersfield Chronicle*, 21 March 1857; and cf. *Huddersfield Examiner*, same date, for less sympathetic account of Akroyd.   [57] Cf. Joyce, *Work, Society and Politics*.
[58] *Bradford Observer*, 6 Sept. 1849.
[59] *Blackburn Standard*, 22 Feb. 1860, obituary of Robert Hopwood.

Plate 5 Edward Akroyd, founding of all Souls Church, Halifax

olence represented a claim for its continuance. The retirement of a long-serving manager at Dean Mills, near Bolton, gave occasion for an address praising his fairness and respect for workers' moral independence: 'When Sunday came every one knew that he was entirely his own master – he might go to what place of worship he thought proper without incurring the frown of his manager.'[60] 'He' might of course have gone to no place of worship at all, but the sensible manager was not to know, or to pretend not to know, about that. Events in the employer family were particularly significant occasions for treats and loyal addresses. Visiting the north Wales retirement home of Oldham Whittaker (of Hurst Mill, near Ashton), his former employees expressed the hope that the son would follow in the path of his father, 'so that they would feel as proud of the son as they did of the father'. In reply, Whittaker alluded to the slogan on one of the banners, 'our interests are one', and to the looming cotton famine: 'both should be prepared, in time of depression, to make sacrifices', just as the preceding prosperity had been shared.[61]

Secondly, it is important to understand these occasions as performances, generally of a highly structured kind, inscribed in the spaces of organised leisure. As in any performance, there might be more or less genuine enthusiasm. The difference made by a competent and decent boss, or simply by grudging affection based on longstanding association, should not be entirely discounted; but the language of publicly displayed gratitude was too widespread and standardised to reflect such individual circumstances. The state of mind of the participants was not necessarily the main point, provided they knew the script and were prepared to speak it. Moreover that script was by no means exceptionally 'deferential', as compared to the language routinely expected of applicants for employment, charitable aid or other favours.[62] The language of loyal addresses shows affinities to that of 'respectable dissent', in Rose's apt phrase, the gentlemanly, rational negotiation apparent in wage-bargaining and popular politics in this period.[63] It constituted a ritual reminder, materialised in the silverware and vellum scrolls, of a set of expectations, conditioned by economic insecurity and asymmetries of power. The symbolic investment in events in the employer's family deserves attention. At one level this reflects the widespread rhetorical appeal to 'family', as an area of experiences and feelings shared by decent people of all classes, and as a metaphor for moralised authority softened by mutual affection. But there

[60] 'Testimonial on retirement of Mr Wilkinson', 5 May 1860, Haggas Bryan Coll., Bolton Archives, ZHB/1/13.   [61] *Ashton Reporter*, 24 Aug. 1861.
[62] See, e.g., model letters in *The Lady's Letter Writer* (Warne's Useful Books, 187?).
[63] Rose, 'Respectable men'.

is also a specific industrial dimension, representing an imagined stability in the face of economic fluctuations, and more specifically the vulnerability of the family firm to succession crises.

Paternalism and deference may appear as striking features of employment relations, relative to more recent periods, or to earlier moments of Chartist insurgency. This was however a qualified paternalism, by comparison with other frequently cited instances. Burawoy for example suggests that a generalised model of paternalism can be applied to large firms in Lancashire, while 'market despotism' is applicable to smaller firms.[64] But these categories oversimplify a more complex range; elements of both paternalism and market despotism were present at all levels. They were however tempered by other features of the industrial culture, embodying the outcomes of conflicts in the first half of the nineteenth century. This included the settlement of working hours and some degree of collective bargaining. Despite the defeat of the Preston lockout, something like standard district wage-rates gradually achieved recognition. Ideas of fair employment were conditioned by this context. Industrial paternalism has some relevance as a feature of employers' perspectives, and of a reassuring image projected to elite opinion. In a fuller account of the social relations and practices in which that image was necessarily embedded, it may be more useful to think of attempts at social and cultural leadership, upheld on certain formal and increasingly ritualised occasions.

Factory act extension

The chorus of public recantations by former opponents of legislation, and mutual self-congratulation on the progress achieved accompanied a series of moves to extend the scope of the factory acts. This had been an aspect of the debate from the early 1830s, with the use of comparative arguments by some leading employers, factory commissioners and their associates.[65] On one hand, this asserted the injustice of focusing on textile factories as peculiarly in need of intervention; on the other, the very possibility of regulating concentrated sites of employment helped project the factory as an enlightened and benign system.

This logic was taken up by Edward Akroyd at the 1857 Social Science Congress. Arguing that the singling out of textile mills had been unjust, Akroyd nevertheless eulogised the effects of legislation, even acknowledg-

---

[64] Burawoy, *Politics of Production*, ch. 2; see also Bendix, *Work and Authority*; D. Reid, 'Schools and the paternalist project at Le Creusot, 1850–1914', *Journal of Social History* 27 (1993)   [65] See above, chapter 3.

ing the 'philanthropic zeal and powerful eloquence' of Sadler and Oastler and the determined stance of the operatives themselves. Akroyd's theme was the educational progress achieved by the factory acts, which he wanted to see extended to 'all classes of work-children throughout the kingdom', so as to secure an 'educated race of operatives' in a competitive world. In this extension of the schooling provisions of the acts 'frivolous and vexatious' regulations were to be avoided. Like so much reform rhetoric, this was an exhortation to voluntary endeavour by enlightened employers, such as those of Birmingham where Akroyd was speaking, as much as a call for any specific legislation. 'Let the various classes of employers . . . enter upon a glorious rivalry, which shall most successfully promote the sound education, the welfare, and the happiness of the work-people.'[66]

Debates about extension initially focused, not on Akroyd's call to regulate all children employed outside the home, but on specific industries. These included bleaching and lacemaking (1860, 1861), whose close linkages to textiles put them high on the agenda; various other trades (including percussion cap manufacture, potteries, lucifer match-making, paper-staining and fustian-cutting) were regulated by the 1864 Act, either because they were regarded as particularly dangerous to health and morals, or because of petitioning from employers and workers. General extension, to most major industries and all premises with more than fifty employed, followed in 1867.[67] All these measures excluded processes carried on in private dwellings, while extending regulation to a wider range of formally defined workplaces. The earlier measures applied to textiles provided a general model for this legislation, but with important modifications and exemptions, particularly provisions in several trades to de-regulate male hours at age sixteen. Arguments for extension generally took the form of enquiries into the numbers of women and children employed, the state of education, health and morals, and the possibilities of more regular working and improved machinery. Counter-arguments emphasised the peculiarities of the trade, market conditions and the threat of undercutting by foreign competitors or by sectors outside the scope of regulation, especially where domestic manufacture co-existed with factory production.

There was protracted controversy in bleaching. The ten-hour day for bleachworks was raised at a short-time meeting in Bolton in 1850 by

---

[66] E. Akroyd, MP, 'On factory education and its extension', *Transactions of the National Association for the Promotion of Social Science* 1 (1857), pp. 151–64.

[67] See Hutchins and Harrison, *History of Factory Legislation*, chs. 7, 8; 'Tabular analysis of varieties of the existing factory acts', Royal Commission on Factory and Workshop Acts, PP 1876 XXIX, appendix H, pp. 213–17, provides a useful summary.

William Milton, Anglican incumbent of St Paul's, a church closely associated with Ainsworth's bleachworks at Haliwell. He was supported by the merchant-manufacturer Robert Heywood, who was anxious to refute the charge of 'having humanity at a small cost, in as much as he had no factory and would not be affected'. In reply, J. H. Ainsworth (who was among the local notables supporting the ten-hour movement for factories) argued that the 'peculiarities' of the trade were 'such as almost to prevent employers from being their own masters, and therefore from controlling the hours of labour'. The matter was then dropped, on a point of order.[68] Milton's public criticism of conditions in bleaching was one of several quarrels with his patron, and he was forced to resign at about this time, accusing Ainsworth of despotic behaviour: 'a new thing that a poor parish priest should resist a power hitherto popularly supposed . . . to be irresistible'. Ainsworth claimed that it was liturgical irregularities and Milton's difficult personality that had led to the breach; at any rate he advertised for a successor 'whose doctrines are Evangelical, and in accordance with the plain teaching of the Catechism on the subject of baptism'.[69]

Whatever the reasons for this incident, Ainsworth was certainly active in organising the bleachers' lobby, briefing witnesses to refute the statements of his former parish priest.[70] The bleachworks' proprietors constituted a fairly tight grouping of employers, probably engaged in oligopolistic competition, and their lobby was effective in delaying regulation.[71] Debate centred on the relations between bleachers and merchants, the bleachers arguing that as 'servants of the public' (i.e. merchants) they were obliged to work irregular hours to meet orders at short notice. Against this, commissioner Tremenheere represented legislation as a salutary stimulus to more rational commercial and managerial practices. The merchants themselves claimed they could adjust to longer order times; work might be lost to the particular bleacher, but not to the Lancashire trade. As one Manchester spinner and commission agent put it: 'Taking it for granted (as the spinners and manufacturers do not complain) that the Factory Act works well . . . I do not know any sufficient reason why the same principle should not regulate bleach, finish and dye works'; regular hours and day-work made stricter management possible, 'instead of, as now, the operatives playing often in the day, and then working during the night'.[72] Tremenheere's enquiry took place in 1854,

[68] *Bolton Chronicle*, 9 March 1850.
[69] Press-cuttings, filed with visitation return for St Paul's, Haliwell, Rushton Collections, Manchester Archives, F942.72.R.121, vol. 22, p. 43.
[70] Correspondence in Ainsworth Papers, Bolton Archives, ZAH/3/2.76–80.
[71] Howe, *Cotton Masters*, pp. 17–8, 190–2.
[72] Bleachworks Commission, PP 1854–5 XVIII, pp. vi, viii–x, 36–7.

when the outcome of the factory question was in fact still rather less certain than these comments would suggest; the controversy about fencing machinery also contributed to an anti-regulation backlash.[73] At any rate, the bleaching masters' lobby won the parliamentary votes, even if they lost the arguments, and legislation was delayed until 1860.

Tremenheere also conducted the enquiry into laceworks. Here the desirability of legislation was held to have been established by the Children's Employment Commission of the 1840s, but had to be balanced against the extent of mechanisation and the difficulty of regulating out-work. In the context of the 1830s and 40s, the exposure of this evil and the impossibility of doing anything about it could be adduced as another example of the superiority of the factory; lace-runners figured in a stock list of juvenile and female employments worse than factory work.[74] By 1861 the further progress of machinery made regulation feasible, but the benefits had to be carefully balanced against the difficulties and costs. 'That caution is imperatively demanded in dealing with this question will be evident from the amount of capital invested in the lace manufacture . . . and from the competition with foreign countries to which the trade is exposed.'[75] Here again there is the familiar link between more regular working, machinery and tighter discipline. Time spent waiting to change the bobbins could be reduced by installing extra sets of bobbins. William Felkin, a leading figure in the Nottingham trade, argued that the going about at all hours occasioned by out-work and the complex interlocking of production, finishing and warehousing should be brought under control, 'parental and other control being, under existing arrangements, very slight, and evils of a very grave nature arising in consequence'.[76] Arguments for regulation had some support from leading manufacturers like Felkin. While male workers' representatives pressed for extension of the factory acts without modification, Tremenheere trod what he regarded as a judicious course, advocating factory act extension with modifications.

In other industries, such as those of Birmingham, the model of the demarcated, regulated workplace was still harder to apply. In Birmingham percussion cap manufacture (one of the city's many specialisms), the manufactories were 'cramped, crowded and ill arranged', a point reinforced by a recent explosion at one such establishment; the commissioners had difficulty in gaining admittance to some premises. Their reports follow the familiar rhetorical strategy of finding a contrast-

[73] Howe, *Cotton Masters*, pp. 188–9.
[74] See, e.g., Factory Comm., First Report, p. 51; Kestner, *Protest and Reform*, pp. 96–101.
[75] Report on . . . Lace Manufacture, PP 1861 XXII, p. 6.   [76] Ibid., p. 60.

ing case of a model, well-regulated establishment, Messrs Eley, located off Greys Inn Road in London: 'These premises are . . . as to the new, i.e. the greater part, very large and airy and nicely kept', with 'extensive and various' machinery, cloak-rooms, wash-rooms and canteens. Girls were employed in preference to boys because they were more careful, did not smoke and older workers could be hired for the same pay as a younger boy.[77]

The commissioners attempted to make sense of the diversity of the Birmingham metal trades by distinguishing 'manufactures carried on almost exclusively in large factories' from workshop trades, identifying the former as the sites of improvement. At one brass foundry, railway demolitions and slum clearances had 'given the opportunity for providing new and convenient buildings . . . [with] separate closets for men and boys, quite apart from the females'; even without these advantages, much could be achieved, as at Josiah Mason, steel pen manufacturer, a 'healthy work-place' despite its location 'in a crowded and poor part of the town'.[78]

The impact of extended legislation is beyond the scope of this study. Enforcement was inevitably uneven, partly because the inspectors' expanded duties were not matched by any commensurate increase in staff or other resources.[79] The practical effects of legislation probably depended on a negotiated convergence of workers' pressure-groups, a segment of employers and state agencies, similar to that painfully achieved in textiles at an earlier period. As in that earlier struggle, the very unevenness of conditions could be used to project the large enterprise under enlightened management as the site of improvement. In his study of Birmingham and the West Midlands (1929), Allen argues on familiar lines that the factory acts had encouraged mechanisation and provided 'a strong inducement to the men to modify their habits of irregular work . . . while the employer for his part received an incentive to take a greater interest in the discipline of his factory'.[80] However this was, as Allen acknowledges, a protracted process. The final quarter of the nineteenth century saw new projects of more systematic intervention in the working-class home and family life, including a rhetorical focus on the evils of married women's employment in the discussions surrounding the 1874

---

[77] Children's Employment Commission, First Report, PP 1863 XVIII, pp. 107, 112–13.
[78] Children's Employment Commission, Third Report, PP 1864 XXII, pp. xiii, 67; and cf. Behagg, *Politics and Production*; D. Reid, 'The decline of Saint Monday', *Past & Present* 71 (1976).
[79] G. Barnsby, *Social Conditions in the Black Country, 1800–1900* (Wolverhampton, 1988), pp. 170–3; Bartrip, 'British government inspection', esp. p. 163.
[80] G.C. Allen, *The Industrial Development of Birmingham and the Black Country, 1860–1927* (London, 1929), pp. 176–7; see also Reid, 'Decline of Saint Monday'.

Factory Act.[81] The establishment of School Boards, itself subject to wide local variations, may have been a more effective agency in encouraging regular school attendance. From a necessary evil, or even a desirable condition, the waged work of school-age children came to be viewed as a danger and a disgrace.[82]

The debates of the 1860s were a relatively low-key affair, replaying the rhetorical moves of the ten-hours struggle in more muted tones. 'Child labour, it seemed, could be taken out of politics, and handed over to administrative processes.'[83] The foregoing discussion has been particularly concerned with the way that the imagery of orderly progress associated with the factory settlement in textiles served as a reference-point for constructing the problems of other sectors. The legislation itself was adapted and modified. Most significant were modifications allowing teenaged males to work men's hours from the age of sixteen in various trades.[84]

Factory act extension probably had a stronger and more direct effect in reinforcing the exclusion of women than applied in textiles, partly because of varying labour-force compositions, partly perhaps because of connections between gender and male working-class claims to citizenship that formed part of the context of the later legislation. In lacemaking, the effect of special exemptions for males over sixteen was to reinforce male control of machine-minding, while women were engaged in winding bobbins and removing the completed lace from the machines; in Edinburgh, female compositors were confined to the book trade by restrictions on their hours.[85] In heavy industry, the gendered form of factory legislation reinforced the exclusion of women and the male bonding aspect of socialisation into work.

Extolling the benefits of the factory acts, Thomas Wood, the skilled engineer son of a handloom weaver, recalled his spell as a factory child, when 'there were no inspectors, no public opinion to put down flagrant cases of oppression'; now the law protected those unable to protect themselves, 'when that point is reached it ceases to interfere'.[86] Skilled men in trades like printing or engineering believed they could bargain for themselves over hours, if necessary by strike action. In this context factory act extension reinforced gendered work identities and the new social subject of the respectable working man as citizen, enfranchised in 1867 and 1884.

---

[81] J. Lewis, 'The working-class wife and mother and state intervention, 1870–1918', in J. Lewis (ed.), *Labour and Love: Women's Experience of Home and Family, 1850–1940* (Oxford, 1986); Rose, *Limited Livelihoods*, pp. 59–75.

[82] Cunningham, *Children of the Poor*, chs. 7, 8.   [83] Ibid., p. 165.

[84] See 'Tabular analysis', cited above, n. 67.

[85] Rose, *Limited Livelihoods*, p. 26; S. Reynolds, *Britannica's Typesetters: Women Compositors in Edinburgh* (Edinburgh, 1989), pp. 70, 84.

[86] *Autobiography of Thomas Wood*, p. 7.

Conclusion

No one has ever been able to get up in Parliament or out and say, 'Here is your miserable textile industry, your deplorable cotton trade, drooping and ruined all because of Factory Acts – let us repeal them forthwith.'[1]

Hutchins and Harrison could claim to write from the vantage-point of a half-century or more of practical experience, which apparently provided triumphant refutation of the prophecies of doom uttered by hard-line opponents of factory legislation. Their study was first undertaken at an Edwardian peak of British textile production, and was informed by a perspective of Fabian self-confidence about the direction, if not the exact rate, of further progress.

The consensus they evoked was, if anything, reinforced through the long decline of the textile industries. Contraction was managed by short-time operation, work-sharing and cartels.[2] John Walton argues that this eased the impact of decline and sustained the 'values, attitudes and allegiances' of a distinct regional culture, characterised by a 'blend of individualistic opportunism and collectivist mutual assistance, of thrift and hedonism'. This was, Walton suggests, a defensive, perhaps parochial, culture, but, for those able to claim a place in it, it made for more humane and tolerable responses to economic adversity.[3] The processes of struggle and negotiation examined in this book were therefore to establish patterns of considerable duration. In different forms, they applied not just to textiles but also to other industries. The battles over factory legislation have been considered here as a central episode in the formation of distinctive industrial cultures, based on the process of 'learning to cope with the industrial revolution'.[4]

This experience also provided material for an international debate. In several other industrialising societies, struggles over control at work and the intensity of labour came to centre on the regulation of work-time, and

---

[1] Hutchins and Harrison, *History of Factory Legislation*, p. 121.
[2] Fowler and Wyke (eds.), *Barefoot Aristocrats*, chs. 9, 11; Walton, 'The north west', pp. 408–14. [3] Walton, 'The north west', p. 414. [4] Ibid., p. 413.

its formal demarcation from 'free time'.[5] *De te fabula narratur,* 'the story is about you', Marx, in prophetic mode, warned his German readers.[6] And German commentators were to pay close attention to the British story of factory legislation, trade unionism and other institutional responses to the social strains of industrialism.[7] The work of Kay and other socio-medical commentators had close parallels in investigations of French textile towns; British experience was to provide a reference-point in debates surrounding the comprehensive but ineffectual child labour law of 1841.[8]

The strongest echoes were perhaps across the Atlantic. Ten-hours campaigns in New England in the 1840s provide interesting parallels to, and divergences from, those in Britain.[9] Unlike their counterparts in the United Kingdom, artisans in American cities were able to exert direct political leverage to push for restrictions on hours; such limitations could be represented as essential to the maintenance of republican virtue and a free society of small producers in town and country. In the 1840s, women mill-workers played an active part, on their own behalf and on their own initiative. They too claimed the ground of republican virtue and independence as 'daughters of freemen'. Thomas Dublin has argued that the concentration of unmarried women workers, recruited from New England farm families and lodged in company boarding-houses, encouraged collective action as much as identification with the employer.[10] There was no real British equivalent to the scale, integrated production facilities and labour recruitment practices of Lowell (though it was often lauded as a model for emulation by visiting British commentators, and inspired attempts to establish properly regulated lodging-houses for young women in the very different environment of Bradford).[11] Working-class women in Lancashire and the West Riding were certainly active supporters of short-time committees, Chartism and industrial disputes (including resistance to extended hours), but formal leadership and

---

[5] See esp, Cross (ed.), *Worktime and Industrialization.*
[6] Marx, *Capital,* vol. *I,* p. 90.
[7] G. von Schulze-Gaevenitz, *Social Peace: A Study of the Trade Union Movement in England* (1893); E.E. von Plener, *The English Factory Legislation* (English edn, 1873).
[8] K. Lynch, 'The problem of child labor reform and the working-class family in France during the July monarchy', *Proceedings of the Western Society for French History* 5 (1977); 'Les enfants du capital', *Les Révoltes Logiques* 3 (1976), esp. pp. 46–7; Reddy, *The Rise of Market Culture,* ch. 6.
[9] T. Dublin, *Women at Work: The Transformation of Work and Community in Lowell, Massachussetts, 1826–1860* (New York, 1979); T. Murphy, 'Work, leisure and moral reform: the ten-hour movement in New England, 1830–1850', in Cross (ed.), *Worktime and Industrialization;* D.R. Roediger and P.S. Foner, *Our Own Time: A History* of *American Labor and the Working Day* (London and New York, 1989), ch. 3.
[10] Dublin, *Women at Work.*   [11] Koditschek, *Class Formation,* pp. 549–50.

public representation remained firmly under male control. Finally, it is important to note the transatlantic resonances of the language of 'slavery'; the daughters of freemen were also daughters of white men.[12] Denunciations of 'white slavery' in factories constructed class issues in racial terms, on both sides of the Atlantic.

The British experience was marked by a particular relation between male workers' demands for a shorter working day and moral campaigns for legislative protection of 'dependent' women and juveniles. Regulation of hours in the textile districts was achieved by a combination of informal localised pressure, strikes and crowd actions, public campaigning and coalitions with concerned philanthropists. This was of particular signifi-cance at a period when formal trade unionism was still relatively weak and had only gained minimal and grudging recognition. The playing out of the factory question in some ways foreshadowed the pattern of tripartite negotiation between labour, employers and the state. At the same time, organised male workers needed the support of a broader-based move-ment, expressed through more open and fluid forms of campaigning, to press their claims.

This process had inherent tensions and ambiguities, and I have tried to tease out some of its complexities. As I have argued, neither a blanket conception of protective legislation as exclusionary in intention and effect, nor its reduction to a tactical move in some long game of class con-flict, can do justice to the situation. Alice Kessler-Harris has argued that, in the United States, increasing emphasis on the 'protective' aspects of legislation could compromise the radical challenge of longstanding labour struggles to reduce working hours.[13] This is also relevant for the British case, especially in the period of greater stability from the 1850s. There may be other stories to tell about the popular victories represented by factory reform in the textile districts. Employers recouped the conces-sions made by means of tighter control and intensified labour, and the burdens of this fell disproportionately on the very workers to whom pro-tection was extended, semi-skilled women and young people. I do not want to deny that factory legislation also benefited these less advantaged categories of worker, merely to suggest that its benefits were unevenly distributed. It is important to listen for the silences in the civic celebration that marked the industrial truces negotiated by reasonable men.[14] And extension of legislation beyond textiles, in the context of the liberal

[12] Roediger, *Wages of Whiteness*.
[13] A. Kessler-Harris, *Out to Work: A History of Wage-earning Women in the United States* (New York, 1982); and cf. K.K. Sklar, '"The greater part of the petitioners are female": the reduction of women's working hours in the paid labor force 1840–1917', in Cross (ed.), *Worktime and Industrialization*.   [14] Rose, 'Respectable men'.

citizenship offered to respectable and independent working men, did have quite direct exclusionary effects in a number of important trades.

The attempt to regulate hours and other work-practices thus had varied and contested meanings. For working-class activists, regulation meant preservation or restoration of independence, an assertion of rights as freemen. The limiting of hours was an attempt to control the work environment, the amount of effort exchanged for wages. This would in turn enable working men to protect the children who figured so prominently in the public debate. For some middle-class reformers regulation meant a rationalised and improved factory system, and a systematic approach to the schooling of poor children. The forms of regulation set in place necessarily entailed the renegotiation and transformation of both these perspectives. The vision of enhanced control over working life remained elusive, and particularly so for women workers who were the object of protection. The imposition of restricted hours nevertheless became embedded as a symbol of successful popular campaigning to moralise the marketplace.

I have emphasised the diverse resources of language that entered into this process, and the discursive slippages in the use of particular languages in new contexts. Political economy and its discourse of market relations had shifting and uncertain boundaries, even (or especially) in the minds of its most committed adherents. The negotiation of these meanings to constitute a relatively stable and robust framework of employment relations helped shape an industrial culture of some duration. The perspectives of workers, employers and other interested parties were active constituents of that culture.

The title of this book draws attention to two key terms in this cultural definition of industrial work. I have argued that, whatever its impact on rates of economic growth, the contemporary attention focused on the factory was itself an important element of historical change. The factory was represented as a particularly significant type of workplace, with certain essential common features (powered machines, a systematised division of labour, concentrated employment of women and children, etc.); quite diverse production sites and labour processes could be assimilated to this image. The image was reinforced by state officials concerned to formalise the boundaries of the workplace and to categorise workers. At the same time, journalism, fiction and other modes of representation engaged in parallel mappings of the 'manufacturing districts'. Industrial England became established as an imagined place, a 'strategic space' in the circuits of accumulation and exchange.[15] Industrialisation is therefore

---

[15] For the concept of 'strategic space', see Lefebvre, *The Production of Space*.

to be seen as a process of cultural change, the production of new meanings and practices, as much as of commodities.

In this process markets themselves, and especially labour markets, were culturally constructed. This is perhaps of some relevance for current arguments about de-regulation. The climate has changed radically since Hutchins and Harrison wrote the words quoted at the opening of this conclusion. Recently, politicians have got up, with monotonous predictability, to blame economic problems on over-regulation, the excesses of trade union power and the 'nanny state'. If history has a lesson to offer it would be that regulation, in the sense of guarantees to underwrite expectations that participants bring to specific market transactions, is inescapable. This is particularly the case for the contractual relations of wage-labour, with their potentially open-ended character. As the gothic imagery of some critics of the factory system might suggest, it is bits of people's lives that are sold on labour markets, sometimes on quite destructive terms. De-regulation is simply an attempt to shift the framework, often at considerable human cost.

The entrepreneurial feast of de-regulation is haunted by the need for regulation. Some of the issues uncannily echo those considered in this book. The Institute of Directors recently complained of the potential cost to employers of a legal precedent awarding damages for breakdown in health caused by excessive work-loads; such costs would, it seems, be a disincentive to the hiring of extra workers. Meanwhile, a bus operator, himself a beneficiary of the de-regulation of passenger transport, nonetheless felt alarm at the anarchic competition that ensued: 'the free market has gone too far'.[16]

But, if some of these dilemmas seem to echo those of the 1830s and 1840s, to cite these instances is also to draw attention to shifts in economic structure and work-practices, as well as in the ideological leanings of governments. The further lesson of history would be that, if regulation is necessarily embedded in the working of markets, it is inherently unstable and difficult to sustain. All markets, however localised and protected, are part of a potentially infinite network of markets, and are liable to disruption by new competition or simply unforeseen circumstances (a war here, or harvest failure there). Formalised rule-setting processes are generally two steps behind these shifting conditions; the time it takes to

[16] B. Clement, 'Stress takes toll of social workers', and C. Woolmar, 'On the buses . . . it's war', *The Independent*, 18 November 1994, pp. 7, 21; and see also interview with Ann Robinson, *New Times*, 12 November 1994, p. 2. These items were gleaned from a casual reading; almost any week's newspapers would yield numerous others. For the implications of recent trends, see C. Tilly, 'Globalization threatens labor's rights', with responses by I. Wallerstein, A.R. Zolberg, E.J. Hobsbawm, L. Beneria, *International Labor and Working-Class History*, no. 47 (1995).

obtain recognition of occupation-related diseases, such as mule-spinners' cancer, is a case in point.[17] New processes or materials (for example the mineral oils associated with these cancers), as much as new production sites, are part of a shifting industrial frontier. Here, the rights of property, managerial prerogative and the sanctity of free contract reign supreme, and campaigning for regulation is uphill work.

The Victorian factory acts, with their long persistence in the legal and customary working practices of British industry, attempted to regulate employment by fixing its boundaries in time and space. This mode of regulation has become more problematical, as the sites of waged work have multiplied and franchising and sub-contract arrangements have extended. The protective nation-state, the privileged arena of nineteenth-century struggles over industrial relations, has diminished purchase on the workings of a transnational economy. New forms of labour market will require new kinds of regulation. But regulation will surely remain necessary, if working lives are to be at all bearable.

[17] Fowler and Wyke (eds.), *Barefoot Aristocrats*, ch. 10.

Select sources and bibliography

MANUSCRIPT COLLECTIONS

Ashworth Papers, Lancashire RO.
Balme Collection, Bradford Archives.
Chadwick Papers, University College, London.
Fielden Papers, John Rylands University Library, Manchester.
Fielden Papers, West Yorkshire RO.
Greg Papers, Manchester Archives.
Haggas Bryan Collection, Bolton Archives.
Heywood Papers, Bolton Archives.
Home Office Papers (factory inspection and social disturbances), HO 45, LAB 15, PRO.

PARLIAMENTARY PAPERS

OO Labour of Children in Factories, 1831–2 XV.
RC Employment of Children in Factories, 1833 XX, XXI, 1834 XIX, XX.
SC Regulation of Mills and Factories, 1840 X.
Reports of Factory Inspectors, 1834 XLIII, 1835 XI, 1836 XLV, 1837 XXXI, 1837–8, XXVIII, XLV, 1839 XIX, 1840 XXIII, 1841 X, 1841, sess. 2, VI, 1842 XXII, 1843 XXVII, 1844 XXVIII, 1845 XXV, 1846 XX, 1847 XV, 1847–8 XXVI, 1849 XXII, 1850 XXIII, 1851 XXIII, 1852 XXI, 1852–3 XL, 1854 XIX.
Bleachworks Commission, 1854–5 XVIII.
Report on...Lace Manufacture, 1861 XXII.
Children's Employment Commission, 1863 XVIII, 1864 XXII.

COLLECTIONS OF PAMPHLETS, BROADSIDES AND EPHEMERA

Extensive reference has been made to the Oastler collection of 'White Slavery' Tracts, Goldsmiths' Library, University of London, and also to collections in various reference libraries, especially the bound volumes of pamphlets in Manchester Central Library, and broadsides in the Cassidy Coll., Tameside Archives, Stalybridge. For Nonconformist tracts and periodicals, Dr Williams Library, London. Many items consulted, but not specifically listed below, are in these collections. C. Driver, *Tory Radical: The Life of Richard*

Oastler (New York, 1946), has a listing of the Oastler pamphlets and other relevant material.

NEWSPAPERS AND PERIODICALS

Anti-Slavery Reporter.
Ashton Chronicle.
Ashton Reporter.
Blackburn Standard.
Bolton Chronicle.
Bradford Observer.
Chambers Edinburgh Journal.
The Champion of What is True and Right.
Christian Observer.
Halifax Guardian.
Illustrated London News.
Leeds Mercury.
McDouall's Chartist and Republican Journal.
Manchester and Salford Advertiser.
The Nonconformist.
North of England Medical and Surgical Journal.
Penny Magazine.
The Poor Man's Advocate.
The Ten Hours Advocate.
The Voice of the West Riding.

NOVELS AND POETRY

Note: dates of original publication in book form are given first, followed by edition consulted where applicable.

Brontë, C., *Shirley* (1849; and Everyman edn, 1908, etc.).
Gaskell, E., *Mary Barton* (1848; and Penguin edn, Harmondsworth, 1970).
     North and South (1855; and Penguin edn, Harmondsworth, 1970).
Laycock, S., *Warblin's fro' an Owd Songster* (1893).
Maidment, B. (ed.), *The Poorhouse Fugitives: Self-Taught Poets and Poetry in Victorian Britain* (paperback edn; Manchester, 1992).
Stone, E., *William Langshawe the Cotton Lord*, 2 vols. (1842).
Trollope, F., *The Life and Adventures of Michael Armstrong the Factory Boy* (1840; reprint, Cass, London, 1968).

OTHER PRINTED SOURCES

'Alfred' [Samuel Kydd], *The History of the Factory Movement*, 2 vols. (1857).
Baines, E. jnr., *History of the Cotton Manufacture in Great Britain* (1835).
Baker, R., *The Factory Acts Made Easy* (1851 and subsequent edns).
Bazley, T., 'Cotton as an element of industry', in *Lectures on the Results of the Great Exhibition*, 2nd ser. (1852).

Brown, J., *A Memoir of Robert Blincoe* (1832 edn; reprint, Caliban, Firle, Sussex, 1977).

Cooke Taylor, W., *Notes of a Tour in the Manufacturing Districts of Lancashire* (2nd edn, 1842).

Gaskell, P., *Artisans and Machinery* (1836).

Ginswick, J. (ed.), *Labour and the Poor in England and Wales: Letters to the Morning Chronicle, 1849–1851* (London and Totowa, N.J., 1983).

Grant, P., *The Ten Hours Bill: The History of Factory Legislation* (1866).

Greg, W. R., *Essays in Political and Social Science*, 2 vols. (1853).

Hodder, E., *The Seventh Earl of Shaftesbury*, 2 vols. (1886).

James, J., *History of the Worsted Manufacture in England* (1857).

Kay, J.P., *The Moral and Physical Condition of the Working Classes Employed in the Cotton Manufacture in Manchester* (1832).

Kenworthy, W., *Inventions and Hours of Labour: A letter to Master Cotton Spinners, Manufacturers, and Millowners in General* (1842).

[Leech, J.], *Stubborn Facts from the Factories, by a Manchester Operative* (1844).

Lyell, K.M. (ed.), *A Memoir of Leonard Horner*, 2 vols. (privately printed, 1890).

Miall, E., *The British Churches in relation to the British People* (1849).

Montgomery, J., *The Theory and Practice of Cotton Spinning* (1833).

Rogers, J. Guinness, *Autobiography* (1903).

Ure, A., *The Philosophy of Manufactures* (1835).

Wing, C., *Evils of the Factory System* (1837).

UNPUBLISHED THESES

Evans, C., 'The separation of work and home?: the case of Lancashire textiles, 1825–65', PhD, University of Manchester, 1990.

Gaskell, S.M., 'Housing estate development, 1840–1918, with particular reference to the Pennine towns', PhD, University of Sheffield, 1974.

Gunn, S., 'The Manchester middle class, 1850–1880', PhD, University of Manchester, 1992.

Huzzard, S., 'The role of the certifying factory surgeon', MA, University of Manchester, 1976.

Johnstone, C., 'The standard of living of worsted workers in Keighley during the nineteenth century', DPhil, University of York, 1976.

Moore, S., 'Women, industrialisation and protest in Bradford, West Yorkshire, 1780–1845', PhD, University of Essex, 1988.

Peacock, A. E., 'The justices of the peace and the prosecution of the factory acts, 1833–1855', DPhil, University of York, 1982.

Saunders, J.R., 'Working-class movements in the West Riding textile district, 1829–1839', PhD, University of Manchester, 1984.

Smith, L.D.W., 'Textile factory settlements in the early industrial revolution', PhD, University of Aston, 1976.

Sykes, R.A., 'Popular politics and trade unionism in south-east Lancashire, 1829–44', PhD, University of Manchester, 1982.

Walsh, D., 'Working class political integration and the Conservative Party: a study of class relations and party political development in the north-west, 1800–1870', PhD, University of Salford, 1991.

BOOKS AND ARTICLES

Ashton, T. S., *Economic and Social Investigations in Manchester, 1833–1933* (London, 1934).

Bartrip, P., 'British government inspection, 1832–1875: some observations', *Historical Journal* 25, no. 3 (1982).

'Success or failure? The prosecution of the early Factory Acts', *Economic History Review* 38 (1985).

Bartrip, P., and Burman, S.B., *The Wounded Soldiers of Industry: Industrial Compensation Policy, 1833–1897* (Oxford, 1985).

Bartrip, P., and Fenn, P., 'The evolution of regulatory style in the nineteenth-century British factory inspectorate', *Journal of Law and Society* 10 (1983).

Behagg, C., *Politics and Production in the Early Nineteenth Century* (London, 1990).

Bendix, R., *Work and Authority in Industry: Ideologies of Management in the Course of Industrialization* (Harper Torchbook edn, New York and Evanston, 1963).

Berg, M., *The Machinery Question and the Making of Political Economy* (Cambridge, 1980).

The Age of Manufactures 1700–1820 (London, 1985).

'Progress and providence in early nineteenth-century political economy', *Social History* 15 (1990).

Biagini, E.F., and Reid, A.R. (eds.), *Current of Radicalism: Popular Radicalism, Organised Labour and Party Politics in Britain, 1850–1914* (Cambridge, 1991).

Bolt, C., and Drescher, S. (eds.), *Anti-Slavery, Religion and Reform: Essays in Memory of Roger Anstey* (Folkestone, 1980).

Boyson, R., *The Ashworth Cotton Enterprise* (Oxford, 1970).

Burawoy, M., *The Politics of Production: Factory Regimes under Capitalism and Socialism* (London, 1985).

Cain, P.J., and Hopkins, A.G., *British Imperialism: Innovation and Expansion, 1688–1914* (Harlow, 1993).

Carson, W.G., 'The conventionalization of early factory crime', *International Journal of the Sociology of Law* 7 (1979).

'The institutionalisation of ambiguity: the early factory acts', in G. Geis and E. Stotland (eds.), *White-Collar Crime* (Beverley Hills and London, 1980).

Clokie, H.M., and Robinson, J.W., *Royal Commissions of Inquiry* (Stamford, Calif. and London, 1937).

Coats, A.W. (ed.), *The Classical Economists and Economic Policy* (London, 1971).

Corrigan, P. (ed.), *Capitalism, State Formation and Marxist Theory* (London, 1980).

Cottereau, A., 'The distinctiveness of working-class cultures in France', in I. Katznelson and A.R. Zolberg (eds.), *Working-Class Formation: Nineteenth-Century Patterns in Western Europe and the United States* (Princeton, 1986).

Crafts, N.F.R., *British Economic Growth during the Industrial Revolution* (Oxford, 1985).

Cross, G. (ed.), *Worktime and Industrialization: An International History* (Philadelphia, 1988).

Crumpp, W.B., and Ghorbal, G., *History of the Huddersfield Woollen Industry* (Huddersfield, 1935).

Cunningham, H., *Children of the Poor: Representations of Childhood since the Seventeenth Century* (Oxford, 1991).

Davidoff, L., and Hall, C., *Family Fortunes: Men and Women of the English Middle Class, 1780–1850* (London, 1987).

Davis, D.B., 'Reflections on abolitionism and ideological hegemony', *American Historical Review* 92, no. 4 (1987).

Donajgrodzki, A. P. (ed.), *Social Control in Nineteenth-Century Britain* (London, 1977).

Drescher, S., 'Cart whip and billy roller: antislavery and reform symbolism in industrializing Britain', *Journal of Social History* 15 (1981–2).

Driver, C., *Tory Radical: The Life of Richard Oastler* (New York, 1946).

Dutton, H.I., and King, J E., *Ten Per Cent and No Surrender: The Preston Strike, 1853–4* (Cambridge, 1981).

'The limits of paternalism: the cotton tyrants of north Lancashire, 1836–1854', *Social History* 7 (1982).

Eley, G., 'Edward Thompson, social history and political culture', in H.J. Kaye and K. McClelland (eds.), *E. P. Thompson: Critical Perspectives* (Cambridge, 1990).

Farnie, D.A., *The English Cotton Industry and the World Market, 1815–1896* (Oxford, 1979).

Field, S., 'Without the law?: professor Arthurs and the early factory inspectorate', *Journal of Law and Society* 17, no. 4 (1990).

Foster, J., 'The first six factory acts', *Bulletin of the Society for the Study of Labour History* 18 (spring 1969).

Class Struggle and the Industrial Revolution: Early Industrial Capitalism in Three English Towns (London, 1974).

Fowler, A., and Wyke, T. (eds.), *The Barefoot Aristocrats: A History of the Amalgamated Association of Operative Cotton-Spinners* (Littleborough, Lancs., 1987).

Fox, C., *Graphic Journalism in England during the 1830s and 1840s* (New York and London, 1988).

Freifeld, M., 'Technological change and the "self-acting" mule', *Social History* 11 (1986).

Gallagher, C., *The Industrial Reformation of English Fiction: Social Discourse and Narrative Form, 1832–1867* (Chicago, 1985).

Gatrell, V.A.C., 'Labour, power and the size of firms in Lancashire cotton', *Economic History Review* 30 (1977).

'Incorporation and the pursuit of liberal hegemony in Manchester, 1790–1839', in D. Fraser (ed.), *Municipal Reform and the Industrial City* (Leicester, 1982).

Gordon, L., *Charlotte Brontë: A Passionate Life* (Vintage paperback edn, London, 1995).

Gray, R., 'Factory legislation and the gendering of jobs in the north of England, 1830–1860', *Gender & History* 5 (1993).

Gregory, D., *Regional Transformation and Industrial Revolution: A Geography of the Yorkshire Woollen Industry* (London and Basingstoke, 1982).

Hall, C., *White, Male and Middle Class: Explorations in Feminism and History* (Cambridge, 1992).

Harper, S., *Picturing the Past: The Rise and Fall of the British Costume Film* (London, 1994).

Henriques, U.R.Q., 'An early factory inspector: James Stuart of Dunearn', *Scottish Historical Review* 50, no. 1 (1971).

Before the Welfare State: Social Administration in Early Industrial Britain (London, 1979).

Hilton, B., *The Age of Atonement: The Influence of Evangelicalism upon Social Thought, 1785–1865* (paperback edn, Oxford, 1991).

Howe, A., *The Cotton Masters, 1830–1880* (Oxford, 1984).

Huberman, M., 'The economic origins of paternalism: Lancashire cotton spinning in the first half of the nineteenth century', *Social History* 12 (1987).

Hudson, P., *The Genesis of Industrial Capital: A Study of the West Riding Wool Textile Industry, c. 1750–1850* (Cambridge, 1986).

The Industrial Revolution (London, 1992).

Hutchins, B.L., and Harrison, A., *A History of Factory Legislation* (3rd edn, London, 1926).

Jenkins, D.T., 'The validity of the factory returns, 1833–1850', *Textile History* 4 (1973).

Jennings, H., *Pandemonium: The Coming of the Machine as Seen by Contemporary Observers* (Pan edn, London, 1987).

John, A.V., *By the Sweat of their Brow: Women Workers at Victorian Coal Mines* (paperback edn, London, 1984).

Jones, G. Stedman, *Languages of Class* (Cambridge, 1983).

Joyce, P., *Work, Society and Politics: The Culture of the Factory in Later Victorian England* (Brighton, 1980).

'Work', in F.M.L. Thompson (ed.), *The Cambridge Social History of Britain, 1750–1950* (Cambridge, 1990), vol. II.

Visions of the People: Industrial England and the Question of Class, 1840–1914 (Cambridge, 1991).

(ed.), *The Historical Meanings of Work* (Cambridge, 1987).

Kestner, J.P., *Protest and Reform: The British Social Narrative by Women, 1827–1867* (London, 1985).

Kirby, R.G., and Musson, A.E., *Voice of the People: John Doherty 1798–1854* (Manchester, 1975).

Kirk, N., *The Growth of Working-class Reformism in Mid-Victorian England* (Beckenham, 1985).

Klingender, F., *Art and the Industrial Revolution* (revised edn, London, 1968).

Koditschek, T., *Class Formation and Urban Industrial Society: Bradford 1750–1850* (Cambridge, 1990).

Lazonick, W., 'Industrial relations and technical change: the case of the self-acting mule', *Cambridge Journal of Economics* 3 (1979).

Lee, C.H., *A Cotton Enterprise: The History of McConnel and Kennedy* (Manchester, 1972).

Lefebvre, H., *The Production of Space*, trans. D. Nicholson-Smith (Oxford and Cambridge, Mass., 1991).

Lloyd-Jones, R., and Le Roux, A.A., 'The size of firms in the cotton industry', *Economic History Review* 33 (1980).

Lloyd-Jones, R., and Lewis, M.J., *Manchester in the Age of the Factory* (London, 1988).

Lown, J., *Women and Industrialisation: Gender at Work in Nineteenth-Century England* (Cambridge, 1990).

Lubenow, W.C., *The Politics of Government Growth: Early Victorian Attitudes to State Intervention, 1833–1848* (Hamden, Conn., 1971).

Maidment, B. (ed.), *The Poorhouse Fugitives* (paperback edn; Manchester, 1992).

Mandler, P., *Aristocratic Government in the Age of Reform: Whigs and Liberals, 1830–1852* (Oxford, 1989).

Marland, H., *Medicine and Society in Wakefield and Huddersfield, 1780–1870* (Cambridge, 1989).

Martin, B., 'Leonard Horner: a portrait of an inspector of factories', *International Review of Social History* 14 (1969).

Marvel, H.P., 'Factory regulation: a reinterpretation of early English experience', *The Journal of Law and Economics* (1977).

Marx, K., *Capital, vol. I* (Pelican edn, Harmondsworth, 1976).

Morgan, C.E., 'Women, work and consciousness in the mid-nineteenth-century English cotton industry', *Social History* 17 (1992).

Morris, R.J., *Class, Sect and Party: The Making of the British Middle Class, Leeds, 1820–1850* (Manchester, 1990).

Mort, F., *Dangerous Sexualities* (London, 1987).

Nardinelli, C., *Child Labor and the Industrial Revolution* (Bloomington and Indianapolis, 1990).

Oakley, J. W., 'Utilitarian, paternalistic or both?: the state in *England and the English*', *Prose Studies* 14, no. 1 (1991).

Peacock, A.E., 'The successful prosecution of the Factory Acts, 1833–55', *Economic History Review* 37 (1984).

Pearson, R., 'Knowing one's place: perceptions of community in the industrial suburbs of Leeds, 1790–1890', *Journal of Social History* 27 (1993).

Reddy, W.R., *The Rise of Market Culture: The Textile Trade and French Society, 1750–1900* (Cambridge, 1984).

Reynolds, J., *The Great Paternalist: Titus Salt and the Growth of Nineteenth-Century Bradford* (London, 1983)

Roberts, D., *Paternalism in Early Victorian England* (London, 1979).

Robson, A.P., *On Higher than Commercial Grounds: The Factory Controversy, 1830–1853* (New York and London, 1985).

Roediger, D.R., *The Wages of Whiteness: Race and the Making of the American Working Class* (London and New York, 1991).

Rose, M.B., *The Gregs of Quarry Bank Mill* (Cambridge, 1986).

Rose, M., Taylor, P., and Winstanley, M., 'The economic origins of paternalism: some objections', *Social History* 14 (1989).

Rose, S. O., *Limited Livelihoods: Gender and Class in Nineteenth-Century England* (London, 1992).

'Respectable men, disorderly others: the language of gender and the Lancashire weavers' strike of 1878 in Britain', *Gender & History* 5 (1993).

Sanderson, M., 'Education and the factory in industrial Lancashire, 1780–1840', *Economic History Review* 20 (1967).

Saville, J., *1848: The British State and the Chartist Movement* (Cambridge 1987).

Scott, J.W., *Gender and the Politics of History* (New York and Oxford, 1988).

Seccombe, W., 'Patriarchy stabilised: the construction of the male breadwinner norm in nineteenth-century Britain', *Social History* 11 (1986).

Seed, J., 'Unitarianism, political economy and the antinomies of liberal culture in Manchester, 1830–1850', *Social History* 7, no. 1 (1982).

'Capital and class formation in early industrial England', *Social History* 18, no. 1 (1993).

Sonenscher, M., 'The *sans-culottes* of the Year II: rethinking the language of labour in revolutionary France', *Social History* 9 (1984).

Sutherland, G. (ed.), *Studies in the Growth of Nineteenth-Century Government* (London, 1972).

Sykes, D.F.E., *History of Huddersfield and its Vicinity* (1898).

Thomas, M.W., *The Early Factory Legislation* (Leigh-on-Sea, 1947).

Thompson, E.P., *The Making of the English Working Class* (Pelican edn, Harmondsworth, 1968).

Customs in Common (London, 1991).

Tiller, K., 'Late Chartism: Halifax 1847–58', in J. Epstein and D. Thompson (eds.), *The Chartist Experience* (London, 1982).

Turley, D., *The Culture of English Anti-slavery, 1780–1860* (London, 1991).

Uglow, J., *Elizabeth Gaskell* (paperback edn, London, 1994).

Valverde, M., '"Giving the female a domestic turn": the social, legal and moral regulation of women's work in British cotton mills, 1830–1850', *Journal of Social History* 21 (1988).

Vernon, J. *Politics and the People: A Study in English Political Culture, c. 1815–1867* (Cambridge, 1993).

von Tunzelmann, G.N., *Steam-Power and British Industrialisation to 1860* (Oxford, 1978).

Walby, S., *Patriarchy at Work* (Cambridge, 1986).

Walton, J.K., 'The north west', in F.M.L. Thompson (ed.), *The Cambridge Social History of Britain, 1750–1850* (Cambridge, 1990), vol. I.

Ward, J.T., *The Factory Movement, 1830–1855* (London, 1962).

Weaver, S.A., *John Fielden and the Politics of Popular Radicalism, 1832–1847* (Oxford, 1987).

Wilson, R.G., *Gentlemen Merchants* (Manchester, 1971).

Wolff, J., and Seed, J. (eds.), *The Culture of Capital* (Manchester, 1988).

Index

Abram, W. A., 222
Accrington, 13
Adventures of Michael Armstrong, 143, 144–9
Ainsworth, J. H. (Haliwell bleachworks), 231
Akroyd, E. (Halifax worsted manufacturer), 224, 226, 229–30
'Alfred', *see* Kydd, S.
Allen, G. C., 233
Altar of the Household, The, 115–16, 118–19
'alternative political economy', 28–9, 36, 54; *see also* political economy
Althorp, Lord, 62
Anglican, 52, 98, 111–12, 224; *see also* Evangelical, religion
Anti-Corn Law League, 191
anti-slavery, 38–41, 43–5, 52, 55
Artisans and Machinery, 85
Ashley, Lord: reform campaigns, 54, 57, 58, 218; religion, 57; Select Committee, 1840, 93–4, 95; Ten Hours Bill, 62, 99, 200
Ashton: manufacture, 13; millowners, 182, 203; prosecutions, 167, 168, 185; working hours, 336
Ashworth, H., 103
Ashworths, H. & E. (Bolton spinners), 51, 99, 124, 135, 175, 185, 189
Athenaeum, The, 146, 152, 154

Baines, E., 133–4
Baker, R. (surgeon, factory superintendent), 78, 82, 91–2, 170, 217, 218
Bartrip, P., 86, 165, 186
Bazley, T., 193
Benthamism, 9, 41, 58, 69, 86
Berg, M., 111
Birt, Rev. J. (Baptist), 41, 43
Blackburn: employers, 103, 107, 194; manufacture, 13, 105, 185; prosecutions, 170, 175, 185

Bogart, The, 64
Bolling, E. & W. (Bolton spinners), 50, 183, 189
Bolton: employers, 103, 107, 194,; manufacture, 13, 105; prosecutions, 167, 175
Bradford: employers, 103, 182; prosecutions, 178–9
Brontë, C., 143, 153–7
Brooks, Rev. J. (Unitarian), 71
Bull, Rev. G. S. (Anglican), 52, 54
Burnley, 13
Bury, 167

Calderdale, 26, 63–5, 103, 104
Carlyle, T., 45, 96, 124–5, 127
Carson, W. G., 165
Chadwick, E.: factory commission, 69, 71–2, 82, 87–9; social reform, 68–9, 80, 92; Ten Hours Bill, 1847, 191
Chalmers, T. (Scottish Evangelical), 65, 120
Chambers' Journal, 136
Chartism, 35, 38, 96, 140, 142, 191, 202, 203, 205–6
Cheetham, J., 203
Cheshire, 12
children: Factory Commission, 1833, 72; Factory Committee, 1840, 95; images of child labour, 139; in the labour force, 15–16, 25–7, 62–3, 68, 105–7; middle-class, 84; in reform campaigns, 29–30, 31–4, 43, 47, 54, 62, 67; working-class, 62–3
Children's Employment Commission, 1840, 95
Christian Observer, 57
citizenship, 26, 29, 44, 127–9, 209, 234, 237–8
class, 10, 211; *see also* gender, labour, middle classes, working classes
Cobbett, William, 39, 45

merchanting, 106–7
Methodist, 52
Miall, E. (editor *The Nonconformist*), 114,
  118, 184, 221
middle classes: anti-slavery, 40–2, 47;
  culture, 76, 97–8, 109–10;
  industrialisation, 2; masculinity, 90; *see
  also* employers, 'experts', liberalism,
  men, women
Mill, J. S., 5
mills, 105–6
Mines Act (1842), 8
Montagu, F., 148
Monthly Repository, 55, 57
Morning Chronicle, 136
Morpeth, Lord, 55
mule spinning, 24, 36, 105, 180, 214

national identity, 210–12
Nonconformist, The, 114, 117, 124–5, 184
Nonconformity: anti-slavery, 37–8, 40–2;
  Congregationalist, 111, 112–14, 222–4;
  ministers, 113; political economy, 114;
  reform campaigns, 37–8, 52; Unitarians,
  112; *see also* Evangelical, religion
North and South, 143, 153–8

Oastler, R.: language, 43, 53–4, 96, 186
politics, 52, 54; populism, 61, 186–7;
reform campaigns, 25, 34, 49, 51–3, 63–5;
  religion, 57; statue, 220–1
Oldham, 105, 167, 194, 195

parliamentary inquiry, 59–61, 65, 66; *see
  also* Factory Acts, Factory Bill, Factory
  Commission, 'experts'
paternalism: deference, 226, 228; employer
  responsibilities, 122, 125–6, 129–30,
  221–2; family, 48–9; gender, 128; liberal
  discourse, 48–50, 127, 128, 130;
  management, 122–3; patrician, 48,
  123–4; reform campaigns, 52–3, 126;
  religion, 112, 120–1; *see also* employers,
  family, works outings
Peacock, A. E., 165–7, 171
Penny Magazine, 138
Pilkington Bros. (Blackburn cotton
  manufacturer), 175, 189, 222–3
political economy, 5, 67, 72, 100, 110, 213,
  238; *see also* 'alternative political
  economy'
Poor Man's Advocate, The, 28, 29
Preston dispute, 1853–4, 202, 205,
  206
professions, 72–6; *see also*, culture,
  'experts', medical men, middle classes

race, 39–40, 45–6
radicalism: anti-slavery, 38, 39; in reform
  campaigns, 7, 29, 36, 184, 203–6; Tory
  alliance, 49, 52–3; working classes,
  27–8
Reach, A., 136
religion: business, 118–19; class relations,
  116–17; employers, 111–21, 181, 182–3;
  middle-class, 110; political economy,
  111; reform campaigns, 52, 57–8;
  sermons, 116–17; ten-hours movement,
  192
respectability, working-class men, 27–8,
  35
Rice, D., 42
Ripponden, 63
Roberton, J. (surgeon), 85
Robson, A. P., 5, 209
Rochdale, 167, 195
Rose, S. O., 219, 228

Saddleworth, 175, 178, 185
Sadler, M. T.: parliamentary committee of
  1832, 23, 25, 30, 34, 57, 68; reform
  campaigns, 39; ten-hours movement, 57;
  see also short-time committees
Saunders, R. J. (factory inspector), 125,
  169, 192
Saville, J., 203
Scotland, 92–3
Seed, J., 122
Select Committee, 1832, *see* Sadler
Select Committee, 1840, 93–95,
Shaftesbury (Seventh Earl of), *see* Ashley
Shirley, 154–5, 156
short-time committees, 59–60, 65–7, 93,
  198, 204–5
short-time movement, 5, 23, 36–7, 61, 187;
  see also ten-hours movement
slavery: language, 42, 44, 45–7; in reform
  campaigns, 32, 38–41; *see also* anti-
  slavery
Smith, A., 43
Smith, S. (surgeon), 76–7
'Society for Improving the Condition of
  Factory Children', 56
spinners, 198–9, 201
Stalybridge: employers, 194; industrial
  structure, 13, 106; prosecutions, 167,
  168; working hours, 195, 203
state: expansion of, 9–10, 61; intervention,
  5, 86–7, 188; *see also* liberalism, middle
  classes, political economy
Statistical Society, Manchester, 71, 100,
  163–4
Statute of Artificers, 61

Printed in the United Kingdom
by Lightning Source UK Ltd.
662